The Singer's Repertoire

Singer's Repertoire

Part I
Coloratura Soprano
Lyric Soprano and
Dramatic Soprano

Second Edition

by

Berton Coffin

The Scarecrow Press, Inc.
New York   1960

To

Valorie Goodall

friend and artist

Foreword

"The Singer's Repertoire" in its second edition has been divided into four parts. Part I includes songs for Coloratura Soprano, Lyric Soprano and Dramatic Soprano. Part II includes songs for Mezzo Soprano and Contralto. Part III includes songs for Lyric Tenor and Dramatic Tenor and Part IV includes songs for Baritone and Bass. This has been thought to be a service to the individual singer who is primarily interested only in that material which is suitable for his particular voice.

Several of the song lists have been augmented and duets, trios, songs of limited range and chamber operas for two, three or four voices have been added. Intentionally no lists have been made of "easy" songs since this has been felt to be a misnomer. That which is easy for one is not necessarily easy for another. Young singers may have short ranges but they frequently have very fine tastes, possibly some language background and even fairly good musicianship due to previous instrumental study. Hence, instead of a list of "easy" songs, the compiler has listed a broad spectrum of songs with limited range.

"The Singer's Repertoire" is an effort to aid all singers and teachers of singing in their repertoire problems. The singer at no stage in his career is free from this problem. In the beginning he has to select the suitable songs for his vocal powers and development. As he becomes a successful amateur singer he secures various engagements which are always presenting new song needs. Should he become a professional singer the needs will be multiplied many times with a changing repertoire required season after season. Should he become a teacher of singing or a vocal coach he will have hundreds of potential singers, each one with different needs. Therefore, no matter with what phase of vocal work one is concerned, the repertoire problem is always present and one's storehouse is always changing, always being added to.

"The Singer's Repertoire" has profited in its growth and development by the advice, counsel and criticism of many experienced singers and many noted teachers of singing. From these discussions, four repertoire aids appear to be paramount:

vii

1. Aids for program building (for this problem the guide lists recital songs in the various languages; songs for opening and closing recitals; and songs by classification.

2. Aids for training repertoire (this problem has been approached by indexing technical characteristics of songs).

3. Aids for specific or seasonal occasions (see Christmas, Easter, Wedding and Patriotic lists).

4. Aids in sacred repertoire (hundreds of songs have been studied and those appropriate are listed).

The above aids are based on contemporarily performed songs and arias as programmed in countless recitals, in recordings, and in the media of radio and television. This mass of material has been interpolated into appropriate listings. The compiler has not assumed the position of musical analyst except for the sacred listing and in augmenting the smaller lists. Questions have not been asked as to why certain songs are sung or not sung; if the song has been found in the above mentioned sources, it is listed, otherwise it is not included in this volume. This book is based on the preselection of songs sung by noteworthy or accepted singers, and is not a compendium of all vocal repertoire which would surely approximate 100,000 song titles. It is merely a distribution of some 8,000 songs into 818 lists for the nine voice classifications rather than an annotated bibliography of songs. For each voice classification there are 71 - 92 lists whereby the characteristics of various songs are shown. It is well known to all teachers that a matching of song traits to the strengths and limitations of any singing personality will assure the individual's best success. This is a very difficult thing to do and it is hoped the problem will be made easier by the multiple listings of this work.

Due to the large number of programs examined, all voices should be represented in proportion to their natural distribution. The largest segments will be the lyric soprano and baritone because there are more of these voices; the smallest segments will be the coloratura soprano, dramatic tenor and bass since these voices occur less frequently. The compiler has made no attempt to classify voices in this study but has merely listed the songs according to the voice classification stated on the programs.

A work of this kind can never be complete in contemporary song (although publication in this field is lamentably limited)   since new songs are appearing and others are falling into disuse.   However, the classic, romantic and impressionistic repertoire is now relatively stable.   These songs comprise the living repertoire of today.

Boulder, Colorado

Table of Contents

xi

Repertoire for the Lyric Soprano Voice

Repertoire for the Dramatic Soprano Voice

Directions for Use

All songs are listed alphabetically by composer with the song listings alphabetized under each composer. The lists are to be read in the following manner: first, the composer's name is given, then the title, then the opera, operetta, cantata, oratorio, if it is an aria. In cases where a solo instrument accompanies the voice and piano that instrument has been indicated.

Next are shown the keys HML. The last letter of the key is important: should it be L - the low range is shown; if the last is M, the medium range is shown; and if it is H - the high. BF-EF indicates a range of B flat to E flat (CS-FS would indicate C sharp to F sharp). The three letters at the extreme right of page are a code for the publisher (code at front of book, i.e. GSC indicates G. Schirmer; SC indicates Schott). Where a dagger (†) appears the song is published by more than one firm.

The Miscellaneous listings are total lists including songs other than those found in the American, British, French, German and Italian listings. However, if there is a void in any of these lists (American, British, French, German, Italian), those songs will be included in the Miscellaneous list. Latin songs always appear in the Miscellaneous lists as do the Portuguese, Hungarian, Hebrew, etc.

This book does not include popular music as such but does have a separate listing of the lighter numbers which are frequently needed. These songs are found under the heading - Songs of Popular Appeal.

The Handel songs are found in the British, German and Italian lists; Wagner in the German and French; and Mozart in the Italian, German and French. American compositions are found in the American lists regardless of whether French, German or Italian texts are used. Likewise English composers are in the English lists.

The classical Italian arias are listed under song rather than opera because the works are no longer staged and they are thought of as song literature.

Publisher Code

† – Published by more than one company

A

ABC – ABC Music Corp.
AHC – Asherberg, Hopwood and Crew
AMI – Amici
AMM – American Music
AMP – Associated Music Publishers
ARR – Arrow Music Press
ASB – Ashbrook
ASC – Arthur P. Schmidt
ASH – Ashdown
AUG – Augener
AXE – Axelrod

B

BAF – Bayley and Ferguson
BAR – Barenreiter
BER – Berlin
BES – Bessel
BIR – Birchard
BLO – C. A. Blodgett
BMI – Broadcast Music, Inc.
BOH – Boosey and Hawkes
BOO – Boosey
BON – Bongiovani
BOS – Boston
BOT – Bote and Bock
BRA – Brandus and Cie
BRE – Bregeman
BRH – Breitkof and Haertel
BRM – Barton and Mead
BRO – Broude
BVC – Bregman, Vocco and Conn

C

CAR – Cardilli
CFI – Carl Fischer
CHA – Chappel
CHE – Chester
CHM – Champagne
CHO – Choudens
CMC – Composers Music Corp.
CMP – Composers Press
CNN – Conn
CRA – Cramer
CRF – Crawford
CRZ – Cranz
CSC – Cos Cob
CST – Costallet
CUR – Curwen

D

DBH – Desylvia, Brown and Henderson
DES – DeSantis
DIT – Ditson
DRE – Dreiklang
DUR – Durand

E

ECS – E. C. Schirmer
ELK – Elkin
ELV – Elkan-Vogel
ENO – Enoch
ESC – Eschig

xix

F

FAM - Famous
FEI - Feist
FLA - Flammer
FOE - Foetisch
FOX - Fox
FRA - Frank
FRL - Forlivesi
FRS - Forster
FST - Forsyth
FTZ - FitzSimmons

G

GAL - Galaxy
GAM - Gamble Hinged (GAH)
GER - Gershwin
GLO - Glocken Verlag
GOL - Goldsea
GOT - Goodwin and Tabb
GRA - H. W. Gray
GSC - G. Schirmer

H

HAC - Hachette
HAM - Hamelle
HAN - Hansen
HAR - Harms
HEU - Heugel
HHE - Hinds, Haydn and Eldredge
HNR - Heinrichofen
HNZ - Hunzinger
HOM - Homeyer
HRM - Harmonia (HMP)
HSC - Hans Schneider

I

INT -- International

J

JCH - John Church

JFI - J. Fischer
JOB - Jobert
JUR - Jurgenson
JWI - J. Williams

K

KAL - Kalmus
KIS - Kistner
KSS - Kustner and Siegel

L

LAC - Lacour
LED - Leduc
LEE - Leeds
LEM - Lemoine

M

MAR - Marks
MAT - Mathot
MCG - MacGimsey
MCR - McLaughlin, Reilly
MER - Mercury
MET - Methuen
MLR - Miller
MLS - Mills
MOR - Morris, E. H.
MOV - Movietone
MUP - Music Press

N

NAG - Nagel Verlag
NEM - New Music
NOR - Norsky Verlag
NOV - Novello

O

OCT - Octava Music Co.
OXF - Oxford

P

PAR - Paragon
PEE - Peer
PET - Peters
PON - William Pont
PRE - Presser
PRM - Paramount
PRO - Prowse
PTR - Paterson

R

RBR - Riker, Brown and
      Wellington
REM - Remick
RIC - Ricordi
ROB - Robbins
ROG - Winthrop Rogers
ROM - Roma
ROU - Rouart, Lerolle
ROW - Row

S

SAL - Salabert
SC - Schott
SCH - Schlesinger
SEN - Senart
SHA - Shapiro
SHU - Schuberth
SIM - Simroch
SIR - Sirene
SON - Sonzogno
SOU - Southern Music Co.
SPA - Spada
STB - Stainer Bell
SUM - Summy

T

TEM - Templeton
TRA - Transcontinental

U

UME - Union Musical Española
UNI - Universal

V

VIC - Victoria
VLP - Valley Press

W

WEI - Weinberger
WHB - Whitney Blake
WHI - White Smith
WIL - Williamson
WIT - Witmark
WLL - Willis
WOO - Wood
WOR - Words and Music
WTR - Weintraub

Z

ZER - Zerboni

Part I

American Recital Songs

Coloratura Soprano

Alberti	Oriental serenade	H	CS–A	CFI
Bacon	Is there such a thing as day?	M	DS–FS	AMP
Barber	Monks and raisons	M	DF–E	GSC
-----	Nuovoletta	H	BS–BS	GSC
-----	Secrets of old	LH	EF–G	GSC
-----	Sleep now	MH	EF–AF	GSC
-----	The daisies	M	C–F	GSC
Beach	Fairy lullaby			ASC
Boyd	Adoration	H	C–A	GAL
Granscombe	At the postern gate	MH	DF–AF	ASC
Burleigh	By the pool at the third roses	H		RIC
Buzzi-Peccia	Little birdies			
-----	Under the greenwood tree	LMH	EF–A	DIT
Cadman	I hear a thrush at eve			MOR
-----	Joy	MH	E–A	GSC
-----	Welcome, sweet wind	H	E–B	GSC
Carpenter	Serenade	LH	CS–A	GSC
Chanler	Wind			GSC
Charles	A wish	LH	E–GS	GSC
-----	And so, goodbye	LH	EF–AF	GSC
-----	Let my song fill your heart	LH	EF–AF	GSC
-----	The white swan	HL	C–F	GSC
Clough- Leighter	My lover he comes on the skee	HM	D–F	BOS
Cottenet	Red, red rose	H	D–BF	CFI
Cowles	Desire	H	F–A	GSC
Creston	Bird of the wilderness	MH	FS–A	GSC
Crist	By a silent seashore	H	CS–GS	GSC
-----	Into a ship dreaming	LMH	EF–GS	CFI
-----	O come hither	HM	B–GS	CFI
-----	White hours like snow	HL	CS–BF	CFI
Curran	Bird songs	MH	EF–AF	GSC
Davis	Nancy Hanks	H	D–G	GAL
Dougherty	Primavera	H	C–BF	GSC
Duke	A piper	H	CS–B	GSC

25

(Duke)	Bells in the rain	H	E-GS	CFI
-----	Little elegy	H	FS-A	GSC
Edmunds	Fare you well	MH	F-AF	ROW
-----	Milk maids	M	DF-F	MER
Ganz	The angels are stooping	MH	GF-A	GSC
Gaynor	May magic			
-----	Pierrot	H	E-B	BOS
Giannini	Tell me, o blue, blue sky	H		RIC
Gilberte	Two roses	LMH	CS-G	CFI
Grant- Schaeffer	The cuckoo clock	H	EF-BF	SUM
Griffes	Elves	H	F-AF	GSC
-----	In a myrtle shade	H	FS-A	GSC
-----	The rose of the night	H	CS-A	GSC
-----	Thy dark eyes to mine	H	EF-AF	GSC
-----	To-night			
-----	Upon their grave	M	C-G	GSC
-----	Waikiki	H	DS-GS	GSC
Hageman	At the well	LH	EF-AF	GSC
-----	Me company along	LH	F-BF	CFI
-----	Music I heard with you	MH	E-A	GAL
Harmati	Spring night			
Harris	Winter	H	F-A	GAL
Horsman	The bird of the wilder- ness	LMH	DF-BF	GSC
-----	Thus wisdom sings	H	EF-A	GSC
Josten	Cupid's counsel	H	EF-AF	GSC
Kramer	Swans	HL		RIC
La Forge	Bird song	H		RIC
-----	Come unto these yellow sands	H	FS-B	GSC
-----	Cupid captive	H		GAL
-----	Pastorale			
-----	The sand			
Lubin	The piper	H	C-A	GSC
Mana-Zucca	Fluttering birds	H	EF-BF	GSC
-----	Sleep, my darling			CNG
-----	There's joy in my heart			CNG
Miller	The blue bell			
-----	The bumblebee			
Naginski	Look down, fair moon			
Nevin	Good night, good night beloved	LH	E-FS	BOS
Nordoff	Fair Annette's song			AMP
-----	Serenade	H	CS-FS	AMP
-----	There shall be more joy	M	CS-FS	AMP
Parker	The lark now leaves her watery nest	LH		JCH
Popper	Gavotte	H	D-B	GSC

26

Proctor	I light the blessed candles	H	DF-A	GSC
Rorem	Alleluia			
-----	The silver swan	H	F-C	PEE
Rybner	Pierrot	HL		GSC
Sacco	Rapunzel	MH	FS-BF	GSC
Saminsky	Queen Estherka's laugh	H	D-A	CFI
Spross	Will o' the wisp			JCH
Thomson	Preciosilla	H	EF-A	GSC
Treharne	A widow bird sat mourning	H	FS-AF	BOS
Vanderpool	Values			WIT
Vene	Age and youth	H	E-A	RIC
-----	The rats	H	E-A	RIC
Ware	By the fountain			FLA
-----	This day is mine	MH	EF-AF	BOS
Warren	Down in the glen	H	F-A	GSC
-----	My lady Lo-Fu			DIT
-----	Snow towards evening	LH	EF-AF	GSC
-----	Who calls?	LH	E-A	CFI
Watts	Joy	HL	D-F	GSC
-----	Stresa	H	EF-BF	DIT
-----	The little shepherd's song	H	G-BF	RIC
-----	The poet sings	MH	EF-AF	DIT
Woodman	Love's in my heart	LH	F-BF	GSC

British Recital Songs

Coloratura Soprano

Anon	Willow song from Otello			GSC
Arne, M.	The lass with the delicate air	MH	D-G	†
Arne, T.	Where the bee sucks	HM		†
Aylward	Deep in my heart	LMH		CHA
Bainton	The nightingale near the house			CUR
Bantock	A feast of lanterns	HM	D-F	GAL
Dax	I heard a piper piping	LH	D-G	CFI
-----	O green grow the rushes	MH	EF-BF	OXF
-----	Shieling song	H	CS-A	CHE
Bayly	I'd be a butterfly			
Benedict	The carnival of Venice	H	D-EF	GSC
-----	The gypsy and the bird	H	D-E	GSC
-----	The wren Flute	H	F-C	PRE
Benjamin	The piper			BOO
Besley	Listening	H	E-AF	CUR
Bishop	Echo song Flute	H	D-C	GSC
-----	Love has eyes	M		†

27

(Bishop)	Should he upbraid	H		†
Bliss	Three jolly gentlemen	H		†
Brahe	Piper from over the hill			
Brewer	The fairy pipers	HML		BOH
Bridge	Adoration	H		ROG
Brown	Shepherd thy demeanor vary!			BOO
Clarke	Shy one	HL	BF-G	BOH
Coleridge- Taylor	Willow song	MH		CRA
Edmunds	I know my love	HL	BF-EF	ROW
-----	The faucon	M	D-F	MER
Forsyth	Dew fairy			
-----	The stranger Organ	H	A-B	GRA
German	Charming Chloe	HML		NOV
Gibbs	To one who passed whistling through the night	H	F-G	CUR
Goossens	The fan song			
Head	A piper	HL		BOO
Holst	A little music	H		AUG
Horn	Cherry ripe	M	D-G	†
Ireland	Bed in summer			CUR
Lehmann	Snake charmer			BOO
Mallinson	My heart, the bird of the wilderness	H	DF-AF	CRA
Quilter	Love's philosophy	LMH	D-A	BOO
-----	To daisies			BOO
Ronald	Down in the forest	HML	C-D	ENO
Sharp	My mother did so before me			MEU
Stanford	Sea wrack	H	EF-A	STB
Taylor	O can ye sew			
Walton	Sunset			
Warlock	Pretty ring time	H	D-G	CFI
-----	The passionate shepherd	HM		ELK

French Recital Songs

Coloratura Soprano

Anon	Dites, que faut-il faire?			
Bachelet	Chère nuit	H	DF-BF	GSC
Bizet	Douce mer			GSC
-----	Le matin			GSC
-----	Vielle chanson	H	EF-A	GSC
Boieldieu	Essayons's il se peut de parler			LEM

28

Busser	La meilleure pensée			DUR
Chaminade	L' été	MH	E-A	†
Charpentier	Les chevaux de bois	H	E-A	HEU
-----	Les yeux de Berthe			HEU
-----	Serenade à Watteau			
Chausson	Sérénade			
Dalcroze	Le coeur de ma mie	HML		†
-----	L' oiseau bleu			CFI
Debussy	Apparition			DUR
-----	Beau soir	LH	C-FS	†
------	Chevaux de bois	H	C-G	†
-----	Clair de lune	M	CS-FS	JOB
-----	De fleurs	H	C-AF	†
-----	Fantoches	H	D-A	JOB
-----	Green	H	C-AF	†
-----	Harmonie du soir			DUR
-----	Il pleur dans mon coeur	LH	CS-GS	†
-----	L'ombre des arbres			DIT
-----	La mer est plus belle	HL		†
-----	Le faune			DUR
-----	Mandoline	HM	BF-F	†
-----	Noël des enfants qui n'ont plus de maisons			DUR
-----	Nuits d'etoiles	LH	E-A	MAR
-----	Pierrot			DUR
-----	Romance	HM	C-E	†
-----	Rondeau			
-----	Rondel chinois			DUR
-----	Voici que le printemps	LH	CS-G	BOS
Délibes	Coppelia waltz	H	BF-BF	GSC
-----	Jours passés			GSC
-----	Les filles de Cadix	HM	A-A	†
-----	Passepied	LH	DS-CS	GSC
Duparc	Chanson triste	MH	FS-AF	†
-----	Extase	LMH	FS-A	†
-----	L'invitation au voyage	HM	E-F	†
-----	Soupir	HL	CS-F	BOS
Dupont	Chanson des noisettes			HEU
-----	Mandoline			DUR
Fauré	Apres un Rêve	HM	C-F	†
-----	Clair de lune	MH	C-G	†
-----	La fée aux chansons	LH	F-F	†
-----	La lune blanche	HL		†
-----	Les roses D'Ispahan	HM	D-FS	DIT
-----	Nell	LH	FS-AF	†
-----	Notre amour	H	DS-B	†
-----	Rencontre	H	EF-AF	†
-----	Sylvie	HL	E-F	†
-----	Vocalise	H		LED

Fourdrain	Le papillon			RIC
Gounod	Au printemps	LMH	DF-AF	GSC
Grovlez	Guitares et mandolines			DUR
Hahn	Le printemps			
-----	Le rossignol des lilas			
Honegger	Le Delphinium			
Hue	Il a neigé des fleurs	H	EF-AF	
-----	Le passant	H	D-G	†
Jacobson	Song of Marie Antoinette	MH	DS-GS	CFI
Koechlin	L'air	M	F-FS	ROU
-----	La lune	M	C-F	ROU
-----	Le thé	HM	C-E	BOS
Lalo	La chanson d'Alouette	H	EF-B	GSC
Letorey	La fontaine de Caramouet			HAM
Liszt	Comment, disaient-ils	H	C-AF	†
-----	Oh! quand je dors	H	E-A	†
Messiaen	Le sourire	H		DUR
-----	Pourquoi	H		DUR
Milhaud	A une fontaine			
-----	Chansons de Ronsard	H		BOH
-----	Tais-toi, Babillarde	H	G-C	BOH
Moret	Le nélumbo	H	E-DF	HEU
Paladilhe	Le roitelet	MH	DS-GS	GSC
Pierné	Le moulin	ML	C-E	BOS
Poldowski	Dansons la gigue	M	EF-G	MAR
-----	Nocturne	H	DS-GS	CHE
Poulenc	Air champêtre			ROU
-----	Air vif	H	C-AF	ROU
-----	C. (J'ai traversé les ponts de c.)			ROU
-----	Fêtes galantes			SAL
Quilitsky	La rose et le rossignol			
Ravel	D'Anne jouant de l'espinette	H	CS-GS	GSC
-----	Ronde			
Roussel	Coeur en péril			DUR
-----	Sarabande			
Saint-Saëns	Aimons-nous			DUR
-----	Au cimetière			
-----	Le bonheur est une chose légère	H	C-A	CHO
	Violin and piano			
-----	The nightingale and the rose	H	C-D	GSC
Sauguet	Amour			
Severac	Chanson pour le petit cheval			ROU
Szulc	Mandoline	H	D-B	ROU
Vidal	Ariette	LH	F-A	GSC

Vuillermoz	Jardin d'amours			SAL
Weckerlin	Je connais un berger			
	discret	M	EF-EF	BOS

German Recital Songs

Coloratura Soprano

Beethoven	Lied aus der Ferne			
-----	Mit einem gemalten Band			RIC
Brahms	Auf dem Schiffe	LH	GS-A	†
-----	Botschaft	HL	D-F	†
-----	Das Maedchen spricht	H	E-FS	†
-----	Eine gute, gute Nacht			†
-----	Es liebt sich so lieblich			
	im Lenze	LH	D-GS	†
-----	Feldeinsamkeit	HL	C-EF	†
-----	Geheimnis			†
-----	Lerchengesang	LH	FS-GS	†
-----	Maedchenlied	HL		†
-----	Nachtigall	MHL	BF-FS	†
-----	Regenlied	HL	CS-F	†
-----	Vergebliches staendchen	LMH	E-FS	†
-----	Vorueber			†
-----	Wiegenlied			
-----	Wie Melodien zieht es	HL	A-E	†
-----	Wir wandelten	LH	EF-GF	†
Haydn	My mother bids me bind			
	my hair	M	E-E	†
Jensen	Murmuring zephyr	LH	E-AF	GSC
Liszt	Kling leise, mein Lied	HL		†
Loesch	Auf der Kirmes			
Loewe	Canzonetta	MH	B-A	DIT
-----	Niemand hat's gesehen	LM	DS-FS	†
Marx	Marienlied	MH	EF-AF	AMP
-----	Nocturne	H	EF-AF	AMP
-----	Selige Nacht	M	DF-GF	AMP
-----	Und gestern hat er mir			
	Rosen gebracht	H	E-A	AMP
Mendelssohn	Fruehlingslied	H	DS-GS	†
-----	Im Gruenen	H	E-BF	AUG
-----	Neue Liebe	H	CS-A	†
-----	O for the wings of a dove	MLH	D-G	†
-----	O Jugend	H	E-A	†
-----	On wings of song			†
Mozart	Warnung	HM	C-D	

(Mozart)	Wiegenlied	MH	G-G	†
Oboussier	Weine du nicht			
	Oboe and harpsichord			
Proch	Theme and variations	H	C-DF	†
	Flute			
Schubert	An die Laute	LH	D-F	†
-----	An die Nachtigall	H	C-G	†
-----	Auf dem Wasser zu singen	MH	EF-GF	†
-----	Ave Maria	LMH	F-F	†
-----	Das Lied im Gruenen			PET
-----	Das Rosenband			PET
-----	Der Hirt auf dem	H	BF-B	†
	Felsen			
	Clarinet or violoncello			
-----	Der Juengling an der	LH	E-A	†
	Quelle			
-----	Der Knabe			PET
-----	Der Musensohn	LH	FS-G	†
-----	Der Schmetterling	LH	E-F	†
-----	Die Forelle	MLH	EF-GF	†
-----	Die Rose	M	G-FS	PET
-----	Die Spinnerin			†
-----	Geheimes	HL	BF-EF	†
-----	Gott im Fruehling			PET
-----	Gretchen am	H	F-A	†
	Spinnrade			
-----	Klaerchens Lied			
-----	Liebesbotschaft	H	E-G	†
-----	Nachtviolen			PET
-----	Rastlose Liebe	M	B-F	†
-----	Ungeduld	HML		†
-----	Wiegenlied (Op. 98)			†
-----	Wohin?	HL	B-E	†
-----	Auftraege	HL	C-E	†
Schumann				
-----	Der Nussbaum	LMH	D-FS	†
-----	Die Meerfee			
-----	Er ist's	HL	BF-EF	†
-----	Geisternaehe			
-----	Intermezzo	HL	C-D	GSC
-----	Marienwuermchen	HL	D-D	†
-----	Mondnacht	M	E-FS	†
-----	O wie lieblich ist das			
	Maedchen			
-----	Schneegloeckchen	HL		†
-----	Volksliedchen	HL		†
Strauss	All' mein' Gedanken	H	CS-GS	
-----	Barcarolle	H	DF-BF	†
-----	Fruehlingsgedraenge			
-----	Kornblumen	LH	DF-AF	†

(Straus)	Liebeshymnus			†
-----	Mohnblumen			
-----	Schlagende Herzen			†
-----	Schlechtes Wetter			†
-----	Staendchen	HM	A-FS	†
Taubert	Der Vogel im Wald			
Trunk	In meiner Heimat			
Wolf	Ach, im Maien	HL	C-E	†
-----	Bedeckt mich mit Blumen	HL	B-D	†
-----	Das grosse Karussell			
-----	Der Knabe und das Immlein	L	CS-A	†
-----	Fruehling uebers Jahr			PET
-----	Gleich und Gleich			†
-----	Ich hab' in Penna	LH		†
-----	Zum neuen Jahr			PET

Italian Recital Songs

Coloratura Soprano

Arditi	Il bacio	H	CS-B	†
-----	Parla	H	CS-CS	GSC
Bononcini	Deh, più a me non v'ascondete	LH	EF-F	†
-----	Per la gloria	HL	C-EF	†
-----	Più non ti voglio credere	H	D-AF	PET
-----	Si che fedele			DUR
Brogi	Le lucciole			
Buzzeleni	Si che morte			
Caccini	Amarilli, mia bella	ML	C-D	†
-----	Deh, dove son fuggite	M		CUR
-----	Tu ch'hai le penne, amore			
Castelnuovo-Tedesco	Orpheus	H		CHE
Cavalli	Donzelle fuggite	HL	C-EF	†
-----	In amor			DUR
Cesti	Intorno all'idol mio	MH	D-F	†
Cimara	Inutile precauzione Flute			
-----	Scherzo			
-----	Stornellata marinara	HM		RIC
-----	Stornello			BON
Cimarosa	Bel nume che adoro			RIC
D'Astorga	Vo' cercando in queste valli	H	D-G	STB
Defesch	Tu fai la superbetta			GSC

De Luca	Non posso disperar	HL	C-E	GSC
Donaudy	Perduto ho la speranza			
Donizetti	La zingara	H	DS-A	GSC
Gagliano	Dormi amore	HL	CS-E	DIT
Gasparini	Caro laccio, dolce nodo	M	EF-EF	GSC
-----	Lasciar d'amarti			
Gluck	O del mio dolce ardor	LH	D-FS	GSC
-----	Ritorna l'eta dell'oro (Il Trionfo di Clelia)			
Handel	Alma mia (Floridante)	HM	CS-E	†
-----	Care selve (Atalanta)	MH	FS-A	†
-----	Lusinghe più care (Alessandro)	H	D-G	†
-----	Mi restano le lagrime (Alcina)			BOO
-----	Parolette vezzi e squardi			
-----	Qual farfalletta (Partenope)	H	E-A	†
Haydn	Al tuo seno fortunato (Orfeo ed Euridice)			
Jommelli	Chi vuol comprar la bella	H	B-G	GSC
Legrenzi	Che fiero costume	HML	C-D	†
Malipiero	L'eco	H	E-G	CHE
Marchesi	La folletta	M		RIC
Mayr	La biondina in gondoleta			
Mozart	Ridente la calma			BOS
Paisiello	Chi vuol la zingarella	L	C-F	GSC
Paradies	Quel ruscelletto	L	BF-F	CFI
Pergolesi	Dite ch'ogni momento			BOS
-----	Nina	HL	CS-D	DIT
-----	Se tu m'ami	LMH	C-G	GSC
Pizzetti	I pastori			FRL
Porpora	Non più fra sassi			PET
Respighi	Scherzo			BON
-----	Son come farfalletta			BON
Ricci	Domi, domi del bambino			
Rode	Al dolce canto			
Rosa	Star vicino	HL	D-E	†
Rossini	La danza	MH	E-A	†
Santoliguido	Riflessi			FOR
Scarlatti, A.	Cara e dolce rimembranza			
-----	Già il sole dal Gange	LH	EF-F	GSC
-----	Rugiadose odorose	HL	D-E	DIT

34

(Scarlatti, A.)	Sento nel core	M	E-F	†
Sibella	La Girometta	HML	D-E	GSC
-----	O bimba bimbetta	LMH	D-G	GSC
Tirindelli	Primavera			
Tocchi	In riva al fiume			
-----	Serenata			
Tosti	'A vucchella	LH	F-G	RIC
Venzano	Grand waltz			

Russian Recital Songs

Coloratura Soprano

Alabieff	The nightingale	H	EF-C	†
	Flute			
Arensky	The little fish's song	H	D-A	†
-----	Valse	H	DF-GF	GSC
Glazounoff	The nereid	H	FS-A	GSC
Gretchaninoff	Il s' est tu, le charmant	H	EF-G	†
	rossignol			
-----	The snowdrop	HM	BF-F	DIT
Prokofieff	The gray eyed king			
Rachmaninoff	Before my window	HM	C-G	†
-----	Daisies			†
-----	Here beauty dwells	H	D-B	CFI
-----	Into my open window	HL	B-FS	BOS
-----	I wait for thee			
-----	Lilacs	LH	EF-G	†
-----	Oh cease thy singing,	H	E-A	CFI
	maiden fair			
-----	Sorrow in spring	H	D-BF	DIT
-----	The alder tree			
-----	The songs of Grusia	H	E-A	GSC
-----	Vocalise	LH	CS-A	GSC
Rimsky-Korsakov	The nightingale and the	H	FS-FS	DIT
	rose			
Rubinstein	The piper			
Stravinsky	Pastorale			GSC
-----	Russian maiden's song			
Tcherepnin	Quiet night			DIT
Vassilenko	Longing	H	E-A	DIT

Scandinavian Recital Songs

Coloratura Soprano

Bodenhoff	Bølge mod kyst			
Grieg	In the boat	LM	D-ES	†
-----	Pretty Margaret			
-----	Solvejg's cradle song	M	CS-FS	GSC
-----	Solvejg's song	MH	E-A	†
-----	The first meeting			PET
Kjerulf	Synnove's song	M	C-F	GSC
Sibelius	A dragon fly			
-----	From the north	H	DS-G	GSC
Weyse	Den store, stille natt			
-----	Teklas sang			
Winding	Den evige sne			

Spanish Recital Songs

Coloratura Soprano

Alvarez	La partida	HL	DS-E	GSC
Granados	Andalusia			
-----	El majo discreto	H		INT
-----	El tra la la y el punteado			INT
-----	Manañica era			
Lara	Granada			SOU
Lecuona	Lament			
Longas	Lavanderas			
-----	Mi jota			SEN
Nin	Montañesa			AMP
Obradors	Al amor			INT
-----	Coplas de curro dulce			
-----	La mi sola laureola			
Turina	Cantares			UME
-----	Cantilena	M	C-EF	UME
Valverde	Clavelitos	MH	E-F	GSC

Miscellaneous Recital Songs

Coloratura Soprano

Bach-Gounod	Ave Maria			
Bizet	Agnus dei	HLM	C-AF	†
Cherubini	Ave Maria	H	E-A	GSC

36

Chopin	My delight	HL		
-----	The birdling			JCH
Dvořák	The lark			
Mozart	Alleluia	LMH	F-C	

Songs and Arias for Opening Recitals

Coloratura Soprano

Anon	Dites, que faut-il faire?			
Bach, J. S.	Jauchzet Gott in allen			BRO
	Landen			
	(Cantata 51)			
Beethoven	Ich liebe dich	HL	BF-DF	†
Bononcini	Deh, più a me non	LH	EF-F	†
	v'ascondete			
Brahms	Nachtigall	MHL	BF-FS	†
Caccini	Amarilli, mia bella	ML	C-D	†
Cavalli	Donzelle fuggite	HL	C-EF	†
Cimara	Stornellata marinara	HM		RIC
Gluck	O del mio dolce ardor	LH	D-FS	GSC
	(Paride ed Elena)			
-----	Ritorna l'eta			
	dell' oro			
	(Il Trionfo di Clelia)			
Gretry	La fauvette avec ses			LEM
	petits			
	(Zémire et Azor) Flute			
Handel	Care selve	MH	FS-A	†
	(Atalanta)			
-----	Let the bright seraphim	H	E-A	†
	(Samson) Trumpet			
-----	O sleep why dost thou	H	DS-GS	†
	leave me			
	(Semele)			
-----	Sweet bird			NOV
	(L'Allegro) Flute			
Haydn	Al tuo seno fortunato			
	(Orfeo ed Euridice)			
-----	With verdure clad	H	E-BF	GSC
	(The Creation)			
Jommelli	Chi vuol comprar la bella	H	B-G	GSC
Mendelssohn	Fruehlingslied	H	DS-GS	†
Mozart	A questo seno, deh vieni			BOO
-----	Alleluja	LMH	F-C	†
-----	Batti, batti, o bel	H	C-BF	†
	Masetto			
	(Don Giovanni)			
				BOO

37

(Mozart)	Bella mia fiamma, addio			BOO
-----	Mia speranza adorata			
-----	Ridente la calma			BOS
Paisiello	Chi vuol la zingarella	L	C-F	GSC
Pergolesi	A lui donnai			
	(Il Flaminio)			
-----	Se tu m'ami	LMH	C-G	GSC
-----	Stizzoso, mio stizzoso	H	C-AF	†
	(La Serva Padrona)			
Porpora	Non più fra sassi			PET
Rosa	Star vicino	HL	D-E	†
Scarlatti, A.	Cara e dolce			
	rimembranza			
-----	Già il sole dal Gange	LH	EF-F	GSC
-----	Sento nel core	M	E-F	†
Schubert	Gott im Fruehling			PET
-----	Liebesbotschaft	H	E-G	†

American Songs for Closing Recitals

Coloratura Soprano

Branscombe	At the postern gate	MH	DF-AF	ASC
Cadman	Joy	MH	E-A	GSC
Carpenter	Serenade	LH	CS-A	GSC
Charles	And so, goodbye	LH	EF-AF	GSC
-----	Let my song fill your heart	LH	EF-AF	GSC
Clough- Leighter	My lover he comes on the skee	HM	D-F	BOS
Creston	Bird of the wilderness	MH	FS-A	GSC
Dougherty	Primavera	H	C-BF	GSC
Giannini	Sing to my heart a song	H	D-B	ELV
Hageman	At the well	LH	EF-AF	GSC
-----	Me company along	LH	F-BF	CFI
Horsman	The bird of the wilderness	LMH	DF-BF	GSC
La Forge	Cupid captive	H		GAL
Mana Zucca	There's joy in my heart!			CNG
Poldini	Dance of the dolls			CHM
Rorem	Alleluia			
Sacco	Rapunzel	MH	FS-BF	GSC
Saminsky	Queen Estherka's laugh	H	D-A	CFI
Ware	This day is mine	MH	EF-AF	BOS
Warren	Fulfilment	H	D-BF	GAL
-----	Who calls?	LH	E-A	CFI

Watts	Joy	HL	D-F	GSC
-----	Stresa	H	EF-BF	DIT

(See also Folk Songs)

Miscellaneous Songs for Closing Recitals

Coloratura Soprano

Alabieff	The nightingale Flute	H	EF-C	†
Besley	Listening	H	E-AF	CUR
Bliss	Three jolly gentlemen	H		†
Debussy	Chevaux de bois	H	C-G	†
Falla	Polo	HL		AMP
Head	A piper	HL		BOO
Hughes	The leprehaun			
Lara	Granada			
Obradors	Coplas de curro dulce			
Poulenc	Air vif	H	C-AF	ROU
Quilter	Love's philosophy	LMH	D-A	BOO
Ronald	Love, I have won you	HML	EF-EF	ENO
Schubert	Die Forelle	MLH	EF-GF	†
Schumann	Er ist's	HL	BF-EF	†
Strauss, J.	Blue Danube waltz			GSC
Strauss, R.	Staendchen	HM	A-FS	†

Atmospheric Songs and Arias

Coloratura Soprano

Barber	Secrets of old	LH	EF-G	GSC
-----	Sleep now	MH	EF-AF	GSC
Bizet	Douce mer			GSC
Crist	Into a ship dreaming	LMH	EF-GS	CFI
Davis	Nancy Hanks	H	D-G	GAL
Debussy	Nuits d'etoiles	LH	E-A	MAR
Delibes	Pourquoi dans les grands bois (Lakmé)	H	FS-AF	BRO
Duke	Bells in the rain	H	E-GS	CFI
-----	Little elegy	H	FS-A	GSC
Duparc	Soupir	HL	CS-F	BOS
Dvořák	The lark			
Forsyth	The stranger (Organ)	H	A-B	GRA
Ganz	The angels are stooping	MH	GF-A	GSC

39

Gounod	Sérénade	LMH	D-A	GSC
Handel	O sleep why dost thou leave me (Semele)	H	DS-GS	†
Kjerulf	Synnove's song	M	C-F	GSC
Kramer	Swans	HL		RIC
Marx	Marienlied	MH	EF-AF	AMP
Naginski	Look down, fair moon			
Niles	I wonder as I wander	HL	BF-D	GSC
Proctor	I light the blessed candles	H	DF-A	GSC
Rachmaninoff	Lilacs	LH	EF-G	†
Ravel	D'Anne jouant de l'espinette	H	CS-GS	GSC
Reger	The Virgin's slumber song	MMH	G-G	†
Schubert	An die Nachtigall	H	C-G	†
-----	Nachtviolen			PET
Schumann	Der Nussbaum	LMH	D-FS	†

Dramatic Songs and Arias

Coloratura Soprano

Alvarez	La partida	HL	DS-E	GSC
Bainton	The nightingale near the house			CUR
Besley	Listening	H	E-AF	CUR
Burleigh	By the pool at the third roses	H		RIC
Debussy	Chevaux de bois	H	C-G	†
-----	De fleurs	H	C-AF	†
-----	Noël des enfants qui n'ont plus de maisons			DUR
Dougherty	Primavera	H	C-BF	GSC
Geehl	For you alone			SHU
Giannini	Sing to my heart a song	H	D-B	ELV
Grieg	In the boat	LM	D-ES	†
Griffes	The rose of the night	H	CS-A	GSC
-----	Thy dark eyes to mine	H	EF-AF	GSC
-----	Waikiki	H	DS-GS	GSC
Hageman	Christ went up into the hills	LH	EF-AF	CFI
-----	Music I heard with you	MH	E-A	GAL
Handel	Let the bright seraphim (Samson) Trumpet	H	E-A	†
Horsman	The bird of the wilderness	LMH	DF-BF	GSC
Malotte	Among the living	LMH	E-G	GSC
Marx	Selige Nacht	M	DF-GF	AMP
Meyerbeer	Roberto, o tu che odoro	H	C-C	DEI

(Meyerbeer)	(Robert le Diable)			
Mozart	Der Hoelle Rache (Die Zauberfloete)	H	F-F	GSC
-----	Martern aller Arten (Abduction from Seraglio)	H	B-D	†
Poldowski	Dansons la gigue	M	EF-G	MAR
Rachmaninoff	Sorrow in spring	H	D-BF	DIT
Ronald	Down in the forest	HML	C-D	ENO
Severac	Chanson pour le petit cheval			ROU
Vene	Age and youth	H	E-A	RIC
Ware	This day is mine	MH	EF-AF	BOS
Warren	Fulfilment	H	D-BF	GAL

Humorous Songs

Coloratura Soprano

Bach, J. S.	Patron, das macht der Wind (Phoebus and Pan)	M	C-G	GSC
Bax	Oh dear what can the matter be?	M	D-EF	CHE
Bliss	Three jolly gentlemen	H		†
Boieldieu	Essayons s'il se peut de parler			LEM
Brahms	Vergebliches Staendchen	LHM	E-FS	†
Clarke	Shy one	HL	BF-G	BOH
Dalcroze	Le coeur de ma mie	HML		†
Debussy	Voici que le printemps	LH	CS-G	BOS
Duke	A piper	H	CS-B	GSC
Josten	Cupid's counsel	H	EF-AF	GSC
Lehmann	The cuckoo	HH	D-B	BOH
Mopper	The lemon-colored dodo	H	F-BF	BOS
Mozart	Durch Zaertlichkeit (Abduction from Seraglio)			†
-----	Warnung	HM	C-D	
Nordoff	Serenade	H	CS-FS	AMP
-----	There shall be more joy	M	CS-FS	AMP
Paisiello	Chi vuol la zingarella	L	C-F	GSC
Pergolesi	Stizzoso, mio stizzoso (La Serva Padrona)	H	C-AF	†
Pinkham	A partridge in a pear tree	H	D-BF	ROW
Powell	The deaf woman's courtship	M		JFI
Spross	Will o' the wisp			JCH
Strauss, J.	Adele's laughing song	H	D-B	GSC

(Strauss, J.)	(Die Fledermaus)			
Vene	The rats	H	E-A	RIC
Wolf	Jack in the box			
-----	Der Knabe und das Immlein	L	CS-A	†
-----	Ich hab' in Penna	LH		†

Folk Songs (Arr.)

Coloratura Soprano

Bacon	Careless love			
Bax	Oh dear what can the matter be?	M	D-EF	CHE
Britten	O can ye sew cushions?			BOH
-----	The Sally gardens			BOH
Falla	Asturiana	HL		AMP
-----	El pano moruno	HL		AMP
-----	Nana	HL		AMP
-----	Polo	HL		AMP
-----	Seguidilla murciana	HL		AMP
Ferrari	Le jardin d'amour	LM	EF-F	GSC
Hopekirk	Coming through the rye			DIT
-----	Flow gently, sweet Afton			DIT
Hughes	I know my love			BOO
-----	The leprehaun			
Kennedy-Fraser	Isle' of my heart			BOO
-----	Land of heart's desire			BOO
Liebling	Mother dear	H	D-E	GSC
McFeeters	Gentle Mary	H	EF-AF	GSC
Niles	Go 'way from my window	MH	C-G	GSC
-----	I wonder as I wander	HL	BF-D	GSC
-----	If I had a ribbon bow			GSC
Page	The meeting of the waters			DIT
Peel	The early morning			CHA
Powell	The deaf woman's courtship	M		JFI
Siegmeister	He's gone away			
Vaughan Williams	Rolling in the dew			OXF
Weckerlin	Maman, dites-moi	M	E-FS	BOS
-----	Menuet de Martino			
-----	Mon petit coeur soupire			

42

American Songs Employing Agility

Coloratura Soprano

Beach	Fairy lullaby			ASC
Buzzi-Peccia	Under the greenwood tree	LMH	EF-A	DIT
Charles	Let my song fill your heart	LH	EF-AF	GSC
Clough-Leighter	My lover he comes on on the skee	HM	D-F	BOS
Crist	O come hither	HM	B-GS	CFI
Curran	Ho! Mr. Piper	LH	D-G	GSC
Gaynor	Pierrot	H	E-B	BOS
La Forge	Come unto these yellow sands	H	FS-B	GSC
Lubin	The piper	H	C-A	GSC
Manning	Shoes	M	EF-F	GSC
Menotti	Lucy's arietta (The Telephone)			GSC
Nordoff	There shall be more joy	M	CS-FS	AMP
Parker	The lark now leaves her watery nest	LH	D-BF	JCH
Treharne	A widow bird sat mourning	H	FS-AF	BOS

British Songs and Arias Employing Agility

Coloratura Soprano

Arne, M.	The lass with the delicate air	MH	D-G	†
Arne, T.	Where the bee sucks	HM		†
Bainton	The nightingale near the house			CUR
Bax	Shieling song	H	CS-A	CHE
Benedict	The carnival of Venice	H	D-EF	GSC
-----	The gypsy and the bird Flute	H	D-E	GSC
-----	The wren Flute	H	F-C	PRE
Besley	Listening	H	E-AF	CUR
Bishop	Echo song Flute	H	D-C	GSC
-----	Lo! here the gentle lark Flute	H		†
-----	Love has eyes	M		†

43

(Bishop)	Pretty mocking bird Flute	H		†
-----	Should he upbraid	H		†
Bliss	Three jolly gentlemen	H		†
Carey	A pastoral			GSC
German	Charming Chloe	HML		NOV
Gibbs	To one who passed whistling through the night	H	F-G	CUR
Handel	Hallelujah (Esther)	H	E-B	CFI
-----	Let the bright seraphim (Samson) Trumpet	H	E-A	†
-----	Oh, had I Jubal's lyre (Joshua)	H	E-FS	GSC
-----	Rejoice Greatly (The Messiah)	H	E-A	†
-----	What's sweeter than a new blown rose? (Joseph)	H	EF-AF	†
Horn	Cherry ripe	M	D-G	†
Quilter	Love's philosophy	LMH	D-A	BOO
Scott	Blackbird's song			ELK

French Songs and Arias
Employing Agility

Coloratura Soprano

Adam	Ah vous dirais-je maman (Le Toreador) Flute			GSC
Auber	Quel bonheur (Fra Diavolo)			BOO
Bizet	Ouvre ton coeur	MH	DS-GS	†
-----	Vielle chanson	H	EF-A	GSC
Boieldieu	Essayons s'il se peut de parler			LEM
Campra	Charmant papillon (Les Fêtes Venitiennes)	MH	D-G	GSC
Chaminade	L'été	MH	E-A	†
Dalcroze	L'oiseau bleu			CFI
David	Charmant oiseau (La Perle du Bresil)	M	D-E	†
Debussy	Fêtes galantes	LH	CS-A	†
Delibes	Bell song (Lakmé)	MH	E-DS	†
-----	Chant de l'almée	H	D-E	GSC
-----	Les filles de Cadix	HM	A-A	†
-----	Passepied	LH	DS-CS	GSC

44

Dupont	Chanson des noisettes			HEU
Falla	Polo	HL		AMP
Ferrari	Le jardin d'amour	LM	EF-F	GSC
Gounod	Je veux vivre (Roméo et Juliette)	H	F-C	†
-----	Mon coeur ne peut changer! (Mireille)			GSC
-----	O légère hirondelle (Mireille)	H	FS-D	CFI
-----	Sérénade	LMH	D-A	GSC
Grétry	Je ne le dis qu'à vous (La Fausse Magie)			LEM
-----	La fauvette avec ses petits (Zémire et Azor) Flute			LEM
-----	Plus de dépit (Les Deux Avares)			LEM
Isouard	Non, je ne veux pas chanter (Le Billet de Loterie)			LEM
Massé	Air du rossignol (Les Noces de Jeannette) Flute			
-----	Sa couleur est blonde et vermeille (Galathée)			JCH
Massenet	Gavotte (Manon)			†
Meyerbeer	La, la, la air cheri (L'Etoile du Nord) Two flutes			BRA
-----	Shadow song (Dinorah)	H	DF-D	†
Milhaud	Tais-toi, Babillarde	H	G-C	BOH
Offenbach	Les oiseaux dans la charmille (Tales of Hoffman)	H	EF-EF	†
Poulenc	Air vif	H	C-AF	ROU
Ravel	Air du feu (L'Enfant et les Sortilèges)			DUR
Saint-Saëns	The nightingale and the rose	H	C-D	GSC
Thomas	Je connais un pauvre enfant (Mignon)	H	C-B	|
-----	Je suis Titania (Mignon)	H	C-EF	GSC
Vidal	Ariette	LH	F-A	GSC

German Songs and Arias
Employing Agility

Coloratura Soprano

Bach, J. S.	Jauchzet Gott in allen Landen (Cantata 51)			BRO
Beethoven	Mit einem gemalten Band			RIC
-----	O waer'ich schon mit dir vereint (Fidelio)			†
Brahms	Botschaft	HL	D-F	†
-----	Das Maedchen spricht	H	E-FS	†
Eckert	Swiss echo song	H	A-B	GSC
Haydn	My mother bids me bind my hair	M	E-E	†
-----	On mighty pens uplifted soars (The Creation)	H	E-A	†
Loewe	Niemand hat's gesehen	LM	DS-FS	†
Marx	Und gestern hat er mir Rosen gebracht	H	E-A	AMP
Mozart	Ach, ich liebte (Abduction from Seraglio)			†
-----	Der Hoelle Rache (Die Zauberfloete)	H	F-F	†
-----	Durch Zaertlichkeit (Abduction from Seraglio)			†
-----	Martern aller Arten (Abduction from Seraglio)	H	B-D	†
Proch	Theme and variations Flute	H	C-DF	†
Schubert	Auf dem Wasser zu singen	MH	EF-GF	†
-----	Der Hirt auf dem Felsen (Clarinet or violoncello	H	BF-B	GSC
-----	Liebesbotschaft	H	E-G	†
-----	Ungeduld	HML		†
Schumann	Auftraege	HL	C-E	†
Strauss, J.	Adele's laughing song (Die Fledermaus)	H	D-B	GSC
-----	Blue Danube Waltz			GSC
-----	Czardas (Die Fledermaus)			BOO
-----	Tales from the Vienna forest	H	EF-C	GSC
-----	Voci di primavera	LMH	EF-C	GSC
Strauss, R.	Staendchen	HM	A-FS	†
Weber	Truebe Augen (Der Freischuetz)			GSC

Italian Songs and Arias
Employing Agility

Coloratura Soprano

Arditi	Il bacio	H	CS-B	†
-----	Parla	H	CS-CS	GSC
Bellini	Ah! non credea mirarti			GSC
	(La Sonnambula)			
-----	Son vergin vezzosa	H	E-B	GSC
	(I Puritani)			
Bononcini	Deh, più a me non	LH	EF-F	†
	v'ascondete			
-----	Per la gloria	HL	C-EF	†
Cimarosa	Perdonate signor mio			RIC
	(Il Matrimonio Segreto)			
Defesch	Tu fai la superbetta			GSC
Donizetti	Chacun le sait	H	C-A	RIC
	(La Fille du Régiment)			
-----	Mad scene	H	FS-C	†
	(Lucia di Lammermoor)			
	Flute			
-----	O luce di quest' anima	H	C-E	GSC
	(Linda di Chamounix)			
-----	Prendi, prendi per mei			BRO
	sei libero			
	(L'Elisir d'Amore)			
-----	Quel guardo			BRO
	(Don Pasquale)			
Handel	Lusinghe più care	H	D-G	†
	(Alessandro)			
-----	Qual farfalletta	H	E-A	†
	(Partenope)			
Jommelli	Chi vuol comprar la bella	H	B-G	GSC
Mozart	Batti, batti, o bel	H	C-BF	†
	Masetto (Don Giovanni)			
-----	Ma che vi fece, o stelle			PET
-----	Mia speranza adorata			
-----	Misera, dove son			BOO
Paradies	Quel ruscelletto	L	BF-F	CFI
Porpora	Non più fra sassi			PET
Rossini	La danza	MH	E-A	†
-----	La pastorella delle Alpi	H	E-C	CFI
Scarlatti, A.	Già il sole dal Gange	LH	EF F	GSC
-----	Rugiadose odorose	HL	D-E	DIT
	(Il Pirro e Demetrio)			
Sibella	O bimba bimbetta	LMH	D-G	GSC
Veracini	Pastorale	MH	C-G	BOO
	(Rosalinda)			

47

Verdi	Ah fors' è lui	H	C-DF	†
-----	(La Traviata) Merce, dilette amiche	MH	A-CS	GSC
-----	(I Vespri Siciliani) Saper vorreste	H	D-B	GSC
-----	(Un Ballo in Maschera) Tacea la notte placida	H	D-DF	†
-----	(Il Trovatore) Volta la Terrea	H	D-BF	GSC
	(Un Ballo in Maschera)			

Miscellaneous Songs and Arias
Employing Agility

Coloratura Soprano

Alabieff	The nightingale	H	EF-C	†
	Flute			
Alvarez	La partida	HL	DS-E	GSC
Chopin	My delight	HL		
Falla	Nana	HL		AMP
-----	Seguidilla murciana	HL		AMP
Glazounoff	La primavera d'or	H	D-BF	GSC
Granados	El majo discreto	H		INT
Mozart	Alleluja	LMH	F-C	†
-----	Et incarnatus est			PET
	(C Minor Mass)			
Rimsky Korsakov	Hymn to the sun	H	FS-B	GSC
	(Le Coq d'Or)			
Rossini	Inflammatus			GSC
	(Stabat Mater)			
Stravinsky	Pastorale			GSC
Thrane	Norwegian echo song	H	D-B	GSC
Turina	Cantares			UME
-----	Cantilena	M	C-EF	UME

American Songs Employing
Crescendo and Diminuendo

Coloratura Soprano

Bacon	Is there such a thing as	M	DS-FS	AMP
	day?			
Barber	Secrets of old	LH	EF-G	GSC
-----	Sleep now	MH	EF-AF	GSC
-----	The daisies	M	C-F	GSC

48

Beach	Fairy lullaby			ASC
Carpenter	When I bring to you coloured toys	LM		GSC
Duke	Bells in the rain	H	E-GS	CFI
Lubin	The piper	H	C-A	GSC
Niles	I wonder as I wander	HL	BF-D	GSC
Nordoff	Fair Annette's song			AMP
-----	Serenade	H	CS-FS	AMP
Ware	By the fountain			FLA
Watts	Wings of night	LH	CS-G	GSC

British Songs and Arias Employing Crescendo and Diminuendo

Coloratura Soprano

Bantock	A dream of spring	H		CHE
Clarke	Shy one	HL	BF-G	BOH
Gibbs	To one who passed whistling through the night	H	F-G	CUR
Handel	As when the dove (Acis and Galatea)	H	D-G	†
-----	O sleep why dost thou leave me (Semele)	H	DS-GS	†
-----	Sweet bird (L' Allegro) Flute			NOV
-----	What's sweeter than a new blown rose? (Joseph)	H	EF-AF	†
Horn	Cherry ripe	M	D-G	†
Ireland	Bed in summer			CUR
Quilter	Dream valley	H	EF-GF	ROG
-----	To daisies			BOO

French Songs and Arias Employing Crescendo and Diminuendo

Coloratura Soprano

Auber	Quel bonheur (Fra Diavolo)			BOO
Bachelet	Chère nuit	H	DF-BF	GSC
Bizet	Vielle chanson	H	EF-A	GSC
Dalcroze	Le coeur de ma mie	HML		†
-----	L'oiseau bleu			CFI
David	Charmant oiseau (La Perle du Brésil)	M	D-E	†
Debussy	Green	H	C-AF	†

49

(Debussy)	Voici que le printemps	LH	CS-G	BOS
Duparc	Chanson triste	MH	FS-AF	†
-----	L'invitation au voyage	HM	E-F	†
Fauré	Clair de lune	MH	C-G	†
-----	Les roses d'Ispahan	HM	D-FS	†
-----	Nell	LH	FS-AF	†
-----	Sylvie	HL	E-F	†
Gounod	Le jour se lève			CHO
	(Mireille)			
Grétry	Je crains de lui			LEM
	(Richard Coeur-de-Lion)			
-----	Plus de dépit			LEM
	(Les Deux Avares)			
Hahn	Le rossignol des lilas			
Herold	Air de Nicette			BRA
	(Le Pré aux Clercs)			
Lalo	La chanson d'Alouette	H	EF-B	GSC
Liszt	Comment, disaient-ils?	H	C-AF	GSC
Massé	Air du rossignol			
	(Les Noces de Jeannette)			
	Flute			
Massenet	Gavotte (Manon)			†
-----	Je suis encore toute			HEU
	étourdie (Manon)			
Meyerbeer	Nobles seigneurs, salut!	LH	C-C	†
	(Les Huguenots)			
Saint-Saëns	Le bonheur est une chose	H	C-A	CHO
	légère			
	Violin and piano			

German Songs and Arias Employing Crescendo and Diminuendo

Coloratura Soprano

Beethoven	Mit einem gemalten			RIC
	Band			
-----	O waer' ich schon mit dir			†
	vereint (Fidelio)			
Brahms	Geheimnis			†
-----	Wie Melodien zieht es	HL	A-E	†
Haydn	On mighty pens uplifted	H	E-A	†
	soars (The Creation)			
Liszt	Kling' leise, mein Lied	HL		†
Mendelssohn	O for the wings of a dove	MLH	D-G	†
Mozart	Durch Zaertlichkeit			†
	(Abduction from Seraglio)			
Schubert	An die Laute	LH	D-F	†

(Schubert)	Auf dem Wasser zu singen	MH	EF-GF	†
-----	Das Lied im Gruenen			PET
-----	Das Rosenband			PET
-----	Der Knabe			PET
-----	Der Musensohn	LH	FS-G	†
-----	Der Schmetterling	LH	E-F	†
-----	Geheimes	HL	BF-EF	†
-----	Gott im Fruehling			PET
-----	Gretchen am Spinnrade	H	F-A	†
-----	Hark! hark! the lark	LMH	F-G	†
-----	Liebesbotschaft	H	E-G	GSC
-----	Wiegenlied (op. 98)			†
Schumann	Der Nussbaum	LMH	D-FS	†
-----	Die Meerfee			
-----	Intermezzo	HL	C-D	†
-----	Lieder der Braut	H	D-A	†
-----	Marienwuermchen	HL	D-D	†
-----	Schneegloeckchen	HL		†
-----	Volksliedchen	HL		†
Strauss	All' mein' Gedanken	H	CS-GS	
-----	Barcarolle	H	DF-BF	†
-----	Schlagende Herzen			†
Wolf	Der Knabe und das Immlein	L	CS-A	†
-----	Fruehling uebers Jahr			†
-----	Gleich und gleich			†

Italian Songs and Arias Employing Crescendo and Diminuendo

Coloratura Soprano

Bononcini	Per la gloria	HL	C-EF	†
-----	Si che fedele			DUR
Cavalli	In amor (Eritrea)			DUR
Cesti	Intorno all'idol mio (Orontea)	MH	D-F	†
De Luca	Non posso disperar	HL	C-E	GSC
Donizetti	Chacun le sait (La Fille du Régiment)	H	C-A	RIC
Handel	Mi restano le lagrime (Alcina)			BOO
Mozart	L'amero, saro costante (Il Re Pastore) Violin or flute	H	D-B	GSC
Pergolesi	Se tu m'ami	LMH	C-G	GSC
Scarlatti, A.	Sento nel core	M	E-F	†

51

Miscellaneous Songs Employing
Crescendo and Diminuendo

Coloratura Soprano

Arensky	The little fish's song	H	D-A	†
Dvořák	Songs my mother taugh me			†
Gretchaninoff	The snowdrop	HM	BF-F	DIT
Grieg	In the boat	LM	D-ES	†
-----	Solvejg's song			
Lilljebjorn	When I was seventeen			RIC
Rachmaninoff	Daisies			†
-----	Lilacs			
-----	Oh cease thy singing, maiden fair	H	E-A	CFI
-----	The songs of Grusia	H	E-A	GSC
-----	Vocalise	LH	CS-A	GSC
Stravinsky	Pastorale			GSC
Turina	Cantilena	M	C-EF	UME

American Songs Employing Piano Singing

Coloratura Soprano

Barber	Sleep now	MH	EF-AF	GSC
Burleigh	By the pool at the third roses	H		RIC
Crist	White hours like snow	HL	CS-BF	CFI
Davis	Nancy Hanks	H	D-G	GAL
Duke	Bells in the rain	H	E-GS	CFI
-----	Little elegy	H	FS-A	GSC
Ganz	The angels are stooping	MH	GF-A	GSC
Giannini	Tell me, o blue, blue sky	H		RIC
Griffes	In a myrtle shade	H	FS-A	GSC
-----	Thy dark eyes to mine	H	EF-AF	GSC
Kramer	Swans	HL		RIC
Manning	Shoes	M	EF-F	GSC
Niles	I wonder as I wander	HL	BF-D	GSC
Nordoff	Serenade	H	CS-FS	AMP
Watts	Stressa	H	EF-BF	DIT
-----	The little shepherd's song	H	G-BF	RIC

British Songs Employing Piano Singing

Coloratura Soprano

Arne, M.	The lass with the delicate air	MH	D-G	†

Bainton	The nightingale near the house			CUR
Bax	I heard a piper piping	LH	D-G	CFI
-----	Shieling song	H	CS-A	CHE
Brewer	The fairy pipers	HML		BOH
Clarke	Shy one	HL	BF-G	BOH
Gibbs	To one who passed whistling through the night	H	F-G	CUR
Head	A piper	HL		BOO
Ronald	Down in the forest	HML	C-D	ENO
Warlock	Pretty ring time	H	D-G	CFI

French Songs and Arias Employing
Piano Singing

Coloratura Soprano

Bizet	Douce mer			GSC
Dalcroze	Le coeur de ma mie	HML		†
Debussy	Clair de lune	M	CS-FS	JOB
-----	Fantoches	H	D-A	JOB
-----	Green	H	C-AF	†
-----	Harmonie du soir			DUR
-----	Il pleure dans mon coeur	LH	CS-GS	†
-----	L'ombre des arbres			†
-----	La mer est plus belle	HL		†
-----	Mandoline	HM	BF-F	†
-----	Nuits d'etoiles	LH	E-A	MAR
-----	Voici que le printemps	LH	CS-G	BOS
Delibes	Sous le ciel tout étoile (Lakmé)			HEU
Duparc	Extase	LMH	FS-A	†
-----	Soupir	HL	CS-F	BOS
Dupont	Mandoline			DUR
Fauré	Après un rêve	HM	C-F	†
-----	Clair de lune	MH	C-G	†
-----	La lune blanche	HL		†
-----	Notre amour	H	DS-B	†
-----	Sylvie	HL	E-F	†
Gounod	Sérénade	LMH	D-A	GSC
Grétry	Je ne fais semblant de rien (L'Ami de la Maison)			LEM
-----	Rose chérie (Zémire et Azor)			LEM
Hahn	Le rossignol des lilas			
Koechlin	L'air	M	F-FS	ROU
-----	La lune	M	C-F	ROU
-----	Le thé	HM	C-E	BOS

53

Liszt	Comment, disaient-ils?	H	C-AF	†
-----	Oh! quand je dors	H	E-A	†
Moret	Le nélumbo	H	E-DF	HEU
Poulenc	Air champêtre			ROU
-----	C. (J'ai traversé les ponts de C.)			ROU
Rabey	Tes yeux Violin and piano	H	EF-G	DUR
Ravel	D'Anne jouant de l'espinette	H	CS-GS	GSC
Saint-Saëns	Le bonheur est une chose H légère Violin and piano		C-A	CHO
Weckerlin	Je connais un berger discret	M	EF-EF	BOS
-----	Maman, dites-moi	M	E-FS	BOS

German Songs Employing
Piano Singing

Coloratura Soprano

Beethoven	Ich liebe dich	HL	BF-DF	†
Brahms	Auf dem Schiffe	LH	GS-A	†
-----	Botschaft	HL	D-F	†
-----	Das Maedchen spricht	H	E-FS	†
-----	Eine gute, gute Nacht			†
-----	Geheimnis			†
-----	Lerchengesang	LH	FS-GS	†
-----	Vergebliches Staendchen	LHM	E-FS	†
Jensen	Murmuring zephyr	LH	E-AF	GSC
Liszt	Kling' leise, mein Lied	HL		†
Marx	Marienlied	MH	EF-AF	AMP
-----	Selige Nacht	M	DF-GF	AMP
Schubert	An die Laute	LH	D-F	†
-----	Auf dem Wasser zu singen	MH	EF-GF	†
-----	Ave Maria	LMH	F-F	†
-----	Das Rosenband			PET
-----	Der Schmetterling	LH	E-F	†
-----	Du bist die Ruh	LMH	EF-AF	†
-----	Geheimes	HL	BF-EF	†
-----	Gott im Fruehling			PET
-----	Liebesbotschaft	H	E-G	GSC
-----	Nachtviolen			PET
-----	Wiegenlied (op. 98)			†
-----	Wohin?	HL	B-E	†
Schumann	Auftraege	HL	C-E	†
-----	Der Nussbaum	LMH	D-FS	†

(Schumann)	Die Meerfee			
-----	Marienwuermchen	HL	D-D	†
-----	Mondnacht	M	E-FS	†
-----	Volksliedchen	HL		†
Strauss, R.	All' mein' Gedanken	H	CS-GS	
-----	Barcarolle	H	DF-BF	†
Trunk	In meiner Heimat			
Wolf	Ach, im Maien	HL	C-E	†
-----	Fruehling uebers Jahr			†
-----	Gleich und gleich			†
-----	Schlafendes Jesuskind	HL	AS-F	†

Italian Songs and Arias Employing
Piano Singing

Coloratura Soprano

Bononcini	Deh, più a me non v'ascondete	LH	EF-F	†
d'Astorga	Vo' cercando in queste valli	H	D-G	STB
Donizetti	Mad scene (Lucia di Lammermoor) Flute	H	FS-C	
Gagliano	Dormi, amore (La Flora)	HL	CS-E	DIT
Gluck	O del mio dolce ardor (Paride ed Elena)	LH	D-FS	GSC
Handel	Care selve (Atalanta)	MH	FS-A	†
Jommelli	Chi vuol comprar la bella	H	B-G	GSC
Mozart	A questo seno, deh vieni			BOO
-----	Deh vieni non tardar (Le Nozze di Figaro)	H	A-A	†
-----	Non so più cosa son (Le Nozze di Figaro)	H	EF-G	†
	Un moto di gioja (Le Nozze di Figaro)			
Pizzetti	I pastori			FRL
Verdi	Addio del passato (La Traviata)			†
-----	Sul fil d'un soffio etesio (Falstaff)	H	DS-A	RIC

Miscellaneous Songs Employing
Piano Singing

Coloratura Soprano

Arensky	Valse	H	DF-GF	GSC
Dvořák	Songs my mother taught me			
Gretchaninoff	Hushed the song of the nightingale			DIT
Grieg	In the boat	LM	D-ES	†
-----	Solvejg's song	MH	E-A	†
Lie	Soft-footed snow	HM		DIT
Rachmaninoff	Before my window	HM	C-G	†
-----	Here beauty dwells	H	D-B	CFI

American Songs Employing
Rapid Enunciation

Coloratura Soprano

Bacon	Four songs	H	DF-G	MUP
Beach	The year's at the spring			ASC
Clough-Leighter	My lover he comes on the skee	HM	D-F	BOS
Curran	Ho! Mr. piper	LH	D-G	GSC
Griffes	Elves	H	F-AF	GSC
Hageman	At the well	LH	EF-AF	GSC
Hageman	Miranda	HL		GAL
Josten	Cupid's counsel	H	EF-AF	GSC
Manning	Shoes	M	EF-F	GSC
Spross	Will o' the wisp			JCH

British Songs Employing
Rapid Enunciation

Coloratura Soprano

Bantock	A feast of lanterns	HM	D-F	GAL
Bartlet	Whither runneth my sweetheart?			BOO
Bax	Oh dear, what can the matter be?	M	D-EF	CHE
Bishop	Love has eyes	M		†

56

(Bishop)	Pretty mocking bird Flute	H		†
Brewer	The fairy pipers	HML		BOH
German	Charming Choe	HML		NOV
Head	A piper	HL		BOO
Holst	A little music	H		AUG
Hughes	Hey diddle diddle			CRA
Morley	It was a lover and his lass			DIT

French Songs and Arias Employing Rapid Enunciation

Coloratura Soprano

Auber	L' eclat de rire (Manon Lescaut)			DUR
Dalcroze	L'oiseau bleu			CFI
Debussy	Chevaux de bois	H	C-G	†
-----	Fantoches	H	D-A	JOB
-----	Fêtes galantes	LH	CS-A	†
-----	Green	H	C-AF	†
-----	Mandoline	HM	BF-F	†
-----	Voici que le printemps	LH	CS-G	BOS
Delibes	Les filles de Cadox	HM	A-A	†
Dupont	Chanson des noisettes			HEU
Fauré	Notre amour	H	DS-B	†
-----	Sylvie	HL	E-F	†
Ferrari	Le Jardin d'amour	LM	EF-F	GSC
Hue	A des oiseaux	H	E-G	†
Koechlin	La lune	M	C-F	ROU
Milhaud	Tais-toi, Babillarde	H	G-C	BOH
Poldowski	Dansons la gigue	M	EF-G	MAR
Severac	Chanson pour le petit cheval			ROU
Vuillermoz	Jardin d' amours			SAL
Weckerlin	Maman, dites-moi	M	E-FS	BOS

German Songs and Arias Employing Rapid Enunciation

Coloratura Soprano

| Bach, J. S. | Patron, das macht der Wind (Phoebus and Pan) | M | C-G | GSC |
| Brahms | Das Maedchen spricht | H | E-FS | † |

(Brahms)	Vergebliches Staendchen	LHM	E-FS	†
Mendelssohn	Im Gruenen	H	E-BF	AUG
-----	Neue Liebe	H	CS-A	†
Mozart	Warnung	HM	C-D	
-----	Welche Wonne, welche Lust (Abduction from Seraglio)			†
Schubert	Das Lied im Gruenen			PET
-----	Der Musensohn	LH	FS-G	†
-----	Der Schmetterling	LH	E-F	†
-----	Die Forelle	MLH	EF-GF	†
-----	Ungeduld	HML		†
-----	Wohin?	HL	B-E	†
Schumann	Auftraege	HL	C-E	†
-----	Volksliedchen	HL		†
Strauss	Staendchen	HM	A-FS	†
Wolf	Ich hab' in Penna	LH		†

Italian Songs and Arias Employing
Rapid Enunciation

Coloratura Soprano

Bononcini	Si che fedele			DUR
Cavalli	Donzelle fuggite	HL	C-EF	†
Cimarosa	Perdonate signor mio (Il Matrimonio Segreto)			RIC
De Luca	Non posso disperar	HL	C-E	GSC
Durante	Danza, danza fanciulla gentile			†
Legrenzi	Che fiero costume	HML	C-D	†
Mozart	Non so più cosa son (Le Nozze di Figaro)	H	EF-G	†
Paisiello	Chi vuol la zingarella	L	C-F	GSC
Pergolesi	A Serpina penserete (La Serva Padrona)			
------	Stizzoso, mio stizzoso (La Serva Padrona)	H	C-AF	†
Rossini	La danza	MH	E-A	†
Tosti	'A vucchella	LH	F-G	RIC

Miscellaneous Songs Employing
Rapid Enunciation

Coloratura Soprano

Falla	Seguidilla Murciana	HL		AMP

Grieg	In the boat	LM	D-ES	†
-----	My Johann			
-----	With a water lilly			†

American Songs Employing
Sustained Singing

Coloratura Soprano

Bacon	Is there such a thing as day?	M	DS-FS	AMP
Barber	Sleep now	MH	EF-AF	GSC
Burleigh	By the pool at the third roses	H		RIC
-----	Were you there?	HML		RIC
Charles	And so, goodbye	LH	EF-AF	GSC
Crist	White hours like snow	HL	CS-BF	CFI
Ganz	The angels are stooping	MH	GF-A	GSC
Giannini	Tell me, o blue, blue sky	H		RIC
Griffes	In a myrtle shade	H	FS-A	GSC
-----	The rose of the night	H	CS-A	GSC
-----	Thy dark eyes to mine	H	EF-AF	GSC
Hageman	Music I heard with you	MH	E-A	GAL
Horsman	The bird of the wilderness	LMH	DF-BF	GSC
Kramer	Swans	HL		RIC
Sacco	Rapunzel	MH	FS-BF	GSC
Watts	Stresa	H	EF-BF	DIT
-----	The poet sings	MH	EF-AF	DIT

British Songs and Arias Employing
Sustained Singing

Coloratura Soprano

Bax	I heard a piper piping	LH	D-G	CFI
Britten	The Sally gardens			BOH
Handel	How beautiful are the feet of them (The Messiah)	H		†
-----	I know that my Redeemer liveth (The Messiah)	MH	E-GS	†
-----	O sleep why dost thou leave me (Semele)	H	DS-GS	†
-----	Sweet bird (L' Allegro) Flute			NOV
Purcell	Cease, o my sad soul			
-----	Had I but love			DUN
Quilter	To daisies			BOO

59

Ronald	Down in the forest	HML	C-D	ENO
-----	Prelude			ENO
-----	O lovely night	HML		BOO

French Songs and Arias Employing Sustained Singing

Coloratura Soprano

Bachelet	Chère nuit	H	DF-BF	GSC
Bizet	Comme autrefois dans la nuit sombre (Les Pêcheurs des Perles)			CHO
-----	Douce mer			GSC
-----	O dieu Brahma (Les Pêcheurs des Perles)	H	B-D	GSC
Debussy	Beau soir	LH	C-FS	†
-----	Clair de lune	M	CS-FS	JOB
-----	De fleurs	H	C-AF	†
-----	Harmonie du soir			DUR
-----	Il pleure dans mon coeur	LH	CS-GS	†
-----	L'ombre des arbres			†
-----	Nuits d'etoiles	LH	E-A	MAR
-----	Romance	HM	C-E	†
Délibes	Jours passés			GSC
-----	Sous le ciel tout étoile (Lakmé)			HEU
Duparc	Chanson triste	MH	FS-AF	†
-----	Extase	LMH	FS-A	†
-----	L'invitation au voyage	HM	E-F	†
-----	Soupir	HL	CS-F	BOS
Fauré	Après un rêve	HM	C-F	†
-----	La lune blanche	HL		†
-----	Les Roses d'Ispahan	HM	D-FS	†
-----	Rencontre	H	EF-AF	†
-----	Vocalise	H		LED
Gounod	Le jour se lève (Mireille)			CHO
Grétry	Rose chérie (Zémire et Azor)			LEM
Hahn	Le rossignol des lilas			
Koechlin	L'air	M	F-FS	ROU
Liszt	Oh! quand je dors	H	E-A	†
Massenet	Je suis encore tout étourdie (Manon)			HEU
Meyerbeer	Nobles Seigneurs, salut! (Les Huguenots)	LH	C-C	†

(Meyerbeer)	Roberto, o tu che odoro (Robert le Diable)	H	C-C	DEI
Moret	Le nélumbo	H	E-DF	HEU
Poulenc	C. (J'ai traversé les ponts de C.)			ROU
Rabey	Tes yeux Violin and piano	H	EF-G	DUR
Ravel	D'Anne jouant de l'espinette	H	CS-GS	GSC
Saint-Saëns	Aimons-nous			DUR

German Songs and Arias Employing Sustained singing

Coloratura Soprano

Beethoven	Ich liebe dich	HL	BF-DF	†
Brahms	Feldeinsamkeit	HL	C-EF	†
-----	Lerchengesang	LH	FS-GS	†
-----	Nachtigall	MHL	BF-FS	†
-----	Wie Melodien zieht es	HL	A-E	†
-----	Wir wandelten	LH	EF-GF	†
Haydn	With verdure clad (The Creation)	H	E-BF	†
Loewe	Canzonetta	MH	B-A	DIT
Marx	Marienlied	MH	EF-AF	AMP
-----	Nocturne	H	EF-AF	AMP
-----	Selige Nacht	M	DF-GF	AMP
Mendelssohn	Fruehlingslied	H	DS-GS	†
-----	O for the wings of a dove	MLH	D-G	†
-----	On wings of song			†
Mozart	Ach, ich fuehl's (Die Zauberfloete)	H	CS-BF	†
-----	Wiegenlied	MH	G-G	†
Schubert	An die Nachtigall	H	C-G	†
-----	Ave Maria	LMH	F-F	†
-----	Der Juengling an der Quelle	LH	E-A	†
-----	Du bist die Ruh	LMH	EF-AF	†
-----	Gretchen am Spinnrade	H	F-A	†
-----	Nachtviolen			PET
-----	Wiegenlied (op. 98)			†
Schumann	Der Nussbaum	LMH	D-FS	†
-----	Intermezzo	HL	C-D	GSC
-----	Lieder der Braut	H	D-A	†
-----	Mondnacht	M	E-FS	†
Strauss	Kornblumen	LH	DF-AF	†
-----	Liebeshymnus			†

Trunk	In meiner Heimat			
Wolf	Ach, im Maien	HL	C-E	†
-----	Bedeckt mich mit Blumen	HL	B-D	†
-----	Schlafendes Jesuskind	HL	AS-F	†

Italian Songs and Arias Employing
Sustained Singing

Coloratura Soprano

Braga	Angel's serenade Violin	LH	D-G	†
Caccini	Amarilli, mia bella	ML	C-D	†
Cesti	Intorno all'idol mio (Orontea)	MH	D-F	†
Cimara	Stornellata marinara	HM		RIC
Cimarosa	Bel nume che adoro			RIC
Donizetti	Regnava nel silenzio (Lucia di Lammermoor)	H	CS-D	GSC
Gagliano	Dormi amore (La Flora)	HL	CS-E	DIT
Gluck	O del mio dolce ardor (Paride ed Elena)	LH	D-FS	GSC
Handel	Care selve (Atalanta)	MH	FS-A	†
-----	Mi restano le lagrime (Alcina)			BOO
Mozart	Bella mia fiamma, addio			BOO
-----	Deh vieni non tardar (Le Nozze di Figaro)	H	A-A	†
-----	L'amero, saro costante (Il Re Pastore) Violin or flute	H	D-B	GSC
-----	Ridente la calma			BOS
Pergolesi	Dite ch'ogni momento			BOS
-----	Nina	HL	CS-D	DIT
Pizzetti	I pastori			FRL
Puccini	Musetta's waltz (La Boheme)	H	EF-BF	RIC
Rosa	Star vicino	HL	D-E	†
Rossini	Una voce poco fa (Il Barbiere di Siviglia)	HM	GS-E	GSC
Verdi	Addio del passato (La Traviata)			†
-----	Caro nome (Rigoletto)	H	DS-DS	†

Miscellaneous Songs Employing
Sustained Singing

Coloratura Soprano

Arensky	The little fish's song	H	D-A	†
-----	Valse	H	DF-GF	GSC
Bach-Gounod	Ave Maria			†
Cherubini	Ave Maria	H	E-A	GSC
Dvořák	The lark			
Gretchaninoff	The snowdrop	HM	BF-F	DIT
Grieg	I love Thee	HML	E-F	†
-----	Solvejg's song	MH	E-A	†
Kjerulf	Synnove's song	M	C-F	GSC
Lilljebjorn	When I was seventeen			RIC
Rachmaninoff	Before my window	HM	C-G	†
-----	Daisies			†
-----	Here beauty dwells	H	D-B	CFI
-----	Into my open window	HL	B-FS	BOS
-----	Oh cease thy singing, maiden fair	H	E-A	CFI
-----	Vocalise	LH	CS-A	GSC
Sibelius	From the north	H	DS-G	GSC

American Songs Employing
Spirited Singing

Coloratura Soprano

Brown	Love is where you find it (The Kissing Bandit)			
Buzzi-Peccia	Under the greenwood tree	LMH	EF-A	DIT
Carpenter	Serenade	LH	CS-A	GSC
Charles	Let my song fill your heart	LH	EF-AF	GSC
Clough-Leighter	My lover he comes on the skee	HM	D-F	BOS
Crist	O come hither	HM	B-GS	CFI
Curran	Ho! Mr. Piper	LH	D-G	GSC
Giannini	Sing to my heart a song	H	D-B	ELV
Griffes	Elves	H	F-AF	GSC
Hageman	At the well	LH	EF-AF	GSC
---------	Me company along	LH	F-BF	CFI
Josten	Cupid's counsel	H	EF-AF	GSC
Nordoff	There shall be more joy	M	CS-FS	AMP
Robyn	A heart that's free	MH	EF-AF	FEI
Saar	The little gray dove	MH	D-BF	GSC

63

Sacco	Rapunzel	MH	FS-BF	GSC
Spross	Will o' the wisp			JCH
Vene	The rats	H	E-A	RIC

British Songs and Arias Employing
Spirited Singing

Coloratura Soprano

Bantock	A feast of lanterns	HM	D-F	GAL
Bax	Oh dear what can the matter be?	M	D-EF	CHE
-----	Shieling song	H	CS-A	CHE
Besley	Listening	H	E-AF	CUR
Bishop	Lo! here the gentle lark Flute	H		†
-----	Love has eyes	M		†
-----	Should he upbraid	H		†
Bliss	Three jolly gentlemen	H		†
Brewer	The fairy pipers	HML		BOH
Carey	A pastoral			GSC
German	Charming Chloe	HML		NOV
Handel	Hallelujah (Esther)	H	E-B	CFI
-----	Rejoice greatly (The Messiah)	H	E-A	†
Head	A piper	HL		BOO
Lehmann	The cuckoo	HH	D-B	BOH
Quilter	Love's philosophy	LMH	D-A	BOO
Ronald	Love, I have won you	HML	EF-EF	ENO
Warlock	Pretty ring time	H	D-G	CFI

French Songs and Arias Employing
Spirited Singing

Coloratura Soprano

Auber	L' eclat de rire (Manon Lescaut)			DUR
Bizet	Ouvre ton coeur	MH	DS-GS	†
Chaminade	L'été	MH	E-A	†
Charpentier	Les chevaux de bois	H	E-A	HEU
Debussy	Chevaux de bois	H	C-G	†
-----	Fantoches	H	D-A	JOB
-----	Fêtes galantes	LH	CS-A	†
-----	La mer est plus belle	HL		†
-----	Le faune			DUR

(Debussy)	Mandoline	HM	BF-F	†
-----	Noël des enfants qui n'ont plus de maisons			DUR
Dupont	Mandoline			DUR
Fauré	Notre amour	H	DS-B	†
Gounod	Au printemps	LMH	DF-AF	GSC
-----	Je veux vivre (Roméo et Juliette)	H	F-C	†
-----	O légère hirondelle (Mireille)	H	FS-D	CFI
Grétry	Je ne fais semblant de rein (L' Ami de la Maison)			LEM
-----	La fauvette avec ses petits (Zémire et Azor) Flute			LEM
Hahn	Le printemps			
Isouard	Non, je ne veux pas chanter (Le Billet de Loterie)			LEM
Koechlin	La lune	M	C-F	ROU
-----	Le thé	HM	C-E	BOS
Massé	Sa couleur est blonde et vermeille (Galathée)			JCH
Meyerbeer	Shadow song (Dinorah)	H	DF-D	†
Milhaud	Tais-toi, Babillarde	H	G-C	BOH
Pierné	La moulin	ML	C-E	BOS
Poldowski	Dansons la gigue	M	EF-G	MAR
Poulenc	Air champêtre			ROU
-----	Air vif	H	C-AF	ROU
Ravel	Air du feu (L'Enfant et les Sortilèges)			DUR
Severac	Chanson pour le petit cheval			ROU
Thomas	Je connais un pauvre enfant (Mignon)	H	C-B	†
Vidal	Ariette	LH	F-A	GSC
Vuillermoz	Jardin d'amours			SAL

German Songs and Arias Employing
Spirited Singing

Coloratura Soprano

Bach, J. S.	Jauchzet Gott in allen Landen (Cantata 51)			BRO
-----	Patron, das macht der Wind (Phoebus and Pan)	M	C-G	GSC
Brahms	Auf dem Schiffe	LH	GS-A	†

65

(Brahms)	Botschaft	HL	D-F	†
-----	Das Maedchen spricht	H	E-FS	†
-----	Es liebt sich so lieblich im Lenze	LH	D-GS	†
-----	Vergebliches Staendchen	LHM	E-FS	†
Eckert	Swiss echo song	H	A-B	GSC
Haydn	O how pleasing to the senses (The Seasons)	H		†
Jensen	Murmuring zephyr	LH	E-AF	GSC
Loewe	Niemand hat's gesehen	LM	DS-FS	†
Marx	Und gestern hat er mir Rosen gebracht	H	E-A	AMP
Mendelssohn	Fruehlingslied	H	DS-GS	†
-----	Im Gruenen	H	E-BF	AUG
-----	Neue Liebe	H	CS-A	†
-----	O Jugend	H	E-A	†
Mozart	Ach, ich liebte (Abduction from Seraglio)			†
-----	Martern aller Arten (Abduction from Seraglio)	H	B-D	†
Schubert	Die Forelle	MLH	EF-GF	†
-----	Rastlose Liebe	M	B-F	†
-----	Wohin?	HL	B-E	DIT
Schumann	Auftraege	HL	C-E	†
-----	Er ist's	HL	BF-EF	†
-----	Geisternaehe			
Strauss, J.	Adele's laughing song (Die Fledermaus)	H	D-B	GSC
-----	Tales from the Vienna forest	H	EF-C	GSC
-----	Voci di primavera	LMH	EF-C	GSC
Strauss, R.	Schlechtes Wetter			†
-----	Staendchen	HM	A-FS	†
Wolf	Ach, im Maien	HL	C-E	†
-----	Ich hab' in Penna	LH		†
-----	Zum neuen Jahr			PET

Italian Songs and Arias Employing
Spirited Singing

Coloratura Soprano

Arditi	Il bacio	H	CS-B	
-----	Parla	H	CS-CS	GSC
Bellini	Ah! non credea mirarti (La Sonnambula)			GSC
-----	Son vergin vezzosa (I Puritani)	H	E-B	GSC

66

Cavalli	Donzelle fuggite	HL	C-EF	†
Cimarosa	Perdonate signor mio (Il Matrimonio Segreto)			RIC
D'Astorga	Vo' cercando in queste valli	H	D-G	STB
Donizetti	Prendi, prendi per mei sei libero (L' Elisir d'Amore)			BRO
-----	Regnava nel silenzio (Lucia di Lammermoor)	H	CS-D	GSC
Handel	Lusinghe più care (Alessandro)	H	D-G	†
-----	Qual farfalletta (Partenope)	H	E-A	†
Legrenzi	Che fiero costume	HML	C-D	
Mozart	A questo seno, deh vieni			BOO
-----	Non so più cosa son (Le Nozze di Figaro)	H	EF-G	
-----	Un moto di gioja (Le Nozze di Figaro)			
Paisiello	Chi vuol la zingarella	L	C-F	GSC
Pergolesi	Stizzoso, mio stizzoso (La Serva Padrona)	H	C-AF	†
Porpora	Non più fra sassi			PET
Respighi	Scherzo			BON
Rossini	La pastorella delle Alpi	H	E-C	CFI
-----	Una voce poco fa (Il Barbiere di Siviglia)	HM	GS-E	GSC
Scarlatti, A.	Già il sole dal Gange	LH	EF-F	GSC
Veracini	Pastorale (Rosalinda)	MH	C-G	BOO
Verdi	Merce, dilette amiche (I Vespri Siciliani)	MH	A-CS	GSC

Miscellaneous Songs Employing
Spirited Singing

Coloratura Soprano

Alabieff	The nightingale Flute	H	EF-C	†
Dvořak	The lark			
-----	Tune thy fiddle gypsy			SIM
Falla	El paño moruno	HL		AMP
-----	Seguidilla murciana	HL		AMP
Glazounoff	La primavera d'or	H	D-BF	GSC
Granados	El majo discreto	H		INT
Grieg	My Johann	H		†

67

Rachmaninoff	Sorrow in spring	H	D-BF	DIT
Thrane	Norwegian echo song	H	D-B	GSC
Turina	Cantares			UME
Turina	Madrigal	H	D-BF	UME

Songs and Arias Employing Staccato

Coloratura Soprano

Arne, M.	The lass with the delicate air	MH	D-B	
Arne, T.	Where the bee sucks	HM		†
Delibes	Bell song (Lakmé)	MH	E-DS	†
-----	Les filles de Cadix	HM	A-A	†
-----	Passepied	LH	DS-CS	GSC
Dupont	Chanson des noisettes			HEU
Gaynor	Pierrot	H	E-B	BOS
Grieg	Solvejg's song	MH	E-A	†
Handel	Oh, had I Jubal's lyre (Joshua)	H	E-FS	†
Haydn	My mother bids me bind my hair	M	E-E	†
La Forge	Come unto these yellow sands	H	FS-B	GSC
Liadoff	The musical snuff box	H	CS-D	GSC
Mozart	Der Hoelle Rache (Die Zauberfloete)	H	F-F	†
Offenbach	Les oiseaux dans la charmille (Tales of Hoffman)	H	EF-EF	†
Saminsky	Queen Estherka's laugh	H	D-A	CFI
Scarlatti, A.	Rugiadose odorose (Il Pirro e Demetrio)	HL	D-E	DIT
Schubert	Der Juengling an der Quelle	LH	E-A	†
Sibella	La Girometta	HML	D-E	GSC
-----	O bimba bimbetta	LMH	D-G	GSC
Strauss	Zerbinetta's aria (Ariadne auf Naxos)			BOO
Thomas	Je suis Titania (Mignon)	H	C-EF	†
Verdi	Tacea la notte placida (Il Trovatore)	H	D-DF	†
Watts	The little shepherd's song	H	G-BF	RIC
Weckerlin	Maman, dites-moi	M	E-FS	BOS

American and British Songs
of Popular Appeal

Coloratura Soprano

Arne, M.	The lass with the delicate air	MH	D-G	†
Benedict	The carnival of Venice	H	D-EF	GSC
-----	The gypsy and the bird Flute	H	D-E	GSC
-----	The wren Flute	H	F-C	PRE
Besley	The second minuet	HL		BOO
Bishop	Echo song Flute	H	D-C	GSC
-----	Lo! here the gentle lark Flute	H		†
- ----	Love has eyes	M		†
-----	Pretty mocking bird Flute	H		†
Buzzi-Peccia	Little birdies			
-----	Under the greenwood tree	LMH	EF-A	DIT
Cadman	Joy	MH	E-A	GSC
Carey	A pastoral			GSC
Charles	And so, goodbye	LH	EF-AF	GSC
-----	Let my song fill your heart	LH	EF-AF	GSC
Clarke	Shy one	HL	BF-G	BOH
Curran	Dawn	LMH	E-BF	GSC
----	Ho! Mr. Piper	LH	D-G	GSC
D'Hardelot	Because	MH	E-G	CHA
Dostal	I am in love			
Friml	L'amour, toujours, l'amour			HAR
Gaynor	May magic			
German	Who'll buy my lavender	HML		BOO
Giannini	Sing to my heart a song	H	D-B	ELV
Grothe	I am dreaming about one only			
Kaufman	In your eyes I find all my fortune			
Lehmann	The cuckoo	HH	D-B	BOH
Manning	Shoes	M	EF-F	GSC
Melichar	I was never in love as much as today			WEI
-----	This is the finest day in my life			
Mopper	The lemon-colored dodo	H	F-BF	BOS
Poldini	Dance of the dolls			CHM
Rasbach	Promise	LH	AF-BF	GSC

Robyn	A heart that's free	MH	EF-AF	FEI
Ronald	Down in the forest	HML	C-D	ENO
-----	O lovely night	HML		BOO
Rybner	Pierrot	HL		GSC
Saar	The little gray dove	MH	D-BF	GSC
Scott	Blackbird's song			ELK
Silesu	Love, here is my heart	M		FEI
Spross	Will o' the wisp			JCH
Ware	By the fountain			FLA
-----	This day is mine	MH	EF-AF	BOS
Warren	Fulfilment	H	D-BF	GAL
-----	If you feel like singing			WAR
-----	My lady Lo-Fu			DIT
Wolf	Jack in the box			
Woodman	A birthday	LH	F-BF	GSC
-----	Love's in my heart	LH	F-BF	GSC

(See also Humorous Songs, Negro Spirituals,
Folk Songs, Operetta Songs and Opera Arias.)

Miscellaneous Songs of
Popular Appeal

Coloratura Soprano

Acqua	Chanson provencale	H	D-BF	GSC
-----	Villanelle	H	EF-D	GSC
Adam	Variations on a nursery theme			GSC
Alabieff	The nightingale Flute	H	EF-C	†
Alvarez	La partida	HL	DS-E	GSC
Arditi	Il bacio	H	CS-B	†
-----	Parla	H	CS-CS	GSC
Bach-Gounod	Ave Maria			†
Bizet	Agnus Dei	HLM	C-AF	†
-----	Ouvre ton coeur	MH	DS-GS	†
Braga	Angel's serenade Violin	LH	D-G	†
Buzzi-Peccia	El morenito	LMH	F-G	GSC
Cavalli	Donzelle fuggite	HL	C-EF	†
D'Albert	Zur Drossel sprach der Fink			
Dalcroze	Le coeur de ma mie	HML		†
Délibes	Chant de l' almée	H	D-E	GSC
-----	Coppelia waltz	H	BF-BF	GSC
-----	Les filles de Cadix	HM	A-A	†
-----	Passepied	LH	DS-CS	GSC

70

Denza	Funiculi, funicula			†
Eckert	Swiss echo song	H	A-B	GSC
Freire	Ay, ay, ay	LH		RIC
Glazounoff	La primavera d'or	H	D-BF	GSC
Gounod	Au printemps	LMH	DF-AF	GSC
-----	Sérénade	LMH	D-A	GSC
Grieg	Solvejg's song	MH	E-A	†
Hue	A des oiseaux	H	E-G	†
Lara	Granada			SOU
Lecuona	Andalucia			MAR
Liadoff	The musical snuff box	H	CS-D	GSC
Lilljebjorn	When I was seventeen			RIC
Mendelssohn	On wings of song			†
Moret	Le nélumbo	H	E-DF	HEU
Mozart	Alleluja	LMH	F-C	†
Pestalozza	Ciribiribin			DIT
Proch	Theme and variations	H	C-DF	†
	Flute			
Rabey	Tes yeux	H	EF-G	DUR
	Violin and piano			
Rimsky-Korsakov	The nightingale and the	H	FS-FS	DIT
	rose			
Rossini	La danza	MH	E-A	†
-----	La pastorella delle Alpi	H	E-C	CFI
Saint-Saëns	La libellule	H	C-D	DUR
Schubert	Ave Maria	LMH	F-F	†
-----	Hark! hark! the lark	LMH	F-G	†
Sibella	La Girometta	HML	D-E	GSC
Sleczynski	Vienna, city of my dreams			HAR
Strauss, J.	Blue Danube waltz			GSC
-----	Kaiser waltz			
-----	Tales from the Vienna	H	EF-C	GSC
	forest			
-----	Voci di Primavera	LMH	EF-C	GSC
-----	Wein, Weib und Gesang			
-----	Wiener Blut			
Thrane	Norwegian echo song	H	D-B	GSC
Tosti	'A vucchella	LH	F-G	RIC
Veracini	Pastorale	MH	C-G	BOO
	(Rosalinda)			
Weber	Invitation to the dance	H	EF-EF	GSC
Yradier	La paloma	HL	BF-EF	GSC

(See also Humorous Songs, Negro Spirituals,
Folk Songs, Operetta Songs and Opera Arias.)

Coloratura Soprano

Adam	Ah vous dirais-je maman (Le Toreador) Flute			GSC
Auber	L'eclat de rire (Manon Lescaut)			DUR
-----	Quel bonheur (Fra Diavolo)			BOO
Bizet	Comme autrefois dans la nuit sombre (Les Pêcheurs des Perles)			CHO
-----	O dieu Brahma (Les Pêcheurs des Perles)	H	B-D	GSC
Campra	Charmant papillon (Les Fêtes Vénitiennes)	MH	D-G	GSC
David	Charmant oiseau (La Perle du Brésil)	M	D-E	†
Delibes	Bell song (Lakmé)	MH	E-DS	†
-----	Pourquoi dans les grands bois (Lakmé)	H	FS-AF	BRO
-----	Sous le ciel tout étoile (Lakmé)			HEU
-----	Tu m'as donné le plus doux rêve (Lakmé)			BRO
Gounod	Je veux vivre (Roméo et Juliette)	H	F-C	†
-----	Le jour se lève (Mireille)			CHO
-----	Mon coeur ne peut changer! (Mireille)			GSC
-----	O légère hirondelle (Mireille)	H	FS-D	CFI
Grétry	Je crains de lui (Richard Coeur-de-Lion)			LEM
-----	Je ne fais semblant de rein (L'Ami de la Maison)			LEM
-----	Je ne le dis qu'à vous (La Fausse Magie)			LEM
-----	La fauvette avec ses petits (Zémire et Azor) Flute			LEM
-----	Plus de dépit (Les Deux Avares)			LEM
-----	Rose chérie (Zémire et Azor)			LEM
Lecocq	Le punch scintille (Girofle)			

Massé	Air du rossignol (Les Noces de Jeannette) Flute			
-----	Cours mon aiguille dans le laine (Les Noces de Jeanette)			
-----	Sa couleur est blonde et vermeille (Galathée)			JCH
Massenet	Gavotte (Manon)			†
-----	Je suis encore tout etourdie (Manon)			HEU
-----	Sévillana (Don Cesar da Bazan)			HEU
Meyerbeer	La, la, la air cheri (L'Etoile du Nord) Two flutes			BRA
-----	Nobles Seigneurs, salut! (Les Huguenots)	LH	C-C	†
-----	Roberto, o tu che adoro (Robert le Diable)	H	C-C	DEI
-----	Shadow song (Dinorah)	H	DF-D	†
Offenbach	Les oiseaux dans la charmille (Tales of Hoffman)	H	EF-EF	†
Ravel	Air du feu (L'Enfant et les Sortilèges)			DUR
Thomas	Je connais un pauvre enfant (Mignon)	H	C-B	†
-----	Je suis Titania (Mignon)	H	C-EF	†

Arias from German Operas

Coloratura Soprano

Beethoven	O waer' ich schon mit dir veroint (Fidelio)			†
Mozart	Ach, ich fuehl's (Die Zauberfloete)	H	CS-BF	†
-----	Ach, ich liebte (Abduction from Seraglio)			†
-----	Der Hoelle Rache (Die Zauberfloete)	H	F-F	†
-----	Durch Zaertlichkeit (Abduction from Seraglio)			†
-----	Martern aller Arten (Abduction from Seraglio)	H	B-D	†

73

(Mozart)	Welche Wonne, welche Lust (Abduction from Seraglio)			†
Strauss, R.	Zerbinetta's aria (Ariadne auf Naxos)			BOO
Weber	Truebe Augen (Der Freischuetz)			GSC

Arias From Italian Operas

Coloratura Soprano

Bellini	Ah! non credea mirarti (La Sonnambula)			GSC
-----	Qui la voce (I Puritani)	H	EF-DF	GSC
-----	Son vergin vezzosa (I Puritani)	H	E-B	GSC
Donizetti	Chacun le sait (La Fille du Régiment)	H	C-A	RIC
-----	Il faut partir (La Fille du Régiment)	H	E-C	GSC
-----	Mad scene (Lucia di Lammermoor) Flute	H	FS-C	†
-----	O luce di quest' anima (Linda di Chamounix)	H	C-E	GSC
-----	Prendi, prendi per mei sei libero (L' Elisir d'Amore)			BRO
-----	Quel guardo (Don Pasquale)			BRO
-----	Regnava nel silenzio (Lucia di Lammermoor)	H	CS-D	GSC
-----	Salut à la France (La Fille du Régiment)			NOV
Flotow	Qui sola, vergin rosa (Martha)			BRO
Gagliano	Dormi amore (La Flora)	HL	CS-E	DIT
Giordano	Brilla sulla mia fronte (Il Re)			SON
Mascagni	Flammen perdonami (Lodoletta)			SON
Mozart	Batti, batti, o bel Masetto (Don Giovanni)	H	C-BF	†
-----	Deh vieni non tardar (Le Nozze di Figaro)	H	A-A	†

(Mozart)	L'amero, saro costante (Il Re Pastore) Violin or flute	H	D-B	GSC
-----	Non so più cosa son (Le Nozze di Figaro)	H	EF-G	†
-----	Un moto di gioja (Le Nozze di Figaro)			
Pergolesi	A lui donnai (Il Flaminio)			
-----	Stizzoso, mio stizzoso (La Serva Padrona)	H	C-AF	†
Ponchielli	La madre mia (Lina)			
Puccini	Musetta's waltz (La Boheme)	H	EF-BF	RIC
Rossini	Sombre forêt (Guillaume Tell)			
-----	Una voce poco fa (Il Barbiere di Siviglia)	HM	GS-E	GSC
Verdi	Addio del passato (La Traviata)			†
-----	Ah fors'è lui (La Traviata)	H	C-DF	†
-----	Caro nome (Rigoletto)	H	DS-DS	†
-----	Merce, dilette amiche (I Vespri Siciliani)	MH	A-CS	GSC
-----	Saper vorreste (Un Ballo in Maschera)	H	D-B	GSC
-----	Sul fil d'un soffio etesio (Falstaff)	H	DS-A	RIC
-----	Tacea la notte placida (Il Trovatore)	H	D-DF	†
-----	Volta la terrea (Un Ballo in Maschera)	H	D-BF	GSC
Zandonai	Paolo datemi pace (Francesca da Rimini)			RIC

Miscellaneous Opera Arias

Coloratura Soprano

Gershwin	Summertime (Porgy and Bess)	
Granados	Descúbrase el pensamiento (Goyescas)	GSC
Menotti	Lucy's arietta (The Telephone)	

Rimsky-Korsakov	Hymn to the sun (Le Coq d'Or)	H	FS-B	GSC
-----	Martha's air (The Tsar's Bride)			
-----	Song of India (Sadko)	LH	D-G	GSC

Arias From Oratorios and Latin Works

Coloratura Soprano

Beethoven	O praise him (Mount of Olives)			
Gaul	These are they (The Holy City)	H	E-GS	GSC
Handel	Hallelujah (Esther)	H	E-B	CFI
-----	How beautiful are the feet of them (The Messiah)	H		†
-----	I know that my Redeemer liveth (The Messiah)	MH	E-GS	†
-----	Let the bright seraphim (Samson) Trumpet	H	E-A	†
-----	Oh, had I Jubal's lyre (Joshua)	H	E-FS	†
-----	O sleep, why dost thou leave me? (Semele)	H	DS-GS	†
-----	Rejoice greatly (The Messiah)	H	E-A	†
-----	Sweet bird (L'Allegro) Flute			NOV
-----	What's sweeter than a new blown rose? (Joseph)	H	EF-AF	†
Haydn	O how pleasing to the senses (The Seasons)	H		†
-----	On mighty pens uplifted soars (The Creation)	H	E-A	†
-----	With verdure clad (The Creation)	H	E-BF	GSC
Mozart	Et incarnatus est (C Minor Mass)			PET
Rossini	Inflammatus (Stabat Mater)			GSC

Cantata Arias

Coloratura Soprano

Bach, J. S.	Hoert doch der sanften Floeten (Cantata 206) 3 Flutes and continuo			
-----	Patron, das macht der Wind (Phoebus and Pan)	M	C-G	GSC
-----	Sheep may safely graze (Cantata 208) 2 Flutes and continuo	LM	EF-GF	GAL

Operetta, Musical Comedy or Show Songs

Coloratura Soprano

Brown	Love is where you find it (The Kissing Bandit)			
Coward	I'll follow my secret heart (Conversation Piece)	M	A-FS	CHA
-----	I'll see you again (Bitter Sweet)	M	C-F	HAR
Friml	Donkey Serenade (The Firefly)			WIT
Herbert	Kiss me again (Mlle. Modiste)	LHM	CS-A	WIT
-----	Romany life (The Fortune Teller)			WIT
Herold	Air de Nicette (Le Pré aux Clercs)			BRA
Kern	All the things you are (Very Warm for May)	M	BF-F	HAR
-----	I dream too much (I Dream Too Much)			CHA
-----	I'm the echo (I Dream too Much)			CHA
Milloecker	Komm, mia bella (Gasparone)	M		SC
Romberg	One kiss (New Moon)			HAR
-----	Romance (The Desert Song)	H	D-BF	HAR
Strauss, J.	Adele's laughing song (Die Fledermaus)	H	D-B	GSC

(Strauss, J.)	Czardas			BOO
	(Die Fledermaus)			
--------	One thousand and one			
	nights (Indigo)			
-----	Southern Roses			
	(Spitzentuch der Koenigin)			

Song Cycles (Or groups of songs)

Coloratura Soprano

Alberti	Four sketches from the	HM	C-F	GSC
	Far East			
Berger	Villanescas	H	CS-B	GSC
Debussy	Fêtes galantes	LH	CS-A	†
-----	Proses lyriques	HL		JOB
Falla	Siete Canciones	HL		AMP
Schumann	Lieder der Braut	H	D-A	†
Stravinsky	Three bird songs			
-----	Three Japanese			RUM
	lyrics for Voice, piano,			
	string quartets, 2 flutes,			
	and 2 clarinets			

Solo Cantatas

Coloratura Soprano

Bach, J.S.	Jauchzet Gott in allen	BRO
	Landen (Cantata 51)	
Scarlatti, A.	Solitude ameni apriche	
	Collinette	

(See Solo Cantatas of Pergolesi, Handel and Scarlatti,
Kirchenkantaten of Buxtehude and Symphoniae Sacrae
of Schuetz.)

Concert Arias

Coloratura Soprano

Mozart	A questo seno, deh vieni	BOO
-----	Bella mia fiamma, addio	BOO
-----	Ma che vi fece, o stelle	PET
-----	Mia speranza adorata	
-----	Misera, dove son	BOO
-----	Non temer amato bene	BOO

Christmas Songs

Coloratura Soprano

Benjamin	Before dawn			CUR
Black	In the sky a wondrous star	H	DF-AF	GRA
Dickinson	The shepherds' story	H		GRA
Dougherty	The first Christmas	H	D-A	GSC
Forsyth	The Child Jesus Organ	H	EF-B	GRA
Hageman	Christmas eve	HML	BF-EF	GAL
Handel	How beautiful are the feet of them (The Messiah)	H		†
-----	Rejoice greatly (The Messiah)	H	E-A	†
Harris	The holy infant	H	G-AF	GAL
Head	The little road to Bethlehem	MH	EF-AF	BOO
Kaull	Unto you is born a Savior	MH	D-AF	BOS
Martin	The Holy Child	HML	G-G	ENO
McKinney	The Holy Mother sings	MH	AF-AF	JFI
Ohlson	The vigils of Mary	H		GSC
Pinkham	A partridge in a pear tree	H	D-BF	ROW
Reger	The Virgin's slumber song	MMH	G-G	†
Sadero	Fa la nana, bambin			RIC
Schubert	Ave Maria	LMH	F-F	†
Trunk	Mary	HM		AMP
Warren	Christmas candle	HML	D-E	GSC
Wolf	Schlafendes Jesuskind	HL	AS-F	

Easter Songs

Coloratura Soprano

Barnes	Easter	HM	D-EF	GSC
Curran	Crucifixion			
Dennee	Easter song	HM	B-F	ASC
Granier	Hosanna	HH	F-BF	DIT
Hageman	Christ went up into the hills	LH	EF-AF	CFI
Handel	I know that my Redeemer liveth (The Messiah)	MH	E-GS	†
Huhn	Christ is risen	HM	C-E	ASC

79

Lekberg	A ballad of trees and the Master	H	E-A	GAL
Ohlson	The vigils of Mary	H		GSC
Rossini	Inflammatus (Stabat Mater)			GSC
Schubert	Ave Maria	LMH	F-F	†
Scott	Angels roll the rock away	MH	E-G	HUN
Ward Stephens	Christ triumphant	MH	F-AF	CHA

Patriotic Songs

Coloratura Soprano

Alberti	A nation's prayer	H		ELV
Cadman	Glory	H	EF-G	GAL
Dungan	Eternal life	HL		PRE
Howe	To the unknown soldier	H	D-G	GSC
Ward Stephens	Phantom legions	MHH	EF-BF	CHA

Sacred Songs

Coloratura Soprano

Bach, J. S.	Sheep may safely graze (Cantata 208) 2 Flutes and continuo	LM	EF-GF	GAL
Brown	The twenty-third Psalm	LH	E-G	GRA
Campbell-Tipton	I will give thanks unto the Lord	LMH	DF-AF	GSC
Candlyn	Light at evening time	H	FS-GS	GRA
Charles	Love is of God	H	D-G	GSC
Clokey	God is in everything	LH	D-G	JFI
Gaul	These are they (The Holy City)	H	E-GS	GSC
Handel	How beautiful are the feet of them (The Messiah)	H		†
-----	I know that my Redeemer liveth (The Messiah)	MH	E-GS	†
-----	Let the bright seraphim (Samson) Trumpet	H	E-A	†
-----	Praise the Lord (Esther)	H	E-G	

80

Haydn	With verdure clad (The Creation)	H	E-BF	†
Mendelssohn	O for the wings of a dove	MLH	D-G	†
Scott	Come ye blessed	LMH	EF-AF	GSC
Timmings	In the evening it will be light	H		GRA
	Chimes			

Wedding Songs

Coloratura Soprano

Beethoven	Ich liebe dich	HL	BF-DF	†
Clough-Leighter	Possession	MH	DF-AF	GSC
De Koven	Oh promise me (Robin Hood)	HML	C-D	†
D'Hardelot	Because	MH	E-G	CHA
Diggle	A wedding prayer	HM	EF-F	GSC
Geehl	For you alone			SHU
Grieg	I love thee	HML	E-F	†
Ronald	Love I have won you	IIML	EF-EF	ENO
Schubert	Du bist die Ruh	LMH	EF-AF	†
Sowerby	O perfect love	MH	EF-AF	GRA
Willan	O perfect love	HM	E-FS	GRA

Songs and Arias with Added Accompanying Instrument

Coloratura Soprano

Adam	Ah vous dirais-je maman (Le Toreador) Flute			GSC
Alabieff	The nightingale Flute	H	EF-C	†
Bach, J. S.	Hoert doch! der sanften Floeten (Cantata 206) 3 Flutes and continuo			
Benedict	The gypsy and the bird Flute	H	D-E	GSC
Bishop	Echo song Flute	H	D-C	GSC
-----	Lo! here the gentle lark Flute	H		†
-----	Pretty mocking bird Flute	H		†

81

Braga	Angel's serenade Violin	LH	D-B	†
Gretry	La fauvette avec ses petits (Zemire et Azor) Flute			LEM
Handel	Let the bright seraphim (Samson) Trumpet	H	E-A	†
-----	Sweet bird (L'Allegro) Flute			NOV
Massé	Air du rossignol (Les Noces de Jeannette) Flute			
Meyerbeer	La, la, la air cheri (L'Etoile du Nord) Two flutes			BRA
Mozart	L'amero, saro costante (Il Re Pastore) Violin or flute	H	D-B	GSC
Proch	Theme and variations Flute	H	C-DF	†
Rabey	Tes yeux Violin and piano	H	EF-G	DUR
Saint-Saëns	Le bonheur est une chose légère Violin and piano	H	C-A	CHO
Schubert	Der Hirt auf dem Felsen Clarinet or violoncello	H	BF-B	†
Timmings	In the evening it will be light Chimes	H		GRA

American Recital Songs

Lyric Soprano

Alberti	Oriental serenade	H	CS-A	CFI
-----	The gypsy			
-----	Trees	H	C-A	CFI
-----	White swan of Samarkand			
Bacon	As if the sea should part			
-----	Is there such a thing as day?	M	DS-FS	AMP
-----	The Colorado tree			
-----	The dove			
-----	The little stone			
-----	The red rose	M		BOO
-----	Where the bee sucks			
Barber	A nun takes the veil	MH	G-G	GSC

(Barber)	I hear an army	LH	D-AF	GSC
-----	Knoxville, summer of 1915	H		GSC
-----	Monks and raisons	M	DF-E	GSC
-----	Nocturne	HM	CS-FS	GSC
-----	Nuovoletta	H	BS-BS	GSC
-----	Rain has fallen	HM	D-E	GSC
-----	Sleep now	MH	EF-AF	GSC
-----	Sure on this shining night	MH	D-G	GSC
-----	The daisies	M	C-F	GSC
Barnett	Nightingale lane	H	BS-GS	GSC
Bauer	Orientale			
Beach	Ah, love but a day			ASC
-----	Fairy lullaby			ASC
-----	I send my heart up to thee	MH		ASC
-----	June	MH		ASC
-----	The year's at the spring	MH	AF-AF	ASC
Bernstein	I just found out today			
-----	Rabbit at top speed			GSC
Bloch	Psalm 114 (Snatched away by Jahveh)	H	A-A	GSC
-----	Psalm 137 (By the waters of Babel)	H	F-AS	GSC
-----	The shelter	MH	CS-GS	GSC
-----	The vagabond	M	E-E	GSC
Bone and Fenton	Deborah	LM	CS-FS	CFI
-----	Tryst	MH	FS-G	CFI
-----	Wind in the tree tops			
Bowles	Cabin	ML	CS-CS	GSC
-----	Heavenly grass	ML	B-E	GSC
-----	In the woods			AMP
-----	Letter to Freddy	M	EF-EF	GSC
-----	On a quiet conscience	M	C-F	MUP
-----	Once a lady was here	ML	C-EF	GSC
Boyd	Adoration	H	C-A	GAL
Braine	Dawn awakes	HML	A-D	ASC
Branscombe	At the postern gate	MH	DF-AF	ASC
-----	I send my heart up to thee			
Browning	The night is but a mirror			
Burleigh	By the pool at the third roses	H		RIC
-----	The sailor's wife	HM		RIC
Buzzi-Peccia	Under the greenwood tree	LMH	EF-A	DIT
Cadman	I hear a thrush at eve			MOR
-----	Joy	MH	E-A	GSC

Campbell- Tipton	A spirit flower	LHM	B-G	GSC
Carpenter	I am like a remnant of a cloud of autumn	L	BF-F	GSC
-----	If	M	D-E	GSC
-----	Light, my light	M	C-G	GSC
-----	Serenade	LH	CS-A	GSC
-----	Silhouettes	M	C-G	GSC
-----	The sleep that flits on baby's eyes	M	B-FS	GSC
-----	When I bring to you colour'd toys	LM	CS-FS	GSC
Castelnuovo- Tedesco	Heavily arise			
-----	O mistress mine			CHE
-----	Roundel	H		CHE
-----	The horn			CHE
Chadwick	Allah	LH	CS-GS	ASC
Chanler	Grandma			GSC
-----	Sleep			GSC
-----	The lamb	M	C-D	AMP
-----	Wind			GSC
Charles	And so, goodbye	LH	EF-AF	GSC
-----	Dawn	M	BF-F	BOS
-----	Let my song fill your heart	LH	EF-AF	GSC
-----	Night	MH	F-AF	GSC
-----	Remembrance			
-----	Sweet song of long ago	HML	A-D	GSC
-----	When I have sung my songs	HM	BF-EF	GSC
Chasins	Dreams			JFI
Clough- Leighter	My lover he comes on the skee	HM	D-F	BOS
Cottenet	Red, red rose	H	D-BF	CFI
Cowell	St. Agnes morning	M	C-G	MER
Cowles	Desire	H	F-A	GSC
-----	The fragrance of a song	HM	E-F	GSC
-----	The grasshopper			
Creston	Bird of the wilderness	MH	FS-A	GSC
Crist	By a silent seashore	H	CS-GS	GSC
-----	C'est mon ami	LH	CS-G	CFI
-----	Evening	H	C-G	GSC
-----	Into a ship dreaming	LMH	EF-GS	CFI
-----	Knock on the door	H	EF-AF	GSC
-----	Love's offering			
-----	O come hither	HM	B-GS	CFI
-----	The dark King's daughter			JCH

Curran	The two magicians	LH	DS-FS	GSC
Davis	Nancy Hanks	H	D-G	GAL
Deis	Come down to Kew			
Dello Joio	Mill doors	M	D-E	CFI
Diamond	David weeps for Absolom	M	D-A	MUP
-----	Even though the world keeps changing	H	CS-A	CFI
-----	To Lucasta, on going to the wars			
Dittenhaver	Hurdy-gurdy playing in the street	H	DF-AF	GAL
-----	Lady of the amber wheat	H		GAL
-----	Passage	M	C-F	GAL
Dougherty	Beauty is not caused	M		AMP
-----	If love were what the rose is			
-----	Love in the dictionary	M	C-G	GSC
-----	Loveliest of trees	HM	C-E	BOH
-----	Madonna of the evening flowers	M		BOO
-----	Music			
-----	Pianissimo	M	C-G	GSC
-----	Pied beauty			
-----	Portrait	HM	BF-G	GSC
-----	Primavera	H	C-BF	GSC
-----	Song for autumn			
-----	The K'e	M	D-F	GSC
-----	The song of the Jasmin			
-----	Weathers			
Duke	A piper	H	CS-B	GSC
-----	Bells in the rain	H	E-GS	CFI
-----	Capri			
-----	Central Park at dusk	M		BOO
-----	Evening			
-----	Hesperus	H	CS-GS	GSC
-----	I can't be talkin' of love	H	CS-G	GSC
-----	Just spring			
-----	Little elegy	H	FS-A	GSC
-----	My soul is an enchanted boat			
-----	Spray	H	CS-A	BOH
-----	The bird			GSC
-----	The puritan's ballad			
-----	To Karen, singing	M	CS-G	ELV
-----	XXth century	M		VLP
-----	Velvet shoes	H	D-A	ROW
-----	Viennese waltz	H	C-GF	ROW
-----	Voices	H	FS-A	BOH
Dukelsky	Adolescence	MH		CFI

85

Edmunds	Billy boy	ML	BF-EF	ROW
-----	Fare you well	MH	F-AF	ROW
Edwards	Little shepherd's song			MLS
-----	The fisher's widow	ML	G-EF	GSC
Elwell	In the mountains	M	DF-F	BMI
-----	The road not taken	M	B-FS	GSC
-----	The sound of the trees	M		AMP
Engel	Sea shell	M	EF-EF	GSC
Fairchild	A memory			BOS
Fisher	Sigh no more ladies			
Flood	The hermit thrush			
-----	The windows of Sainte Chapelle	H		RIC
-----	White bud			
Gaines	My heart hath a mind			
Ganz	A memory	HM	B-D	GSC
-----	The angels are stooping	MH	GF-A	GSC
Gaynor	May magic			
Giannini	Be still my heart			ELV
-----	Far above the purple hills	LH	CS-A	RIC
-----	Heart cry	H		RIC
-----	Tell me, o blue, blue sky	H		RIC
Gilberte	Two roses	LMH	CS-G	CFI
Golde	Love was with me yesterday	LMH	E-A	CFI
-----	Who knows?	HM	BF-F	GSC
Grant	Looking across	H	D-G	AMP
Grant-Schaeffer	The cuckoo clock	H	EF-BF	SUM
Griffes	By a lonely forest pathway	HML	A-EF	GSC
-----	Elves	H	F-AF	GSC
-----	Evening song	H	DS-GS	GSC
-----	In a myrtle shade	H	FS-A	GSC
-----	Symphony in yellow	M	D-GF	GSC
-----	The dreamy lake	H	BS-GS	GSC
-----	The lament of Ian the proud	MH	DS-AS	GSC
-----	The rose of the night	H	CS-A	GSC
-----	Thy dark eyes to mine	H	EF-AF	GSC
-----	Time was, when I in anguish lay	H	E-GS	GSC
-----	Waikiki	H	DS-GS	GSC
Hadley	Evening song	HM	BF-EF	GSC
-----	My shadow			ASC
Hageman	At the well	LH	EF-AF	GSC
-----	Do no go, my love	HL	B-EF	GSC
-----	Is it you?			
-----	Miranda	HL		GAL

86

(Hageman)	Music I heard with you	MH	E-A	GAL
-----	The donkey			BOO
-----	The night has a thousand eyes	M	C-FS	BOO
Harrington	Alas, that spring should vanish	LH	DF-AF	CFI
Harris	Someone came knocking at my door	M		GAL
Haubiel	I love you	M	B-FS	GSC
-----	To you			CMP
Hindemith	Echo	H	D-FS	AMP
-----	On hearing the last rose of summer	M	D-FS	AMP
-----	The whistling thief	M	E-F	AMP
-----	The wildflower's song	MH	E-G	AMP
Homer	House that Jack built			JCH
Hopkinson	Beneath a weeping willow's shade	H	D-G	†
-----	My days have been so wondrous free	LH	EF-G	
-----	My love is gone to sea	HL	D-E	†
-----	O'er the hills	LH	C-G	†
Horsman	In the yellow dusk	MH	FS-A	GSC
-----	The bird of the wilderness	LMH	DF-BF	GSC
-----	The dream	H	F-G	GSC
-----	Thus wisdom sings	H	EF-A	GSC
Howe	When I died in Berners Street	H	C-G	GSC
Huerter	Pirate dreams	HML		DIT
Ives	Ann Street			
-----	At sea			
-----	Mists			
-----	Two little flowers			
Josten	Cupid's counsel	H	EF-AF	GSC
Kagen	A June day	H	FS-BF	WTR
-----	All day I hear	H	F-FS	WTR
-----	I'm nobody	H	D-G	WTR
-----	Let it be forgotten	M	F-F	WTR
-----	Maybe	H	D-G	WTR
-----	War is kind			
Kernochan	We two together	H	EF-AF	GAL
Kingsford	Wallpaper for a little girl's room	M	BF-F	GSC
Klein	Illusion	M		AMP
-----	Night mist	M		AMP
Klemm	Sounds			DIT
Kramer	Clouds	H		JFI
-----	Pleading	LH	D-GF	JFI
-----	Swans	HL		RIC

(Kramer)	The crystal gazer			DIT
La Forge	Chant de joie libre			
-----	Come unto these yellow sands	H	FS-B	GSC
-----	Cupid captive	H		GAL
-----	Gypsy melodies			
-----	Hills	HL		RIC
-----	Pastorale			
Levitzki	Ah, thou beloved one	H	EF-AF	GSC
Lubin	The piper	H	C-A	GSC
MacDowell	A maid sings light	H	F-G	ASC
-----	As the gloaming shadows creep			
-----	Idyl			
-----	Long ago	HL		ASC
-----	The blue bell			GSC
-----	The sea	HL	D-D	BRH
-----	The swan bent low	LH		ELK
Malotte	A day is born			
-----	Hebrew prayer			
Mana-Zucca	Speak to me			
-----	Spring is whispering			CNG
-----	There's joy in my heart			CNG
Manning	In the Luxembourg gardens	HML	BF-D	GSC
-----	The street fair			
-----	White clouds			DIT
McArthur	Night	H	F-AF	GSC
-----	Spring came	HL	D-F	GSC
McDonald	He is gone	H	DF-BF	ELV
Metcalf	At nightfall	HML	C-DF	ASC
Moore	Sigh no more, ladies			BOO
Mopper	Amelia			
-----	Gray velvet			
-----	Men	M	D-FS	BOS
Naginski	Look down, fair moon			
-----	The pasture	M	BF-EF	GSC
-----	Under the harvest moon	M	D-E	GSC
Nordoff	Fair Annette's song			AMP
-----	Madrigals			
-----	Music I heard with you	H	DS-FS	AMP
-----	Praise			
-----	Serenade	H	CS-FS	AMP
-----	Song	H	DF-A	AMP
-----	Tell me, Thyrsis	H	E-G	AMP
-----	There shall be more joy	M	CS-FS	AMP
-----	This is the shape of the leaf	M	B-E	SC
-----	Willow River	H	D-G	AMP

88

Parker	A gypsy maiden, I			
-----	The lark now leaves her watery nest	LH	D-BF	JCH
Proctor	I heard a bird			
-----	I light the blessed candles	H	DF-A	GSC
Protheroe	Ah, love but a day	LMH	F-AF	GAM
-----	Sing again			
Rasbach	Mountains	LH	DF-AF	GSC
Robinson	The chudder weaver	H	C-G	GSC
Rogers	The last song	MLH	E-AF	GSC
-----	Time for making songs	HM	CS-F	DIT
Rorem	Alleluia			
-----	The silver swan	H	F-C	PEE
Rummel	Ecstasy	LMH	GF-AF	GSC
Russell	Fulfillment	LH	EF-GF	BOS
-----	Harbor night	M	D-F	CFI
Rybner	Pierrot	HL		GSC
Sacco	Let it be forgotten	LH	F-AF	CFI
-----	Little man	LH	D-F	BOS
-----	Mexican serenade	HL	D-EF	BOS
-----	Rapunzel	MH	FS-BF	GSC
-----	The ragpicker	MH	C-AF	GSC
-----	Where the lilac blows	LH	D-G	BOS
Saminsky	Queen Esterka's laugh	H	D-A	CFI
Sargent	Three a. m.	M	DF-E	GSC
-----	Twentieth century	H	EF-GS	LEE
Schneider	Flower rain			SUM
Schuman	Holiday song	M	C-F	GSC
-----	Orpheus with his lute	M	C-FS	GSC
Shepherd	Triptych String quartet	H		GSC
Silberta	Lullaby for Judith			
-----	You shall have your red rose			
-----	Wild geese			
Spencer	For whom the bell tolls	MH	F-AF	BOS
Spross	Ishtar			
-----	Will o' the wisp			JCH
Still	The breath of a rose			
Swanson	Joy	M	BF-EF	LEE
-----	Night song			
-----	The negro speaks of rivers	M		LEE
-----	The valley	L	BF-DF	LEE
Taylor	A song for lovers	MH	D-F	JFI
-----	The rivals	H	E-G	JFI
Thompson	Velvet shoes	M	C-E	ECS
Thomson	Dirge	M	D-F	GSC
-----	Preciosilla	H	EF-A	GSC
-----	The tiger			

89

Tyson	Like barley bending	HL	C-EF	GSC
Vene	Age and youth	H	E-A	RIC
Wagenaar	From a very little sphinx			
Walther	Sometimes	MH	EF-AF	GSC
Ware	This day is mine	MH	EF-AF	BOS
Warner	Hurdy gurdy	M	D-F	CFI
Warren	Down in the glen	H	F-A	GSC
-----	Heather	LH	FS-G	GSC
-----	I saw a little tailor			
-----	Silent noon	HL		DIT
-----	Snow towards evening	LH	EF-AF	GSC
-----	Wander shoes	LH	F-G	FLA
-----	We two	LH	E-A	GSC
-----	White horses of the sea	LH	F-G	GSC
Watts	Hushing song			
-----	Joy	HL	D-F	GSC
-----	Like music on the waters	H		GSC
-----	Pierrot	HM		DIT
-----	Stresa	H	EF-BF	DIT
-----	The little shepherd's song	H	G-BF	RIC
-----	The poet sings	MH	EF-AF	DIT
-----	Transformation	ML	AS-DS	GSC
-----	Wings of night	LH	CS-G	GSC
-----	With the tide	H	DF-A	GSC
Weaver	A book of verses	H	D-AF	GAL
Wolf	Weather forecast	H	EF-GS	GSC
Woodman	Love's in my heart	LH	F-BF	GSC
Worth	Madrigale			
-----	Midsummer	LM	E-A	GSC
Young	The tea-kettle song			

British Recital Songs

Lyric Soprano

Aiken	Sonnet XVIII			
Anon	Have you seen but a white lily grow?	H	E-F	GSC
Arne, M.	The lass with the delicate air	MH	D-G	†
Arne, T.	Blow, blow, thou winter wind	M	C-F	†
-----	In infancy			NOV
-----	Oh come my dearest			
-----	Polly Willis	H	D-G	†
-----	Under the greenwood tree			
-----	Water parted from the sea			GSC
-----	When daisies pied			AUG

90

(Arne, T.)	Where the bee sucks	HM		†
Bainton	The nightingale near the house			CUR
Bantock	A dream of spring	H	E-G	CHE
-----	A feast of lanterns	HM	D-F	GAL
-----	Silent strings	MH	F-G	BOO
-----	The celestial weaver			
Bartlet	Whither runneth my sweetheart			BOO
Bax	Cradle song			CHA
-----	I heard a piper piping	LH	D-G	CFI
-----	O, green grow the rushes	MH	EF-BF	OXF
-----	Shieling song	H	CS-A	CHE
-----	The white peace			CHE
Bayly	I'd be a butterfly			
Benjamin	The piper			BOO
-----	The wasp			CUR
Berners	Lullaby	M	C-G	CHE
-----	The green eyed monster	M	C-G	CHE
Besley	Listening	H	E-AF	CUR
Bishop	Bid me discourse	H	B-A	†
-----	Love has eyes	M		†
-----	Should he upbraid	H		†
Bliss	Simples			
-----	Three jolly gentlemen	II		†
Boyce	Tell me lovely shepherd			AUG
Brewer	The fairy pipers	HML		BOH
Bridge	Adoration	H		ROG
-----	All things that we clasp	HL		BOS
-----	O that it were so	LMH	D-G	CHA
Britten	As it is plenty			
-----	Les illuminations	H		BOH
-----	Let the florid music praise			
-----	Marine			
-----	Nocturne			BOH
-----	Now the leaves are falling fast			
-----	Oh, to vex me			BOO
-----	Royaute			
Brook	At Michael's Gate	H	C AF	CUR
Brown	Shepherd thy demeanor vary!			BOO
Campion	Author of light			
-----	Beauty if thou so much desire			
-----	Fain would I wed			
-----	When to her lute Corinna sings			STB
Clarke	Shy one	HL	BF-G	BOH
Coates	The green hills o' Somerset			

91

Coleridge-Taylor	She rested by the broken brook	HL		DIT
-----	Willow song	MH		CRA
Delius	Cradle song			AUG
-----	In a seraglio garden			
-----	Irmelin rose			BOO
-----	Love's philosophy			†
-----	The nightingale has a lyre of gold			†
-----	The princess			
Dowland	Awake, sweet love	M	E-F	STB
-----	Come again, sweet love	M	D-E	STB
-----	Come away			BOO
-----	Flow, my tears	M	D-E	STB
-----	Shall I sue?			STB
Dunhill	To the Queen of Heaven	M	C-G	GSC
Edmunds	I know my love	HL	BF-EF	ROW
-----	The faucon	M	D-F	MER
Fellows	Willow song			
Forsyth	The stranger Organ	H	A-B	GRA
German	Charming Chloe	HML		NOV
Gibbs	Five eyes	HL	D-D	BOS
-----	Silver		CS-FS	ROG
-----	To one who passed whistling through the night	H	F-G	CUR
-----	Why do I love?			BOO
Green	My lips shall speak the praise	M	E-F	OXF
Handel	Loves' a dear deceitful jewel	LH	F-F	RBR
-----	Pack clouds away			PAT
Harty	Lane o' the thrushes			BOO
-----	The fiddler of Dooney			BOO
Head	A blackbird singing	MH		BOO
-----	A piper	HL		BOO
-----	The dreaming lake	HL		BOO
Henschel	Morning-hymn	MH	DS-GS	†
Holbrooke	The clown's song			
Holst	A little music	H		AUG
Hook	Softly waft, ye southern breezes			GSC
Horn	Cherry ripe	M	D-G	†
-----	I've been roaming	L	B-E	DIT
Ireland	Bed in summer			CUR
Jacob	Laughing song	H	D-G	OXF

92

Johnson	As I walked forth one summer day			DIT
Lehmann	Alas that spring should vanish			GSC
-----	Magdalen at Michael's gate			CHA
-----	Snake charmer			BOO
Linley	O, bid your faithful Ariel fly			BOO
Mallinson	My heart, the bird of the wilderness	H	DF-AF	CRA
Matthews	Night song at Amalfi	H		RLV
Milford	Love on my heart	H	FS-FS	NOV
Morley	It was a lover and his lass	HM		DIT
-----	Love winged my hopes			
Parry	Armida's garden			NOV
-----	The maiden			NOV
-----	Whether I live			NOV
Peel	Lov'liest of trees			
Purcell	Cease, o my sad soul			POT
-----	Come unto these yellow sands			AUG
-----	Here the deities approve			
-----	If music be the food of love	M	D-G	BOO
-----	Man is for woman made			
-----	Not all my torments			NOV
-----	Since from my dear			
-----	Song of Bonvica			NOV
-----	Strike the viol			BAF
-----	The Blessed Virgin's expostulation	H		SC
-----	The fatal hour comes on			
-----	We sing to him			
Quilter	A land of silence			BOO
-----	Blow, blow, thou winter wind	HL	C-E	BOO
-----	Come away, come away death			BOO
-----	Dream valley	H	EF-GF	ROG
-----	Go, lovely rose	LHM	F-GF	CHA
-----	How should I your true love know?			BOO
-----	It was a lover and his lass	HL	CS-E	BOO
-----	Love's philosophy	LMH	D-A	BOO
-----	Take, o take those lips away			BOO
-----	To daisies			BOO
Ronald	Down in the forest	HML	C-D	ENO
-----	Drift down, drift down			BOO

(Ronald)	Love, I have won you	HML	EF-EF	ENO
Rosseter	What then is love but mourning			STB
-----	When Laura smiles	LM	D-E	STB
Scott	Don't come in, sir, please!	HL		GAL
-----	Lullaby	MML	BF-DF	GAL
-----	The unforeseen	HML		GAL
Sharp	My mother did so before me			MEU
Shaw	Song of the Palanquin bearers	LH	E-F	CUR
Stanford	I'll rock you to rest	HML		BOH
-----	Sea wrack	H	EF-A	STB
Stephenson	Love is a sickness	HML	C-D	BOO
-----	Ships that pass in the night	HML	DF-DF	BOO
Taylor	O can ye sew			
-----	The wind mill	M		OXF
Thiman	The silver swan	MH	EF-G	NOV
Vaughan Williams	How can the tree but wither?			OXF
-----	In dreams			
-----	Orpheus with his lute			PRO
-----	Silent noon			GSC
-----	The water mill	L	C-D	OXF
Warlock	Pretty ring time	H	D-G	CFI
-----	Rantum, tantum	H	DF-G	CHE
-----	The distracted maid	H	DF-G	CHE

French Recital Songs

Lyric Soprano

Acqua	Chanson provençale	H	D-BF	GSC
Attaignant	Puisque, voulez-vous que je vous laisse			
Aubert	La lettre			DUR
-----	Vieille chanson espagnole			DUR
Auric	Printemps			DUR
Bachelet	Chère nuit	H	DF-BF	GSC
Bemberg	Chant hindou	HML	A-EF	†
-----	Il neige	H	FS-G	GRU
Berlioz	L'absence	H	CS-FS	GSC
-----	La mort d'Ophélie			CST
-----	Le spectre de la rose			CST
-----	L'isle inconnue			CST

94

(Berlioz)	Villanelle	H	E-FS	†
Bizet	Adieu de l'hôtesse arabe	H	BF-G	†
-----	Agnus Dei	HLM	C-AF	†
-----	Après l'hiver			†
-----	Chanson d'avril	H	BF-G	†
-----	Douce mer			GSC
-----	Ouvre ton coeur	MH	DS-GS	†
-----	Pastorale	H	C-FS	GSC
-----	Vielle chanson	H	EF-A	GSC
Boulanger	Cantique	M	F-F	HAM
Britten	Antique			
Bruneau	Le passepied			
-----	Le sabot de frene			CHO
-----	Les cloches de Nantes			
-----	Les pieds nus			
Busser	Notre Père qui êtes aux cieux			
Campra	Hébé	H		ROU
Chabrier	Les cigales	HML		†
-----	L'île heureuse	M	B-F	†
-----	Villanelle des petits canards	HML	B-E	†
Chaminade	Berceuse	LH	D-G	†
-----	L'été	MH	E-A	†
-----	The silver ring	HM	BF-F	GSC
-----	Tu me dirais	LH	BF-AF	DIT
Chausson	Chanson perpétuelle (String quartet)	H	CS-GS	ROU
-----	Dans la forêt	HL		INT
-----	La fleur des eaux	HL		
-----	L'amour d'Antan	HL		INT
-----	Le colibri (Violin or cello)	M	F-GF	BOS
-----	Le temps des lilas	MH	D-GS	†
-----	Les papillons	M	C-F	GSC
-----	Nocturne	HL		INT
-----	Sérénade			
Couperin	Brunete			
Dalayrac	D'un époux chéri			DUR
-----	Jeune fillette	HL	GS-E	DIT
Dalcroze	Le coeur de ma mie	HML		†
-----	Le petit oiseau			
-----	L'oiseau bleu			CFI
Debussy	Apparition			DUR
-----	Beau soir	LH	C-FS	†
-----	C'est l'extase	LH	CS-A	†
-----	Chevaux de bois	H	C-G	†
-----	Clair de lune	M	CS-FS	JOB
-----	Colloque sentimental			DUR

95

(Debussy)	Crois mon conseil, chère Climène			DUR
-----	De fleurs	H	C-AF	†
-----	De grève	HL		†
-----	De soir	HL		†
-----	En sourdine	M	C-FS	†
-----	Fantoches	H	D-A	JOB
-----	Green	H	C-AF	†
-----	Harmonie du soir			DUR
-----	Il pleure dans mon coeur	LH	CS-GS	†
-----	L'echelonnement des haïes			HAM
-----	L'ombre des arbres			†
-----	La demoiselle Élue			DUR
-----	La flûte de Pan		B-B	†
-----	La lettre de Geneviève			DUR
-----	La mer est plus belle	HL		†
-----	La vierge Erigone			DUR
-----	Le balcon			JOB
-----	Le faune			DUR
-----	Le jet d'eau			DUR
-----	Le tombeau des naïades			JOB
-----	Le angélus			HAM
-----	Les cloches	LH	E-GS	†
-----	Les ingénus			DUR
-----	Mandoline	HM	BF-F	†
-----	Noël des enfants qui n'ont plus de maisons			DUR
-----	Nuits d'etoiles	LH	E-A	MAR
-----	Pantomime			DUR
-----	Paysages belges			JOB
-----	Pierrot			DUR
-----	Placet futile			DUR
-----	Recueillement			DUR
-----	Romance	HM	C-E	†
-----	Voici que le printemps	LH	CS-G	BOS
Delibes	Eglogue			
-----	Les filles de Cadix	HM	A-A	†
-----	Myrto	M	A-FS	GSC
-----	Passepied	LH	DS-CS	GSC
-----	Que l'heure est donc brève			
Duparc	Chanson triste	MH	FS-AF	†
-----	Extase	LMH	FS-A	†
-----	L'invitation au voyage	HM	E-F	†
-----	Phidylé	MH	EF-AF	BOS
-----	Soupir	HL	CS-F	BOS
Dupont	Chanson des noisettes			HEU
-----	Mandoline			DUR
-----	Adieu	MH	F-F	†

(Fauré)	Après un rêve	HM	C-F	†
-----	Au bord de l'eau	HL	C-F	†
-----	Aurore	H	D-G	†
-----	Chanson du pêcheur	H	E-A	HAM
-----	Clair de lune	MH	C-G	†
-----	Dans les ruines d'une abbaye	M	E-FS	†
------	Dolly			HAM
-----	En sourdine	HL	C-EF	†
-----	Hymne	MH	D-G	HAM
-----	Ici-bas!	H	FS-G	†
-----	La fée aux chansons	LH	F-F	†
-----	La lune blanche	HL		†
-----	La rose	H	F-A	MAR
-----	Le parfum impérissable	LH	GF-GF	
-----	Le secret	LH	F-G	†
-----	Les roses d'Ispahan	HM	D-FS	†
-----	Lydia	MH	G-G	†
-----	Mandoline	HL	F-E	†
-----	Nell	LH	FS-AF	†
-----	Notre amour	H	DS-B	†
-----	Rencontre	H	EF-AF	†
-----	Spleen	H	E-FS	MAR
-----	Sylvie	HL	E-F	†
-----	Vocalise	H		LED
Ferrari	Je saute, je danse			
-----	La peureuse			
-----	Le miroir	M	E-F	GSC
-----	Le roi a fait battre tambour			
-----	Les belles manières			
Février	Le printemps			HEU
Fontenailles	Obstination	MH	EF-GF	DUR
Fourdrain	Carnaval	M	C-F	RIC
-----	Celle que je préfère	H		RIC
-----	Chanson norvégienne	H	E-G	RIC
-----	Chevauchée cosaque	H	D-G	RIC
-----	L'oasis			
-----	Le papillon			RIC
Franck	Lied	LH	FS-FS	†
-----	Nocturne	HL		†
Gaubert	Ah, fuyez à présent			
Georges	Hymne au soleil	LH	E-A	HOM
-----	La pluie	HL		INT
Godard	Florian's song	LMH	D-FS	GSC
Gounod	Adore and be still	HL		GSC
-----	Au printemps	LMH	DF-AF	GSC
-----	Au rossignol	LMH	D-G	CHO
-----	Où voulez-vous aller?	H	D-A	GSC

97

(Gounod)	Sérénade	LMH	D-A	GSC
-----	Vénise	HL		INT
Gretry	Comme un eclair			
Grovlez	Guitares et mandolines			DUR
Hahn	À Chloris	H	DS-FS	HEU
-----	En sourdine			HEU
-----	Infidélité	M		HEU
-----	L'air			HEU
-----	L'enamourée			HEU
-----	L'heure exquise	M	DF-F	†
-----	Cimetière de campagne			HEU
-----	Fêtes galantes			
-----	Le printemps			
-----	Le rossignol des lilas			
-----	Mai			HEU
-----	Offrande	M	D-D	†
-----	Paysage	MH	EF-G	HEU
-----	Quand je fus pris au pavillon	M		HEU
-----	Rêverie			HEU
-----	Si mes vers avaient des ailes	HLM	B-FS	†
-----	The rain song			
Hindemith	La belle dame sans merci	MH		SC
Honegger	Amour			
-----	Le grand étang			
-----	Les cloches			SEN
-----	Poème de Verlaine			SAL
-----	Poème de William Aguet			SAL
-----	Psalm 130 (Mimaamaquim)			SAL
-----	Psalm 138 (I will give Thee thanks with my whole heart)			SAL
Hue	A des oiseaux	H	E-G	†
-----	Il a neigé des fleurs	H	EF-AF	
-----	L'âne blanc	H	EF-G	HEU
-----	Les clochettes des muguets	HL	E-GF	INT
-----	Soir païen Flutes			ROU
-----	Vocalise-étude			
Jaubert	La chanson de Tessa			
Koechlin	L'air	M	F-FS	ROU
-----	L'hiver	H	E-G	†
-----	La lune	M	C-F	ROU
-----	La pêche			ROU
-----	Le matin	H		ROU
-----	Le thé	HM	C-E	BOS
-----	Si tu le veux	LH	FS-A	MAR
Lalo	La chanson d'Alouette	H	EF-B	GSC
Laparra	C'est une calme			

98

(Laparra)	Le bonheur			
-----	Le tambour			
-----	Lettre à une espagnole			ENO
Leguerney	Au sommeil			ROU
-----	Genièvres hérissés	H	D-G	ROU
Leroux	Le nil	LH	E-A	†
	Cello or violin			
Letorey	La fontaine de Caramouet			HAM
Liszt	Comment, disaient-ils?	H	C-AF	†
-----	Enfant, si j'étais roi			SC
-----	Oh! quand je dors	H	E-A	†
-----	S'il est un charmant gazon	HL		†
Lully	Au clair de la lune	H	E-D	CFI
Manning	Vielle chanson de chasse			
Martini	Plaisir d'amour	M	BF-EF	GSC
Massenet	Crépuscule	M	D-E	GSC
-----	Elégie	LM	C-GF	GSC
-----	Entchantement	HL		HEU
-----	Ouvre tes yeux bleus	MH	C-G	†
-----	Première danse	H	E-G	GSC
-----	Sérénade du passant!			HEU
Mehul	N'avoir jamais qu'une pensée			
Moret	La lettre			
-----	Le nélumbo	H	E-DF	HEU
Mozart	Dans un bois	H	EF-AF	
-----	Oiseaux, si tous les ans	H	C-G	KAL
Paladilhe	Le roitelet	MH	DS-GS	GSC
-----	Psyché	HM	BF-F	GSC
Paulin	Que deviennent les roses			
Pierné	An album for my little friends			
-----	Ils étaient trois petits chats blancs			MAR
-----	Le moulin	ML	C-E	BOS
Poldowski	Cortège	M	D-FS	CHE
-----	Effet de neige	M	EF-F	CHE
-----	L'heure exquise	LMH	DF-AF	CHE
Poulenc	A sa guitare	M	D-FS	DUR
-----	Air champêtre			ROU
-----	Air grave			ROU
-----	Air romantique			SAL
-----	Air vif	H	C-AF	ROU
-----	Allons plus vite			ROU
-----	Au delà	H	D-G	DUR
-----	Berceuse			ROU
-----	Bleuet	H	FS-GF	DUR
-----	C (J'ai traversé les ponts de C)			ROU

(Poulenc)	Chanson de la fille frivole			ESC
-----	Chanson d'Orkenise			AMP
-----	Cimetière			ROU
-----	Fêtes galantes			SAL
-----	Figure de force			DUR
-----	Fleurs	M	DF-F	ROU
-----	Hôtel			AMP
-----	Il vole			SAL
-----	La petite servante			ROU
-----	Le disparu			ROU
-----	Les chemins de l'amour	M		AMP
-----	Les gars qui vont à la fête	H	C-GF	AMP
-----	Priez pour paix	ML		ROU
-----	Reine des mouettes	M	FF-F	SAL
-----	Sanglots			AMP
-----	Une herbe pauvre	H	E-G	DUR
-----	Violon			ROU
Rabey	Tes yeux (Violin and piano)	H	EF-G	DUR
Rameau	La musette			BOS
-----	Le grillon			DUR
Ravel	Asie	M	BF-G	DUR
-----	D'Anne jouant de l'espinette	H	CS-GS	GSC
-----	D'Anne qui me jecta	HM	CS-FS	GSC
-----	Kaddisch	H	C-G	DUR
-----	La flûte enchantée	M	DS-FS	DUR
-----	Le paon	M	C-F	DUR
-----	Manteau de fleurs	H		INT
-----	Nicolette	L	B-FS	ELK
-----	Ronde			
-----	Sur l'herbe	MH	C-G	DUR
-----	Tout gai!	MH	EF-F	
-----	Trois beaux oiseaux du paradis			DUR
-----	Vocalise en forme de habanera	MH	BF-G	MAR
Rhené-Baton	Berceuse			DUR
Roussel	Jazz dans la nuit	H	C-A	DUR
-----	Le jardin mouillé	M	C-FS	ROU
-----	Response d'une épouse sage			DUR
Saint-Saëns	A swan's song (Harp or piano and cello)	H	D-G	GSC
-----	Aimons-nous			DUR
-----	Guitares et mandolines			DUR
-----	La cloche	LH	DF-AF	†

(Saint Saëns)	La libellule	H	C–D	DUR
-----	Le bonheur est une chose légère (Violin and piano)	H	C–A	CHO
-----	Mai	H	G–FS	DUR
-----	Pourquoi rester seulette	H	D–A	GSC
-----	Une flûte invisible			
Satie	Daphénéo			ROU
-----	Le chapelier			ROU
Severac	Ba, be, bi, bo, bu			ROU
-----	Chanson de Blaisine			
-----	Chanson pour le petit cheval			ROU
-----	Offrande			ROU
-----	Ma poupée chérie			ROU
-----	Ne dérangez pas le monde			ROU
-----	Zon, zon, zon			ROU
Staub	L'heure silencieuse	H	EF–G	DUR
Szulc	Claire du lune	H	E–G	AXE
-----	Hantise d'amour	H	D–BF	GSC
-----	Mandoline	H	D–B	ROU
Vidal	Ariette	LH	F–A	GSC

German Recital Songs

Lyric Soprano

Bach, C.P.E.	Das Gebet			SIM
-----	Passionslied			SIM
-----	The last judgement			
Bach, J. S.	Bist du bei mir	HML	A–EF	†
-----	Come visit ye glowing	H		
-----	Comfort sweet, Lord Jesus comes			OXF
-----	Dir, dir Jehovah			†
-----	Father what I proffer			
-----	Ich halte treulich still			
-----	Komm suesser Tod	MH	C–G	†
-----	Liebster Herr Jesu			BRH
-----	O Jesulein suess			
Beethoven	An die Hoffnung	H	B–A	†
-----	Andenken			†
-----	A song of penitence			
-----	Bitten			†
-----	Busslied			†
-----	Das Geheimnis			
-----	Freudvoll und leidvoll	M	DS–E	†
-----	Ich liebe dich	HL	BF–DF	GSC

(Beethoven)	Mailied			RIC
-----	Mit einem gemalten Band			RIC
-----	Neue Liebe, neues Leben			†
Berg	Die Nachtigall			AMP
Blech	Heimkehr vom Feste			UNI
Brahms	An ein Veilchen	H	DS-GS	†
-----	An eine Aeolsharfe	H	EF-AF	†
-----	Auf dem Schiffe	LH	GS-A	†
-----	Auf dem See	HL	D-F	†
-----	Bei dir sind meine Gedanken	MH	E-FS	†
-----	Blinde Kuh			†
-----	Botschaft	HL	D-F	†
-----	Daemm'rung senkte sich von oben	LH	BF-G	†
-----	Das Maedchen spricht	H	E-FS	†
-----	Dein blaues Auge	MH	BF-G	†
-----	Der Jaeger	HL		†
-----	Der Tod, das ist die kuehle Nacht	L	AF-F	†
-----	Dort in den Weiden	LH	A-A	†
-----	Ein Wanderer	LH	E-AF	†
-----	Eine gute, gute Nacht			†
-----	Erinnerung	H	E-G	†
-----	Es liebt sich so lieblich im Lenze	LH	D-GS	†
-----	Es traeumte mir			RIC
-----	Feldeinsamkeit	HL	C-EF	†
-----	Fruehlingstrost	LH	E-A	†
-----	Geheimnis			†
-----	Immer leiser wird mein Schlummer	LH	DF-A	†
-----	In Waldeseinsamkeit	H	ES-G	†
-----	Juchhe!			†
-----	Lerchengesang	LH	FS-GS	†
-----	Maedchenlied	HL		†
-----	Meerfahrt			†
-----	Mein wundes Herz verlangt			
-----	Meine Lieder	HL	D-DS	†
-----	Nachtigall	MHL	BF-FS	†
-----	O liebliche Wangen	MLH	E-G	†
-----	O wuesst' ich doch den Weg zurueck	H	E-FS	†
-----	Regenlied	HL	CS-F	†
-----	Rote Abendwolken zieh'n	H	EF-AF	†
-----	Ruhe Suessliebchen	HL	BS-E	†
-----	Salamander			†
-----	Salome			†
-----	Sandmaennchen	LH	F-G	†

(Brahms)	Schoen war, das ich dir Weihte			†
-----	Schwesterlein			†
-----	Sonntag	H	D-G	†
-----	Staendchen	HL	BF-E	†
-----	Unbewegte laue Luft			PET
-----	Vergebliches Staendchen			†
-----	Vorueber			†
-----	Waehrend des Regens			†
-----	Wiegenlied			
-----	Wie Melodien zieht es	HL	A-E	†
-----	Wir wandelten	LH	EF-GF	†
Cornelius	Hirschlein ging im Wald			
-----	Im Lenz			
-----	Komm, wir wandeln	H	FS-GS	SC
-----	Moechte im Walde mit dir gehen			
-----	Morgenwind			
Franck, J. W.	Auf, auf, zu Gottes Lob			SIM
Franz	Ach, wenn, ich doch ein Immchen war			
-----	Ein Stuendlein wohl vor Tag			†
-----	Er ist gekommen	HL	EF-F	†
-----	Es hat die Rose sich beklagt	LH	DF-F	†
-----	For music	ML	C-D	†
-----	Gute Nacht	HL		†
-----	Im Herbst	HM	A-F	†
-----	Liebchen ist da!	HL		GSC
-----	Mutter, o sing mich zur Ruh	HL	E-G	†
-----	Sonnenuntergang	HL	CS-FS	DIT
-----	Stille Sicherheit	M	E-F	†
-----	Vergessen	HL		DIT
-----	Voeglein wohin?	HL		GSC
Handel	Dank sei dir, Herr	M	CS-E	†
-----	Das zitternde Glaenzen der spielenden Wellen			
Haydn	Das Leben ist ein Traum			GSC
-----	Der erste Kuss			
-----	My mother bids me bind my hair	M	E-E	†
-----	O tuneful voice			
-----	Pastorella			
-----	She never told her love	HL	B-D	DIT
-----	Sympathy			
-----	The mermaid's song	M	C-F	PRE
Hiller	Sei du mit mir			AMP
Hindemith	Geburt Marias			AMP

(Hindemith)	Pietà from Marienleben			AMP
-----	The moon	M	DS-EF	AMP
Humperdinck	Die Lerche			
Jensen	Am Ufer des Flusses des Manzanares	H	D-FS	GSC
-----	An der Linden			
-----	Fruehlingsnacht	L	D-E	GSC
-----	Murmuring zephyr	LH	E-AF	GSC
-----	Waldesgespraech			
Kienzl	Maria auf dem Berge			
Liszt	In Liebeslust			
-----	Kling'leise, mein Lied	HL		†
Loewe	Canzonetta	MH	B-A	DIT
-----	Der Edelfalk			SC
-----	Der Zahn			SC
-----	Des Glockenthuermers Tochterlein	H	CS-A	SC
-----	Die wandelnde Glocke			SC
-----	Niemand hat's gesehen	LM	DS-FS	†
Mahler	Das Irdische Leben	HL	A-F	INT
-----	Ich atmet' einen linden Duft	HL		INT
-----	Ich ging mit Lust	HL		INT
-----	Liebst du um Schoenheit	HL		INT
-----	Rheinlegendchen	M	B-FS	†
-----	Wer hat dies Liedlein erdacht?	HL	BF-E	INT
Marx	Der bescheidene Schaefer			UNI
-----	Hat dich die Liebe beruehrt	MH	EF-BF	AMP
-----	Marienlied	MH	EF-AF	AMP
-----	Nocturne	H	EF-AF	AMP
-----	Regenlied	LH	E-G	UNI
-----	Selige Nacht	M	DF-GF	AMP
-----	Und gestern hat er mir Rosen gebracht	H	E-A	AMP
-----	Valse de Chopin	M	CS-GS	AMP
-----	Venetianisches Wiegenlied			AMP
-----	Waldseligkeit	H	D-A	UNI
-----	Wie einst			UNI
Mendelssohn	And'res Maienlied			AUG
-----	Bei der Wiege	M	DF-EF	†
-----	Das erste Veilchen	M	F-F	†
-----	Der Mond	HL		†
-----	Die Liebende schreibt	HL		†
-----	Fruehlingslied	H	DS-GS	†
-----	Gruss	M	DS-FS	†
-----	Im Gruenen	H	E-BF	AUG
-----	Minnelied	H	E-G	AUG

(Mendelssohn)	Nachtlied			
-----	Neue Lieb	H	CS-A	†
-----	O Jugend	H	E-A	†
-----	On wings of song			†
-----	Suleika	H	E-GS	†
Mittler	Over the mountains	H		DIT
-----	Soft through my heart	M		AMP
Mozart	Abdenempfindung	M	E-F	
-----	An Chloe	LH	EF-AF	
-----	Das Lied der Trennung			
-----	Das Traumbild			
-----	Das Veilchen	LMH	F-G	†
-----	Der Zauberer	H	F-G	
-----	Die kleine Spinnerin			
-----	Die Verschweigung			
-----	Nehmt meinen Dank			
-----	Sehnsucht nach dem Fruehling			
-----	Trennungslied			
-----	Warnung	HM	C-D	
-----	Wiegenlied	MH	C-G	†
Reger	Des Kindes Gebet	H	F-G	BOT
-----	Friede	H	EF-G	UNI
-----	Mit Rosen bestreut			UNI
-----	Waldeinsamkeit	HML	A-D	BOS
Schoeck	Das bescheidene Wuenschlein			
-----	Die drei Zigeuner			
-----	In der Fremde			
-----	Nachtlied			
-----	Sommerabend			
Schrecker	Wiegenlied der Els			
Schubert	Am Grabe Anselmos	HL	B-EF	†
-----	An den Mond	HL	F-GF	†
-----	An die Laute	LH	D-F	†
-----	An die Nachtigall	H	C-G	†
-----	An die Sonne			†
-----	An eine Quelle			PET
-----	An mein Klavier			PET
-----	Auf dem Strom Horn or violoncello			PET
-----	Auf dem Wasser zu singen	MH	EF-GF	†
-----	Aufloesung	LH	D-A	DIT
-----	Ave Maria	LMH	F-F	†
-----	Ballade			
-----	Danksagung an den Bach	HL	E-F	†
-----	Das Lied im Gruenen			PET
-----	Das Maedchen			PET
-----	Das Wandern	HLM	E-E	†

105

(Schubert)	Das Wirtshaus	HL	C-D	†
-----	Dass sie hier gewesen!			PET
-----	Delphine			PET
-----	Der Blumen Schmerz			PET
-----	Der Einsame	LH	D-G	†
-----	Der Hirt auf dem Felsen Clarinet or violoncello	H	BF-B	
-----	Der Juengling an der Quelle	LH	E-A	†
-----	Der Juengling und der Tod	M	DF-FF	†
-----	Der Knabe			PET
-----	Der Leiermann	ML	C-D	†
-----	Der Morgenkuss			PET
-----	Der Musensohn	LH	FS-G	†
-----	Der Neugierige	HL	CS-EF	†
-----	Der Schmetterling	LH	E-F	†
-----	Der Wachtelschlag	H	DS-FS	PET
-----	Der Wegweiser	L	D-EF	†
-----	Des Fischers Liebesglueck	LH	F-A	†
-----	Des Maedchens	LH	C-E	GSC
-----	Didone's aria			
-----	Die Forelle	MLH	EF-GF	†
-----	Die Gebuesche			PET
-----	Die junge Nonne	LH	C-GF	†
-----	Die Maenner sind mechant			PET
-----	Die Post	HML	BF-EF	†
-----	Die Rose	M	G-FS	PET
-----	Die Taubenpost	HL	D-EF	†
-----	Die Voegel	LH	E-GS	†
-----	Dithyrambe	L	A-D	†
-----	Du bist die Ruh	LMH	EF-AF	†
-----	Ellens zweiter Gesang			PET
-----	Erlafsee	H	E-G	†
-----	Erntelied			PET
-----	Erstarrung	HL	D-F	†
-----	Florio			PET
-----	Freude der Kinderjahre	LH	C-G	†
-----	Fruehlingsglaube	M	EF-F	†
-----	Fruehlingssehnsucht	HL	B-E	†
-----	Fruehlingstraum	HL	C-D	†
-----	Ganymed	LH	EF-G	†
-----	Geheimes	HL	BF-EF	†
-----	Gott im Fruehling			PET
-----	Gretchen am Spinnrade	H	F-A	†
-----	Haenflings Liebeswerbung			PET
-----	Halt!	HL	E-F	†
-----	Heidenroeslein			
-----	Ihr Bild	HL	C-C	†

106

(Schubert)	Im Abendrot	HL	C-D	†
-----	Im Fruehling	LH	D-FS	†
-----	Klaerchens Lied			
-----	La pastorella			SC
-----	Lachen und Weinen	HL	C-EF	†
-----	Letzte Hoffnung	HL		†
-----	Liebesbotschaft	H	E-G	†
-----	Lied der Mignon	HL		†
-----	Lob der Thraenen	LM	F-F	†
-----	Meeresstille	HL	B-D	†
-----	Mein!	HL		†
-----	Mignon	HL		†
-----	Nachtstueck	LH	D-G	†
-----	Nachtviolen			PET
-----	Naehe des Geliebten	HL	D-EF	†
-----	Nur wer die Sehnsucht kennt	LH		†
-----	Rastlose Liebe	M	B-F	†
-----	Seligkeit			
-----	Sprache der Liebe			PET
-----	Staendchen			
-----	Suleika I	LH	DS-G	†
-----	Suleika II	LH	F-BF	†
-----	Ueber allen Zauber Liebe			
-----	Ungeduld	HML		GSC
-----	Verklaerung			PET
-----	Versunken			PET
-----	Viola			
-----	Vor meiner Wiege	HL	C-E	†
-----	Wanderers Nachtlied 2	LH	F-F	†
-----	Wehmuth	HL	B-D	†
-----	Wiegenlied (Op. 98)			†
-----	Wohin?	HL	B-E	†
Schuetz	Eile mich, Gott, zu erretten			BAR
-----	Herr, unser Herrscher!			BAR
Schumann	Abends am Strande			
-----	Abschied vom Walde			
-----	Alte Laute	HL	DF-DF	†
-----	An den Sonnenschein	HL	A-D	†
-----	Auftraege	HL	C-E	†
-----	Dein Angesicht	HL	B-EF	†
-----	Der Himmel hat eine Traene geweint			
-----	Der Nussbaum	LMH	D-FS	†
-----	Der Sandmann	HL	AF-DF	†
-----	Die blume der Ergebung			
-----	Die Lotusblume	HLM	BF-F	†
-----	Die Meerfee			

(Schumann)	Du bist wie eine Blume	HM	F-EF	†
-----	Freisinn			
-----	Fruehlingslust	HL		†
-----	Fruehlingsnacht	L	CS-E	†
-----	Geisternaehe			
-----	Herzeleid			
-----	In der Fremde	HL		†
-----	Intermezzo	HL	C-D	†
-----	Lied der Suleika			
-----	Marienwuermchen	HL	D-D	†
-----	Mein schoener Stern			
-----	Meine Rose			
-----	Mondnacht	M	E-FS	†
-----	O wie lieblich ist das Maedchen			
-----	Roeselein, Roeselein			
-----	Schneegloeckchen	HL		†
-----	Singet nicht in Trauertoenen			
-----	Stille Traenen	HL		†
-----	Volksliedchen	HL		†
-----	Wer machte dich so krank?			
-----	Widmung	HL	BF-F	†
Strauss	Ach Lieb, ich muss nun scheiden	H	D-G	
-----	All' mein' Gedanken	H	CS-GS	
-----	Als mir dein Lied erklang			
-----	An die Nacht			
-----	Beim Schlafengehen			
-----	Breit ueber mein Haupt	LH	GF-AF	†
-----	Das Rosenband			†
-----	Des Dichters Abendgang			†
-----	Die Georgine	LH	B-A	†
-----	Die Nacht	HL		†
-----	Du meines Herzens Kroenelein	HL	CS-E	†
-----	Fruendliche Vision	HL	C-F	†
-----	Fruehling			
-----	Fruehlingsfeier			
-----	Fruehlingsgedraenge			
-----	Fruehlingsstimme			
-----	Hat's gesagt, bleibt's nicht dabei			†
-----	Heimkehr	HL	B-E	†
-----	Heimliche Aufforderung	HL	B-E	†
-----	Ich trage meine minne	M		†
-----	Ich wollt' ein Straeusslein binden			†

(Strauss)	Kling			†
-----	Kornblumen	LH	DF-AF	†
-----	Lied der Frauen			†
-----	Mein Herz ist stumm	LH	EF-AF	
-----	Meinem Kinde			†
-----	Mit deinen blauen Augen	LH	C-GS	DIT
-----	Morgen	HML	E-F	†
-----	Nichts	LH	E-A	†
-----	O suesser Mai			†
-----	Rueckleben			†
-----	Schlagende Herzen			†
-----	Schlechtes Wetter			†
-----	Schoen sind doch kalt die Himmelssterne	H	F-BF	
-----	Schwung			
-----	Seitdem dein Aug' in meines schaute			SC
-----	September			
-----	Traum durch die Daemmerung	HML	BF-EF	†
-----	Waldseligkeit			†
-----	Wiegenlied			
-----	Wie sollten wir geheim sie halten	LH	D-A	
Trunk	Die Allee			
-----	In meiner Heimat			
-----	Mary	HM		AMP
Tunder	Ach Herr, lass deine lieben Engelein			KIS
Wagner	Schlaf, holdes Kind			
Weingartner	Die Post im Walde			
-----	Liebesfeier			
Wetzler	Deiner hellen Stimme			
Wolf	Abschied			†
-----	Ach, des Knaben Augen	HL		†
-----	Ach, im Maien	HL	C-E	DIT
-----	Als ich auf dem Euphrat schiffte			†
-----	Anakreons Grab	HL	D-D	†
-----	An eine Aeolsharfe			†
-----	Auch kleine Dinge	HM	D-E	†
-----	Auf ein altes Bild	HL	E-DS	†
-----	Auf eine Christblume	HL	C-F	†
-----	Auf einer Wanderung	HL		†
-----	Bedeckt mich mit Blumen	HL	B-D	†
-----	Blumengruss	HL	D-E	†
-----	Das verlassene Maegdlein	HL	D-EF	†
-----	Der Gaertner	HL		†
-----	Der Genesene an die Hoffnung	H	BF-AF	PET

(Wolf)	Der Knabe und das Immlein	L	CS-A	†
-----	Die Bekehrte			PET
-----	Die heilige Marie singt			
-----	Die Sproede			†
-----	Die Zigeunerin			†
-----	Du denkst, mit einem Faedchen			†
-----	Elfenlied	HL	D-F	†
-----	Er ist's	H	D-G	†
-----	Frage und Antwort			PET
-----	Fruehling uebers Jahr			†
-----	Fuehr' mich, Kind	H	E-FS	
-----	Ganymed	HL	CS-D	†
-----	Gesang Weylas	HL	DF-F	†
-----	Gesegnet sei das Gruen	HL		†
-----	Gleich und gleich			†
-----	Heb' auf dein blondes Haupt	HL	G-DF	†
-----	Hoch beglueckt in deiner Liebe	HL	DF-F	†
-----	Ich hab' in Penna	LH		†
-----	Ihr jungen Leute			PET
-----	Im Fruehling	HL	BF-F	†
-----	In dem Schatten meiner Locken	M	C-EF	†
-----	Kennst du das Land			†
-----	Lebe wohl	HL	BF-F	†
-----	Liebe mir in Busen zuendet	M	E-F	†
-----	Lied vom Winde			†
-----	Mausfallen Spruechlein	HL	BF-E	†
-----	Morgentau	HL	D-D	†
-----	Nachtzauber	HL	B-E	†
-----	Nimmersatte Liebe	LH	CF-AF	†
-----	Nixe Binsefuss	H	E-G	†
-----	Nun bin ich dein	M	C-F	†
-----	Nun wandre, Maria	HL	EF-D	†
-----	O waer' dein Haus			†
-----	Phaenomen			PET
-----	Rat einer Alten			†
-----	Sie blasen zum Abmarsch			
-----	Storchenbotschaft			PET
-----	Tretet ein, hoher Krieger	HL	B-F	†
-----	Und willst du deinen Liebsten sterben	HL		†
-----	Verborgenheit	HL	B-E	†
-----	Verschwiegene Liebe	LH	DF-FS	†
-----	Waldmaedchen			PET

110

(Wolf)	Wenn du zu den Blumen gehst	HL	B-EF	†
-----	Wer sein holdes Lieb verloren			
-----	Wie glaenzt der helle Mond			†
-----	Zitronenfalter im April	HL		†
-----	Zum neuen Jahr			PET
Wolff	Wer rief dich denn?			

Italian Recital Songs

Lyric Soprano

Abbatini	Quanto è bello il mio diletto			PET
Alfano	Non nascondere il segreto del tuo cuore			
Arditi	Il bacio	H	CS-B	†
Ariosti	Vuoi, che parta (Lucio Vero)			PET
Augustini	Tu non m'intendi amor			
Bassani	Posate, dormite (La Serenata)	H	EF-F	GSC
Bellini	Dolente immagine di fille mia			RIC
Bononcini	Deh, più a me non v'ascondete	LH	EF-F	†
-----	L'esperto nocchiero (Astarte)	HL	B-E	†
-----	Per la gloria	HL	C-EF	†
-----	Più non ti voglio credere Violin	H	D-AF	PET
-----	Si che fedele			DUR
Brogi	Gotine gialle	H		HOM
-----	Le lucciole			
Buzzi-Peccia	Colombetta			RIC
Caccini	Amarilli, mia bella	ML	C-D	†
Caldara	Come raggio di sol	HL	D-F	†
-----	Sebben crudele	HML	E-DS	†
-----	Selve amiche, ombrose piante	HM	E-E	†
Campana	Veglia			
Carissimi	Piangete, ohime			RIC
Casella	Fuor de la bella gaiba			
Castelnuovo-Tedesco	Quattro scherzi per musica			RIC
Cavalli	Donzelle fuggite	HL	C-EF	†

Cesti	Ah, quanto è vero (Il Pomo d'Oro)	HL	F-F	DIT
-----	Che angoscia, che affanno (Il Pomo d'Oro)	HL	C-DF	DIT
-----	Lasciatemi in pace			
Cimara	Filastrocca			
-----	Fiocca la neve	H	G-G	GSC
-----	Ondina			
-----	Scherzo			
-----	Stornello			BON
-----	Trittico primaverile			
Cimarosa	Bel nume che adoro			RIC
Cottone	Ninna, nanna	H	FS-A	MCR
D'Astorga	Qual mai fatale arcano			
-----	Vo' cercando in queste valli	H	D-G	STB
De Luca	Non posso disperar	HL	C-E	GSC
De Meglio	Una tarentella			
Donaudy	Ah mai non cessate			RIC
-----	O del mio amato ben	M	EF-F	RIC
-----	Ognun ripicchia e nicchia			RIC
-----	Quand' il tuo diavol nacque			RIC
-----	Spirate pur, spirate			RIC
Donizetti	La zingara	H	DS-A	GSC
Durante	Vergin, tutta amor	LM	C-EF	†
Falconieri	Non più d'amòre	HL	C-D	DIT
-----	Nudo arciero	HL	AF-AF	DIT
-----	O bellissimi capelli	HL	B-D	†
-----	Occhietti amati	HL	B-D	DIT
-----	Vallanella			
Freschi	Parte il pie			
Gagliano	Dormi, amore	HL	CS-E	DIT
Ghedini	La tortora			
Giordani	Caro mio ben	HML	B-D	†
Gluck	Ah ritorna (Il Trionfo di Clelia)			PET
-----	O del mio dolce ardor (Paride ed Elena)	LH	D-FS	GSC
-----	Spiagge amate (Paride ed Elena)			†
Handel	Affani del pensier (Ottone)			†
-----	Amor commanda (Floridante)	H		†
-----	Bel piacere (Agrippina)			†
-----	Cara sposa (Radamisto)	M	CS-D	
-----	Care selve (Atalanta)	MH	FS-A	†

(Handel)	Caro voi siete all alma (Serse)	H	E-A	CFI
-----	Ch' io mai vi possa (Siroe)			†
-----	Come alla tortorella (Atalanta)	M	B-E	CFI
-----	Deh lasciatemi (Tamerlano)			
-----	Generoso chi sol (Scipione)			GSC
-----	La speranza è giunto in porto (Ottone)			
-----	Lusinghe più care (Alessandro)	H	D-G	†
-----	Mio caro bene (Rodelinda)			OXF
-----	Ne men con l'ombre (Serse)	H	E-A	CFI
-----	Ombre, piante (Rodelinda)	H	FS-A	CFI
-----	Qual farfalletta (Partenope)	H	E-A	†
-----	Rendi' l sereno al ciglio (Sosarme)	LH	EF-F	†
-----	Riportai (Atalanta)			BOO
-----	Se fedele vuoi ch'io ti creda (Orlando)			
-----	Sei, mia gioja (Partenope)			CFI
-----	Sommi Dei (Radimisto)			†
-----	Spietati, io vi giurai (Rodelinda)			BOO
-----	V' adoro pupille (Julius Caesar)			BOO
-----	Vieni o figlio caro e mi consola (Ottone)			†
-----	Voi dolce aurette al cor (Tolomeo)			GSC
Hasse	Nel mirar quel sasso amato			
Haydn	Del mio core (Orfeo ed Euridice)			GSC
-----	Pensi a me			
-----	Un tetto umil			
Jommelli	Chi vuol comprar la bella	H	B-G	GSC
Legrenzi	Bella, moro per te			
-----	Che fiero costume	HML	C-D	†
Lotti	Pur dicesti, o bocca bella	LMH	E-FS	GSC
Malipiero	Ballata	H		CHE
Marcello	O Signor chi sarà			
-----	Un guardo vogli a me	M		BOS
Monteverdi	Lettera amorosa			
-----	Maledetto sia l'aspetto			PET

Mortari	Il mago pistagna			
Mozart	Ridente la calma			BOS
Paisiello	Chi vuol la zingarella	L	C-F	GSC
-----	Nel cor più non mi sento	HL	C-EF	†
Paradies	M'ha preso alla sua ragna	M	EF-F	GSC
-----	Quel ruscelletto	L	BF-F	CFI
Pergolesi	Confusa, smarrita			GSC
-----	Nina	HL	CS-D	DIT
-----	Se tu m'ami	LMH	C-G	GSC
Perti	Canzonetta			
Piccini	Se il ciel mi divide	M	C-F	†
	(Alessandro di Indie)			
Pizzetti	I pastori			FRL
-----	Levommi il mio pensier			RIC
-----	Ninna nanna di uliva			
-----	Quel rosignol che si soave piagne			RIC
Porpora	Non più fra sassi			PET
Quagliati	Apra il suo verde seno	HL	E-CS	DIT
Recli	Bella bellina			
Respighi	Abbandono			BON
-----	Ballata			RIC
-----	Bella porta di rubini			RIC
-----	Crepusculo			
-----	E se un giorno tornasse	M		RIC
-----	Invito alla danza			B ON
-----	La najade ese un giorno tornasse			
-----	Nebbie			†
-----	Nevicata	HM		BON
-----	Notte			BON
-----	Pioggia			BON
-----	Quando nasceste voi			
-----	Scherzo			BON
Rocca	La vocazione di St. Francesco	M	C-F	CHA
Rontani	Or ch'io non segno più	HL	CS-E	DIT
Rosa	Selve, voi che le speranze	MH	D-G	DIT
Rossini	La danza	MH	E-A	†
-----	La promessa			
Sadero	Ero la vo	M		CHE
-----	Fa la nana, bamhin			ZER
-----	I battitori di grano	M		CHE
-----	In mezo al mar	M		CHE
Santoliquido	Io mi levai			
-----	Riflessi			FOR
Sarti	Lungi dal caro bene (Armide)	HL	G-D	GSC
Sartorio	Il mio cor			

Scarlatti, A.	All' acquisto di gloria (Tigrane)	H	C-G	GSC
-----	Col dire a me così			
-----	Già il sole dal Gange	LH	EF-F	GSC
-----	Già mai la lontananza			DUR
-----	La fortuna			BOS
-----	La tua pena			
-----	Labbra gradite			
-----	Quanto è dolce quel velen			
-----	Rugiadose odorose (Il Pirro e Demetrio)	HL	D-E	DIT
-----	Se Florindo è fedele	LM	EF-EF	GSC
-----	Speranza			
-----	Toglietemi la vita ancor			RIC
Scarlatti, D.	Consolati e spara amante	L	BF-E	GSC
-----	Qual farfalletta			
Sgambati	Separazione	LMH	FS-G	GSC
Sibella	Ballata			
-----	La Girometta	HML	D-E	GSC
-----	O bimba bimbetta	LMH	D-G	GSC
-----	O bocca dolorosa	HM	D-F	GSC
Stradella	Così, amor, mi fai languir	HL	F-G	DIT
-----	Per pietà (Il Floridoro)	HM	D-F	DIT
-----	Pietà, Signore	HM	C-F	GSC
-----	Ragion sempre addita	H	E-G	†
Strozzi	Amor dormiglione	HL	B-E	DIT
Tocchi	Ninna, nanna			
Tosti	'A vucchella	LH	F-G	RIC
-----	Mattinata			RIC
-----	Sogno			RIC
Traetta	Ombra cara, amorosa	HL	B-F	†
Vellucci	Che fai tu luna			
Viardot	Fingo per mio diletto			
Vivaldi	Da du venti (Ercole)			
-----	La pastorella sul prima albore			
-----	Un certo no so che	HL	BF-EF	†

Russian Recital Songs

Lyric Soprano

Arensky	By the river			
-----	Revery	MH	DS-FS	DIT
-----	The little fish's song	H	D-A	†
-----	Valse	H	DF-GF	GSC
Borodin	In your far country			
Cui	Poet and critic			

(Cui)	The statue at Czarskoe-Selo	HM	DF-EF	†
-----	Touching the flower			
-----	Twilight			
Dargomijshky	It's all the same to me			
-----	My darling girls			
-----	Parting			
-----	Song of the mermaid			
-----	When the sun is sinking low			
Glazounoff	I am not allowed to go to the river			
-----	Romance orientale			
-----	The nereid	H	FS-A	GSC
Glinka	Ah, kindly star			
-----	How sweet it is to be with you	HM		GSC
-----	The first train			
-----	The journey			
Gretchaninoff	Hushed the song of the nightingale	MH	E-G	DIT
-----	Il s'est tu, le charmant rossignol	H	EF-G	CFI
-----	My native land	L	C-EF	GSC
-----	Over the steppe	LM	C-G	GSC
-----	The skylark			DIT
-----	Wounded birch	HL	B-EF	†
Liadoff	Le lac enchante			
Mednikoff	The hills of Gruzia	H	DS-A	LAC
Medtner	Butterfly			
-----	Roses			
-----	Spanish romance			
-----	The angel			
-----	The ravens			
-----	The singer			
-----	To a dreamer			
-----	Waltz			
-----	Winter evening			
Mussorgsky	In the corner			INT
-----	Night			GSC
-----	The orphan girl			GSC
-----	Tiny star where art thou	LH	DF-F	BOS
Prokofieff	Jewish cradle song			
-----	Snowdrops			GSC
Rachmaninoff	All is so fair			
-----	At night	LH	D-A	BOS
-----	Before my window	HM	C-G	†
-----	Daisies			†
-----	Floods of spring	HL		DIT
-----	God took away from me			GSC

(Rachmaninoff)	Here beauty dwells	H	D-B	CFI
-----	In the silence of night	LH	D-A	GSC
-----	Into my open window	HL	B-FS	BOS
-----	Lilacs	LH	EF-G	†
-----	Melody	H	DS-A	CFI
-----	Midsummer nights	H		BOO
-----	Morning	ML	B-DS	GSC
-----	Oh cease they singing, maiden fair	H	E-A	CFI
-----	O thou billowy harvest field	HL	CS-E	GSC
-----	Sorrow in spring	H	D-BF	DIT
-----	The answer	H		BOO
-----	The coming of spring	LH	DF-AF	BOS
-----	The island	LH	DF-F	†
-----	The soldier's bride			†
-----	The songs of Grusia	H	E-A	GSC
-----	Vocalise	LH	CS-A	GSC
-----	Why wert thou given me			
Rimsky-Korsakov	Hebrew love song	HM		GSC
-----	It is not the wind blowing			
-----	The nightingale and the rose	H	FS-FS	DIT
-----	Zuleika's song			
Rubinstein	Es blinkt der Thau	LH	EF-GF	GSC
-----	Neue Liebe			
-----	Romance			
-----	The lark	LH	EF-G	DIT
-----	The rose			GSC
Scriabin	Soft the rose			
Stravinsky	La rosée sainte			
-----	Pastorale			GSC
-----	Song of the dew			JUR
-----	Spring			
-----	The cloister (La novice)			DIT
-----	Tilibom			
Tchaikovsky	A child's song			
-----	All for you			
-----	At the ball	MH		GSC
-----	At the open window			GSC
-----	Complaint of the bride			
-----	Cradle song	LH	D-G	†
-----	Disappointment			
-----	He loved me so dear	HL		GSC
-----	If I had known			
-----	In this hour of the night	H		GSC
-----	It was early in spring			
-----	Lament			

(Tchaikovsky)	Les Larmes			BES
-----	Serenade			DIT
-----	Song of the gypsy girl			
-----	So soon forgotten			
-----	Why	HL		†
Zimbalist	The folk songs of little Russia			

Scandinavian Recital Songs

Lyric Soprano

Agerby	Havren			
Alfven	Skogen sover			LUN
Alnaes	A leva			
-----	Lykken mellem to mennesker	M	B-FS	HAN
-----	Sidste reis			
Backer				
Gröndahl	In dreaming dance			
-----	Mot kveld			
Bellman	Butterflies at Haga			
-----	Liksom en herdinna			
-----	Undan ur vågen			
Berg	Herdegossen			
Berger	Jungfrun under lind			
Ericksson	Ljus			
-----	Min själ vak upp			
Grieg	A dream			†
-----	Among roses			
-----	By the brook			GSC
-----	En fuglevise			
-----	From Monte Pincio			PET
-----	Greeting			PET
-----	Hope			
-----	I love thee	HML	E-F	†
-----	In the boat	LM	D-EF	†
-----	It was a lovely summer evening			
-----	Kveldsang for Blakken			
-----	Little hut			
-----	Modersorg			
-----	Prinsessen	HL	B-E	†
-----	Snegl, Snegl	M	B-F	HAN
-----	Solvejg's cradle song	M	CS-FS	GSC
-----	Solvejg's song	MH	E-A	†
-----	Springtide	M		DIT
-----	The first meeting			PET

118

(Grieg)	Udvandreren	M	EF-F	HAN
Heise	Loneliness in the forest			
-----	Skovensomhed			
-----	Sol deroppe ganger under lide			
Kilpinen	Der spuk			
-----	Kuessekraut			
-----	Liebessuche			
-----	The cuckoo calls			
Kjerulf	My heart and lute	H		DIT
-----	Synnove's song	M	C-F	GSC
Lange-Mueller	Lykken er ikke gods eller guld			
Lie	Soft-footed snow	HM		DIT
Lindberg	Hur skall man bruden klaeda?			
Nielson	Aebleblomsten			HAN
-----	Havren			
Nystroem	Gubben och gumma			
-----	Kaerlekens visa			
Palmgren	Spring song			
-----	When I first saw your eyes			
-----	Where is the end of the road?			
Peterson-Berger	En visa i folkton			
-----	Till bruden			
-----	Titania			
Rangstroem	A bird flew over the forest			
-----	Avskedet			
-----	Flicken under nymånen			
-----	Pan			
-----	Rondeau			
Sibelius	Black roses	M	A-ES	AMP
-----	But my bird is long in homing			
-----	From the north	H	DS-G	GSC
-----	Illalle			
-----	Ingalill			
-----	Spring is fleeting			DIT
-----	The first kiss	M		AMP
-----	The silent town			AMP
-----	Was it a dream?			BRH
-----	Whisper, reed			
Sinding	Sylvelin	M	E-E	GSC
Sjoegren	Liten prins i vaggan			
Soederberg	Fågelns visa			
Soedermann	Längtan			
-----	Tag emot krandse			

Lyric Soprano

Alvarez	La partida	HL	DS-E	GSC
Berger	They all dance the samba	M	A-FS	GSC
Boero	Serenata			
-----	Serrana			
Freire	Ay, ay, ay	LH		RIC
Fuste	Háblame de amores			REI
Ginastera	Arrorro			RIC
-----	Triste			RIC
Granados	El majo discreto	H		INT
-----	El mirar de la maja			INT
-----	Gracia mía			
-----	Iban al pinar			
-----	Mañanica era			
Grever	Dame tu amor			
-----	Despedida			
Guastavino	La rose y la sauce			RIC
Guridi	Jota castellana			
-----	No quiero tus avellanas			
Lecuona	Desengano			
-----	Mi vida eres tu			MAR
Longas	Lavanderas			
-----	Sevillana			
Mignone	Bella granada			
-----	El clavelito en tus lindos cabellos			
-----	Improviso			
Nin	El amor es como un niño			ESC
-----	El vito			ESC
-----	Granadina			AMP
-----	Malagueña			AMP
-----	Minué cantado			ESC
-----	Montañesa			AMP
-----	Polo			AMP
-----	Villancico catalán			
Obradors	Coplas de curro dulce			
-----	Corazón, por qué pasáis?			
-----	Del cabello mas sutil			RIC
-----	Dos cantares populares			
-----	El vito			
-----	La mi sola laureola			
Padilla	El relicario			GOL
-----	La violetera			HAR
Rogatis	Chacarera			
-----	Gato			

120

(Rogatis)	Vidala			
Sandoval	Copla bailable			
-----	Copla leonesa			
-----	Copla malagueña			
-----	Eres tú			
-----	Sin tu amor	H	E-G	GSC
-----	Zamorana			
Tavares	Bahía			
-----	Benedicto pretinho			
-----	Dansa de caboclo			
Turina	Cantares			UME
-----	Desa el aura			
-----	Farruca	M	A-F	UME
-----	La giralda			
-----	Las locas por amor			UME
-----	Madrigal	H	D-BF	UME
-----	Nunca olvida			
-----	Olas gigantes			
-----	Rima	H	A-A	AMP
-----	Saeta en forma de salve a la Virgen de la esperanza			
-----	Tu pupila es azul			
Yradier	La paloma	HL	BF-EF	GSC

Miscellaneous Recital Songs

Lyric Soprano

Bach-Gounod	Ave Maria			
Bizet	Agnus Dei	HLM	C-AF	
Buchardo	Chilean dance			
Carr	Ave Maria			
Caturia	Bito manue			
Cherubini	Ave Maria	H	E-A	GSC
Chopin	Lithuanian song	ML	C-C	GSC
-----	Mazurka			
-----	My beloved	HL		GSC
-----	My delight	HL		
-----	The maiden's wish	LM	CS-E	GSC
Couperin	Adolescentalus sum ergo Organ, flute and strings			
Dvořák	God is my shepherd			AMP
-----	Hear my prayer, O Lord			AMP
-----	Lord, Thou art my refuge and shield			AMP
-----	Songs my mother taught me	HM	E-E	

121

(Dvořák)	The lark			
-----	The maiden's lament			
-----	The mower			
-----	Tune thy fiddle, gypsy			SIM
-----	Turn Thee to me			AMP
Fernandez	A velha historia			
-----	Cancáo do mar			
-----	Noite de junho			
-----	Samaritana da floresta			
Fisher	Eili, Eili	LMH	E-G	DIT
Franck	Panis angelicus	LM		
Guarnieri	Sae arue			
Janacek	Spring song			
Lecuona	Always in my heart			SOU
Loeffler	Canticum fratris solis			
Mignone	Variations for soprano on popular song luar do sertao			
Mozart	Alleluia	LMH	F-C	
Saint-Saëns	Ave Maria	HM		DIT
Saminsky	Hebrew lullaby	H	D-G	CFI
Schubert	Ave Maria	LMH	F-F	
-----	Salve Regina			
Ticciati	O salutaris hostia			
Villa-Lobos	Bachianas Brazileiras no. 5 8 Celli and bass			AMP
-----	Lundu da marquesa de Santos			
-----	Nhapope			
-----	O canto da nossa terra			
-----	The lost cat			
Weinberger	The way to Emmaus Organ			GRA

British Songs and Arias for
Opening Recitals

Lyric Soprano

Anon	Have you seen but a white lily grow?	H	E-F	GSC
Arne, T.	Oh come my dearest			
-----	Water parted from the sea			GSC
Green	My lips shall speak the praise	M	E-F	OXF
Handel	Have mercy Lord (Te Deum)	HM		†
-----	Let me wander not unseen (L' Allegro)	M	D-G	†

(Handel)	Let the bright seraphim (Samson) Trumpet	H	E-A	†
-----	O sleep why dost thou leave me (Semele)	H	DS-GS	†
-----	Sweet bird (L' Allegro) Flute			NOV
-----	Trip, blithe streamlet (Serse)			
-----	With artful beguiling (Alessandro)			†
Purcell	Fairest Isle (King Arthur)			NOV
-----	Hark, the echoing air (The Fairy Queen)			BAF
-----	Here the deities approve			
-----	If music be the food of love	M	D-G	BOO
-----	Music for a while (Oedipus)	LH		SC
-----	Not all my torments			NOV
-----	We sing to him			

French Songs and Arias for Opening Recitals

Lyric Soprano

Berlioz	Villanelle	H	E-FS	†
Gretry	La fauvette avec ses petits (Zemire et Azor) Flute			LEM
Lully	Chant du Vénus (Revenez Amours) (Thésée)			LEM
Mehul	N'avoir jamais qu une pensée			
Mozart	Dans un bois	H	EF-AF	
Rameau	La musette			BOS
-----	Quand le silence (Air tendre) (Diane et Acteon)			DUR
Severac	Zon, zon, zon			ROU

German Songs and Arias for Opening Recitals

Lyric Soprano

Bach, J. S.	Bist du bei mir	HML	A-EF	†
-----	Ich halte treulich still			

123

(Bach)	Jauchzet Gott in allen Landen (Cantata 51)			BRO
-----	O Jesulein suess			
-----	Seufzer, Traenen, Kummer, Noth (Cantata 21) Oboe			†
Beethoven	Andenken			†
-----	Ich liebe dich	HL	BF-DF	†
Brahms	Ein Wanderer	LH	E-AF	†
-----	Nachtigall	MHL	BF-FS	†
Handel	Dank sei dir Herr (Added to Israel in Egypt)	M	CS-E	†
Haydn	O tuneful voice			
-----	She never told her love	HL	B-D	DIT
-----	Sympathy			
-----	The mermaid's song	M	C-F	PRE
-----	With verdure clad (The Creation)	H	E-BF	†
Mendelssohn	Fruehlingslied	H	DS-GS	†
Mozart	An Chloe	LH	EF-AF	
Schubert	Das Wandern	HLM	E-E	†
-----	Der Wachtelschlag	H	DS-FS	PET
-----	Ganymed	LH	EF-G	†
-----	Gott im Fruehling			PET
-----	Liebesbotschaft	H	E-G	GSC
-----	Verklaerung			PET
Schuetz	Eile mich, Gott, zu erretten			BAR

Italian Songs and Arias for Opening Recitals

Lyric Soprano

Bassani	Posate, dormite (La Serenata)	H	EF-F	GSC
Bononcini	Deh, più a me non v' ascondete	LH	EF-F	†
Caccini	Amarilli, mia bella	ML	C-D	†
Caldara	Sebben crudele	HML	E-DS	†
Carissimi	Lamento della figlia de Jephte (Jepthe)			
Cavalli	Donzelle fuggite	HL	C-EF	†
Cesti	Ah, quanto è vero (Il Pomo d'Oro)	HL	F-F	DIT
-----	Che angoscia, che affanno (Il Pomo d'Oro)	HL	C-DF	DIT
D'Astorga	Qual mai fatale arcano			
Durante	Vergin, tutta amor	LM	C-EF	†

124

Falconieri	O bellissimi capelli	HL	B-D	†
-----	Villanella			
Freschi	Parte il pie			
Gluck	Che fiero momento			HEU
	(Orfeo ed Euridice)			
-----	O del mio dolce ardor	LH	D-FS	GSC
	(Paride ed Elena)			
-----	Spiagge amate			†
	(Paride ed Elena)			
Handel	Affani del pensier			†
	(Ottone)			
-----	Cara sposa	M	CS-D	†
	(Radamisto)			
-----	Care selve (Atalanta)	MH	FS-A	BOO
-----	Ch'io mai vi possa			†
	(Siroe)			
-----	Generoso chi sol			GSC
	(Scipione)			
-----	Ne men con l'ombre	H	E-A	CFI
	(Serse)			
-----	Rendi'l sereno al ciglio	LH	EF-F	†
	(Sosarme)			
-----	Se fedele vuoi ch'io ti			
	creda (Orlando)			
-----	Sei, mia gioja			CFI
	(Partenope)			
-----	Spietati, io vi giurai			BOO
	(Rodelinda)			
-----	V'adoro pupille			BOO
	(Julius Caesar)			
-----	Voi dolce aurette al cor			GSC
	(Tolomeo)			
Hasse	Nel mirar quel sasso amato			
Haydn	Del mio core			GSC
	(Orfeo ed Euridice)			
Jommelli	Chi vuol comprar la	H	B-G	GSC
	bella			
Lotti	Pur dicesti, o bocca	LMH	E-FS	GSC
	bella			
Marcello	O Signor chi sarà			
Mozart	A questo seno, deh vieni			BOO
-----	Ah spiegarti, oh Dio			
-----	Batti, batti, o bel Masetto	H	C-BF	GSC
	(Don Giovanni)			
-----	Bella mia fiamma addio			BOO
-----	Ch'io mi scordi di te			BOO
-----	Parto, parto	H		AMP
	(La Clemenza di Tito)			
	B flat clarinet and piano			

125

(Mozart)	Ridente la calma			BOS
-----	Vado, ma dove			
Paisiello	Chi vuol la zingarella	L	C-F	GSC
-----	Nel cor più non mi sento	HL	C-EF	†
Pergolesi	Se tu m'ami	LMH	C-G	GSC
-----	Stizzoso, mio stizzoso	H	C-AF	†
	(La Serva Padrona)			
Porpora	Non più fra sassi			PET
Sarti	Lungi dal caro bene	HL	G-D	GSC
	(Armide)			
Scarlatti, A.	All' acquisto di gloria	H	C-G	GSC
	(Tigrane)			
-----	Già il sole dal Gange	LH	EF-F	GSC
-----	Già mai la lontananza			DUR
Sgambati	Separazione	LMH	FS-G	GSC
Stradella	Per pietà (Il Floridoro)	HM	D-F	DIT
-----	Pietà, Signore	HM	C-F	GSC
Traetta	Ombra cara, amorosa	HL	B-F	†
Vivaldi	Un certo no so che	HL	BF-EF	GSC

American Songs for Closing Recitals

Lyric Soprano

Bacon	The Colorado tree			
Barber	I hear an army	LH	D-AF	GSC
-----	Sure on this shining night	MH	D-G	GSC
Bernstein	La bonne cuisine	H	B-B	GSC
Branscombe	At the postern gate	MH	DF-AF	ASC
Cadman	Joy	MH	E-A	GSC
Carpenter	Light, my light	M	C-G	GSC
-----	Serenade	LH	CS-A	GSC
Charles	And so, goodbye	LH	EF-AF	GSC
-----	Let my song fill your heart	LH	EF-AF	GSC
-----	Night	MH	F-AF	GSC
-----	When I have sung my songs	HM	BF-EF	GSC
Clough-Leighter	My lover he comes on the skee	HM	D-F	BOS
Creston	Bird of the wilderness	MH	FS-A	GSC
Crist	Knock on the door	H	EF-AF	GSC
Dougherty	Beauty is not caused	M		AMP
-----	Everyone sang			
-----	Portrait	HM	BF-G	GSC
-----	Primavera	H	C-BF	GSC
-----	Song for autumn			

Duke	Evening			
-----	The puritan's ballad			
-----	XXth century	M		VLP
Giannini	Sing to my heart a song	M	D-B	ELV
Golde	Who knows?	HM	BF-F	GSC
Griffes	Evening song			
Hageman	At the well	LH	EF-AF	GSC
-----	Is it you?			
-----	Miranda	HL		GAL
Horsman	The bird of the wilderness	LMH	DF-BF	GSC
Kahn	Spring's in the air	LH	D-A	GSC
Kernochan	We two together	H	EF-AF	GAL
La Forge	Cupid captive	H		GAL
-----	Hills	HL		RIC
-----	Song of the open	MH	EF-AF	GSC
Malotte	A day is born			
Mana-Zucca	There's joy in my heart			CNG
McArthur	Night	H	F-AF	GSC
-----	Spring came	HL	D-F	GSC
Nordoff	Tell me, Thyrsis	H	E-G	AMP
Poldini	Dance of the dolls			CHM
Protheroe	Sing again			
Rasbach	April	LH	EF-G	GSC
Rogers	The last song	MLH	E-AF	GSC
-----	Time for making songs	HM	CS-F	DIT
Rorem	Alleluia			
Rummel	Ecstasy	LMH	GF-AF	GSC
Sacco	Rapunzel	MH	FS-BF	GSC
Saminsky	Queen Estherka's laugh	H	D-A	CFI
Sargent	Twentieth century	H	EF-GS	LEE
Schuman	Holiday song	M	C-F	GSC
Swanson	Joy	M	BF-EF	LEE
Ware	This day is mine	MH	EF-AF	BOS
Warren	Fulfillment	H	D-BF	GAL
-----	Heather	LH	FS-G	GSC
-----	We two	LH	E-A	GSC
-----	White horses of the sea	LH	F-G	GSC
Watts	Joy	HL	D-F	GSC
-----	Stresa	H	EF-BF	DIT
-----	With the tide	H	DF-A	GSC
Worth	Midsummer	LM	E-A	GSC

(See also Negro Spirituals and Folk Songs.)

Miscellaneous Songs for
Closing Recitals

Lyric Soprano

Aiken	Sonnet no. XVIII			
Bizet	Adieu de l'hotesse arabe	H	BF-G	†
Bliss	The buckle			CUR
-----	Three jolly gentlemen	H		†
Brahms	Juchhe!			†
Britten	Les illuminations	H		BOH
Caturia	Bito manue			
Cimara	Canto di primavera		D-G	FRL
Debussy	Chevaux de bois	H	C-G	†
-----	La Demoiselle Elue			DUR
Delius	Love's philosophy			†
Falla	Jota	LH		AMP
-----	Polo	HL		AMP
Gretchaninoff	My native land	L	C-EF	GSC
Grieg	By the brook			GSC
-----	En fuglevise			
Head	A piper	HL		BOO
Henschel	Morning-hymn	MH	DS-GS	†
Jensen	Fruehlingsnacht	L	D-E	GSC
Laparra	Le bonheur			
Lecuona	Desengano			
-----	Mi vida eres tu			MAR
Mortari	Il mago pistagna			
Mozart	Schon lacht der holde Fruehling			
Nin	El vito			ESC
-----	Polo			AMP
Obradors	Chiquitita la novia			
-----	Coplas de curro dulce			
-----	El vito			
Poulenc	Air vif	H	C-AF	ROU
Quilter	Blow, blow, thou winter wind	HL	C-E	BOO
-----	Love's philosophy	LMH	D-A	BOO
Rachmaninoff	Floods of spring	HL		DIT
Respighi	Pioggia			BON
Schubert	Aufloesung	LH	D-A	†
-----	Die Forelle	MLH	EF-GF	†
Schumann	Er ist's	HL	BF-EF	†
-----	Singet nicht in Trauertoenen			
Sibelius	Was it a dream			BRH
Strauss, J.	Blue Danube waltz			GSC
Strauss, R.	Lied der Frauen			†

Turina	Farruca	M	A–F	UME
-----	La giralda			
Warlock	Yarmouth Fair	HL	B–E	CFI
Wolf	Er ist's	H	D–G	†

American Atmospheric Songs

Lyric Soprano

Bacon	Four songs	H	DF–G	MUP
Barber	Rain has fallen	HM	D–E	GSC
-----	Sleep now	MH	EF–AF	GSC
Bone and Fenton	Tryst	MH	FS–G	CFI
Burleigh	Sometimes I feel like a motherless child	HML		RIC
Carpenter	When I bring to you colour'd toys	LM	CS–FS	GSC
Charles	When I have sung my songs	HM	BF–EF	GSC
Crist	Into a ship dreaming	LMH	EF–GS	CFI
Davis	Nancy Hanks	H	D–G	GAL
Dougherty	Lovliest of trees	HM	C–E	BOH
Duke	Bells in the rain	H	E–GS	CFI
-----	Central Park at dusk	M		BOO
-----	I can't be talkin' of love	H	CS–G	GSC
-----	Little elegy	H	FS–A	GSC
-----	The bird			GSC
Flood	The windows of Sainte Chapelle	H		RIC
Ganz	A memory	HM	B–D	GSC
-----	The angels are stooping	MH	GF–A	GSC
Griffes	Symphony in yellow	M	D–GF	GSC
-----	The dreamy lake	H	BS–GS	GSC
Kramer	Pleading	LH	D–GF	JFI
-----	Swans	HL		RIC
MacGimsey	Sweet little Jesus boy	ML	D–D	CFI
McArthur	Night	H	F–AF	GSC
McDonald	He is gone	H	DF–BF	ELV
Naginski	Look down, fair moon			
Niles	I wonder as I wander	HL	BF–D	GSC
Nordoff	Music I heard with you	H	DS–FS	AMP
Proctor	I light the blessed candles	H	DF–A	GSC
Sacco	The ragpicker	MH	C–AF	GSC
Tyson	Like barley bending	HL	C–EF	GSC
Warren	Wander shoes	LH	F–G	FLA
Watts	Wings of night	LH	CS–G	GSC

British Atmospheric Songs

Lyric Soprano

Anon	Have you seen but a white lily grow?	H	E-F	GSC
Bantock	A dream of spring	H	E-G	CHE
Bax	The white peace			CHE
Forsyth	The stranger	H	A-B	GRA
Gibbs	Silver		CS-FS	ROG
Handel	O sleep why dost thou leave me (Semele)	H	DS-GS	†
Hughes	Open the door softly	LMH	G-G	ENO
Quilter	Dream valley	H	EF-GF	ROG
Ronald	Drift down, drift down			BOO
Vaughan Williams	Silent noon			GSC

French Atmospheric Songs

Lyric Soprano

Bizet	Douce mer			GSC
Breville	Prières d'enfant	M	D-F	ROU
Chaminade	The silver ring	HM	BF-F	GSC
Chausson	Les papillons	M	C-F	GSC
Debussy	C'est l'extase	LH	CS-A	†
-----	Les cloches	LH	E-GS	†
-----	Nuits d'etoiles	LH	E-A	MAR
Duparc	Soupir	HL	CS-F	BOS
Fauré	En sourdine	HL	C-EF	†
Ferrari	Le miroir	M	E-F	GSC
Gounod	Sérénade	LMH	D-A	GSC
Hahn	A Chloris	H	DS-FS	HEU
-----	L'heure exquise	M	DF-F	†
-----	Paysage	MH	EF-G	HEU
Leguerney	Genièvres hérissés	H	D-G	ROU
-----	Je vous envoie	H	C-A	ROU
Paladilhe	Psyché	HM	BF-F	GSC
Poulenc	Fleurs	M	DF-F	ROU
Ravel	D'Anne jouant de l'espinette	H	CS-GS	GSC
-----	Le réveil de la mariée	MH	G-F	DUR
-----	Sur l'herbe	MH	C-G	DUR
Roussel	Le jardin mouillé	M	C-FS	ROU
Staub	L'heure silencieuse	H	EF-G	DUR
Szulc	Claire de lune	H	E-G	AXE

German Atmospheric Songs

Lyric Soprano

Haydn	She never told her love	HL	B-D	DIT
Hindemith	The moon	M	DS-EF	AMP
Mahler	Ich ging mit Lust	HL		INT
Marx	Marienlied	MH	EF-AF	AMP
Schubert	An die Nachtigall	H	C-G	†
-----	Nachtviolen			PET
Schumann	Dein Angesicht	HL	B-EF	†
-----	Der Nussbaum	LMH	D-FS	†
Strauss	Die Nacht	HL		†
-----	Traum durch die Daemmerung	HML	BF-EF	†
Wolf	In dem Schatten meiner Locken	M	C-EF	†
-----	Verborgenheit	HL	B-E	†

Miscellaneous Atmospheric Songs

Lyric Soprano

Alnaes	Lykken mellem to mennesker	M	B-FS	HAN
Cui	The statue at Czarskoe-Selo	HM	DF-EF	†
Dvořák	The lark			
Grieg	Snegl, Snegl	M	B-F	HAN
-----	Udvandreren	M	EF-F	HAN
Kjerulf	Synnove's song	M	C-F	GSC
Lie	Soft-footed snow	HM		DIT
Mussorgsky	Tiny star where art thou?	LH	DF-F	BOS
Rachmaninoff	Lilacs	LH	EF-G	†
-----	Morning	ML	B-DS	GSC
Sinding	Sylvelin	M	E-E	GSC

American Dramatic Songs

Lyric Soprano

Barber	I hear an army	LH	D-AF	GSC
Beach	Ah, love but a day			ASC
-----	The year's at the spring	MH	AF-AF	ASC
Bloch	Psalm 114 (Snatched away by Jahveh)	H	A-A	GSC

131

(Bloch)	Psalm 137 (By the waters of Babel)	H	F-AS	GSC
Burleigh	By the pool at the third roses	H		RIC
Campbell-Tipton	A spirit flower	LHM	B-G	GSC
Carpenter	I am like a remnant of a cloud of autumn	L	BF-F	GSC
-----	Light, my light	M	C-G	GSC
Crist	The dark king's daughter			JCH
Diamond	David weeps for Absolom	M	D-A	MUP
Dougherty	Primavera	H	C-BF	GSC
Duke	Capri			
-----	Evening			
-----	Spray	H	CS-A	BOH
Geehl	For you alone			SHU
Giannini	Far above the purple hills	LH	CS-A	RIC
-----	Sing to my heart a song	H	D-B	ELV
Griffes	Evening song	H	DS-GS	GSC
-----	The lament of Ian the proud	MH	DS-AS	GSC
-----	The rose of the night	H	CS-A	GSC
-----	Thy dark eyes to mine	H	EF-AF	GSC
-----	Time was, when I in anguish lay	H	E-GS	GSC
-----	Waikiki	H	DS-GS	GSC
Hageman	Do not go, my love	HL	B-EF	GSC
-----	Music I heard with you	MH	E-A	GAL
Horsman	The bird of the wilderness	LMH	DF-BF	GSC
Kernochan	We two together	H	EF-AF	GAL
La Forge	Song of the open	MH	EF-AF	DIT
MacDowell	The sea	HL	D-D	BRH
Nordoff	Tell me, Thyrsis	H	E-G	AMP
Protheroe	Ah, love but a day	LMH	F-AF	GAM
Rogers	The last song	MLH	E-AF	GSC
-----	Time for making songs	HM	CS-F	DIT
Schuman	Holiday song	M	C-F	GSC
Vene	Age and youth	H	E-A	RIC
Ware	This day is mine	MH	EF-AF	BOS
Warren	Fulfilment	H	D-BF	GAL
-----	We two	LH	E-A	GSC
-----	White horses of the sea	LH	F-G	GSC
Worth	Midsummer	LM	E-A	GSC

British Dramatic Songs

Lyric Soprano

Bainton	The nightingale near the house			CUR
Besley	Listening	H	E-AF	CUR
Bridge	O that it were so	LMH	D-G	CHA
Elgar	Be not extreme, O Lord (Light of Life)			NOV
Handel	Let the bright seraphim (Samson) Trumpet	H	E-A	†
Henschel	Morning-hymn	MH	DS-GS	†
Quilter	Blow, blow, thou winter wind	HL	C-E	BOO
Ronald	Down in the forest	HML	C-D	ENO
-----	Prelude	HML	B-D	ENO

French Dramatic Songs and Arias

Lyric Soprano

Berlioz	Le spectre de la rose			CST
-----	Les nuits d'été			AUG
Bizet	Je dis que rien ne m'épouvante (Carmen)	LH	D-B	†
Chausson	Chanson perpétuelle	H	CS-GS	ROU
Debussy	Air de Lia (L'Enfant Prodigue)	H	E-A	DUR
-----	Chevaux de bois	H	C-G	†
-----	Colloque sentimental			DUR
-----	De fleurs	H	C-AF	†
-----	Noël des enfants qui n'ont plus de maisons			DUR
Duparc	Phidylé	MH	EF-AF	BOS
Fauré	Poème d'un jour			HAM
Fourdrain	Chanson norvégienne	H	E-G	RIC
Gluck	L' ai-je bien entendu? (Iphigenie en Aulide)			†
-----	Non! ce n'est point (Alceste)	H	E-G	†
Gounod	Plus grand, dans son obscurité (La Reine de Saba)	MH	CS-B	†
Hahn	Offrande	M	D-D	†
Halévy	Il va venir (La Juive)	H	D-CF	†
Honegger	Les cloches			SEN

133

(Honegger)	O had I wings like a dove (King David)			CHE
Massenet	Charmes des jours passés (Hérodiade)			HEU
-----	Dis-moi que je suis belle (Thaïs)	H	D-B	HEU
-----	Il est doux, il est bon (Hérodiade)	MH	EF-BF	GSC
-----	L'amour est une vertu rare (Thaïs)			HEU
Meyerbeer	Roberto, o tu che adoro (Robert le Diable)	H	C-C	DEI
Poldowski	L'heure exquise	LMH	DF-AF	CHE
Severac	Chanson pour le petit cheval			ROU

German Dramatic Songs and Arias

Lyric Soprano

Franz	Im Herbst	HM	A-F	†
Mahler	Das Irdische Leben	HL	A-F	INT
Marx	Hat dich die Liebe beruehrt	MH	EF-BF	AMP
-----	Selige Nacht	M	DF-GF	AMP
Mendelssohn	Hear ye, Israel (Elijah)	H	E-A	†
Mozart	Martern aller Arten (Abduction from Seraglio)	H	B-D	†
Schubert	Die junge Nonne	LH	C-GF	†
-----	Erstarrung	HL	D-F	†
-----	Fruehlingstraum	HL	C-D	†
-----	Ganymed	LH	EF-G	†
Strauss, R.	Kling			†
Wolf	Lebe wohl	HL	BF-F	†
-----	Liebe mir in Busen zuendet	M	E-F	†
-----	Nachtzauber	HL	B-E	†

Italian Dramatic Songs and Arias

Lyric Soprano

Boito	Morte di Margherita (L' altra notte) (Mefistofele)	H	D-B	GSC
Carissimi	Piangete, ohime			RIC

134

Catalani	Ebben? Ne andrò lontana	H	E-B	RIC
	(La Wally)			
Cilea	Io son' l' umile ancella	H		AMP
	(Adriana Lecouvreur)			
-----	Poveri fiori			SON
	(Adriana Lecouvreur)			
Cimara	Canto di primavera		D-G	FRL
Durante	Vergin, tutta amor	LM	C-EF	†
Faccio	Sortita d'Ofelia (Amleto)			GSC
Giordano	La mamma morta	H	CS-B	AMP
	(Andrea Chenier)			
Mascagni	Son pochi fiori			GSC
	(L' Amico Fritz)			
Mozart	Or sai, chi l' onore			†
	(Don Giovanni)			
Pergolesi	Confusa, smarrita			GSC
Puccini	Ancora un passo			RIC
	(Madama Butterfly)			
-----	In quelle trine morbide	H	DF-BF	RIC
	(Manon Lescaut)			
-----	Musetta's waltz	H	EF-DF	RIC
	(La Boheme)			
-----	Solo perduta abbandonata			RIC
	(Manon Lescaut)			
-----	Tu, che di gel sei cinta			RIC
	(Turandot)			
-----	Un bel di vedremo	H	DF-BF	RIC
	(Madama Butterfly)			
-----	Vissi d' arte	MH	EF-BF	RIC
	(Tosca)			
Respighi	Nebbie			†
Traetta	Ombra cara, amorosa	HL	B-F	†
Verdi	Ecco l' orrido campo	H	B-C	RIC
	(Un Ballo in Maschera)			

Miscellaneous Dramatic Songs

Lyric Soprano

Alvarez	La partida	HL	DS-E	GSC
Dvořák	Hear my prayer, O Lord			AMP
Granados	La maja dolorosa	M		INT
Gretchaninoff	Over the steppe	LM	C-G	GSC
-----	The skylark			DIT
-----	Wounded birch	HL	B-EF	†
Grieg	A dream			†
-----	In the boat	LM	D-ES	†
-----	Prinsessen	HL	B-E	†

135

Mussorgsky	The orphan girl			GSC
Rachmaninoff	Floods of spring	HL		DIT
-----	God took away from me			GSC
-----	O thou billowy harvest field	HL	CS-E	GSC
-----	Sorrow in spring	H	D-BF	DIT
-----	The soldier's bride			†
-----	To the children	MH	F-G	DIT
Sibelius	Black roses	M	A-ES	AMP
-----	Was it a dream			BRH
Stravinsky	Song of the dew			JUR
-----	The cloister (La novice)			DIT
Tchaikovsky	All for you			
-----	Complaint of the bride			
-----	None but the lonely heart	HLM	C-F	DIT
-----	Why	HL		†
Turina	Madrigal	H	D-BF	UME
-----	Rima	H	A-A	AMP

American Humorous Songs

Lyric Soprano

Bergsma	Six songs	H	E-BF	CFI
Bernstein	I hate music	H	C-A	WIT
-----	I just found out today			
-----	La bonne cuisine	H	B-B	GSC
-----	Rabbit at top speed			GSC
Carpenter	If	M	D-E	GSC
Crist	Chinese mother goose rhymes	H	C-G	CFI
Davis	Deaf old woman			GAL
Dougherty	Love in the dictionary	M	C-G	GSC
-----	Weathers			
Duke	A piper	H	CS-B	GSC
-----	I can't be talkin' of love	H	CS-G	GSC
Griselle and Young	The cuckoo clock	LH	EF-G	GSC
Gruenberg	Animals and insects	H	A-A	UNI
Hadley	My shadow			ASC
Hindemith	The whistling thief	M	E-F	AMP
Josten	Cupid's counsel	H	EF-AF	GSC
Kountz	The little French clock	LH	D-G	GAL
MacDowell	A maid sings light	H	F-G	ASC
Mopper	The lemon-colored dodo	H	F-BF	BOS
Nordoff	Serenade	H	CS-FS	AMP
-----	There shall be more joy	M	CS-FS	AMP

Powell	The deaf woman's courtship	M		JFI
Rich	American lullaby	LH	C-F	GSC
Sacco	Mexican serenade	HL	D-EF	BOS
Sandoval	Theme and 3 variations on "Long ago"	H	CS-B	GSC
Schuman	Holiday song	M	C-F	GSC
Slonimsky	Gravestones at Hancock, New Hampshire	H	D-G	AXE
Spross	Will o' the wisp			JCH
Wolf	Jack in the box			
-----	Weather forecast	H	EF-GS	GSC

British Humorous Songs

Lyric Soprano

Bax	Oh dear, what can the matter be?	M	D-EF	CHE
Bliss	The buckle			CUR
-----	Three jolly gentlemen	H		†
Britten	Oliver Cromwell			BOH
Clarke	Shy one	HL	BF-G	BOH
Gibbs	Five eyes	HL	D-D	BOS
Jacob	Laughing song	H	D-G	OXF
Lehmann	The cuckoo	HH	D-B	BOH
Novello	The little damozel	LHM	C-G	BOO

French Humorous Songs

Lyric Soprano

Chabrier	Villanelle des petits canards	HML	B-E	†
Dalcroze	Le coeur de ma mie	HML		†
Debussy	Voici que le printemps	LH	CS-G	BOS
Monsigny	Il regardait mon bouquet (Le Roi et le Fermier)	H	D-G	GSC
Pierné	Ils etaient trois petits chats blancs			MAR
Ravel	Sur l' herbe	MH	C-G	DUR
Rosenthal	Le marabout			ESC
Satie	Le chapelier			ROU

Lyric Soprano

Bach, J. S.	Patron, das macht der Wind (Phoebus and Pan)	M	C–G	GSC
Blech	Heimkehr vom Feste			UNI
Brahms	Vergebliches Staendchen	LHM	E–FS	†
Loewe	Der Zahn			SC
-----	Des glockenthuermers Tochterlein	H	CS–A	SC
Mahler	Rheinlegendchen	M	B–FS	†
-----	Wer hat dies Liedlein erdacht?	HL	BF–E	INT
Marx	Der bescheidene Schaefer			UNI
Mozart	Durch Zaertlichkeit (Abduction from Seraglio)			†
-----	Warnung	HM	C–D	
Nicolai	Now to my aid fun wit and humor (The Merry Wives)			
Reger	Waldeinsamkeit	HML	A–D	BOS
Schubert	Die Maenner sind mechant			PET
-----	Heidenroeslein			
Strauss, J.	Adele's laughing song (Die Fledermaus)	H	D–B	GSC
-----	Ein Maedchen hat es gar nicht gut (The Gypsy Baron)			CRZ
Wolf	Abschied			†
-----	Der Knabe und das Immlein	L	CS–A	†
-----	Elfenlied	HL	D–F	†
-----	Ich hab' in Penna	LH		†
-----	Nimmersatte Liebe	LH	CF–AF	†
-----	Storchenbotschaft			†
-----	Tretet ein, hoher Krieger	HL	B–F	†

Italian Humorous Songs and Arias

Lyric Soprano

Mozart	Venite inginocchiatevi (Le Nozze di Figaro)	H	D–G	†
Paisiello	Chi vuol la zingarella	L	C–F	GSC
Pergolesi	A Serpina penserete (La Serva Padrona)	HLM	D–F	†
-----	Stizzoso, mio stizzoso (La Serva Padrona)	H	C–AF	†

Rontani	Or ch' io non segno più	HL	CS-E	DIT

American Folk Songs (Arr.)

Lyric Soprano

Bacon	Careless love			GAL
Davis	Deaf old woman			BRO
Endicott	He stole my tender heart away			
Hughes	Birds' courting song			GSC
Johnson	His name so sweet	H	D-D	CFI
Niles	Down in the valley			GSC
-----	Go 'way from my window	MH	C-G	GSC
-----	I wonder as I wander	HL	BF-D	GSC
-----	If I had a ribbon bow			GSC
-----	The blue madonna	H		GSC
Powell	The deaf woman's courtship	M		JFI
-----	The rich old woman	M		JFI
Siegmeister	He's gone away			
Sowerby	He's gone away			
Taylor	Twenty, eighteen	IIM	D-E	JFI
Willan	The little red lark			BOS

British Folk Songs (Arr.)

Lyric Soprano

Bax	Oh dear, what can the matter be?	M	D-EF	CHE
Benjamin	Jan (Creole melody)	M		BOO
-----	Linstead market	M		BOO
Britten	La belle est au jardin d'amour			BOH
-----	Le roi s'en va-t-en chasse			BOH
-----	O can ye sew cushions?			BOH
-----	Quand jétais chez mon pore			
-----	The ash grove			BOH
-----	The Sally gardens			BOH
Gatty	Bendemeer's stream	LMH		BOO
Grainger	The sprig of thyme	LH	E-FS	GSC
Gurney	Down by the Salley gardens			OXF
Hook	Mary of Allendale			BOO
Hopekirk	Coming through the rye			DIT
-----	Flow gently, sweet Afton			DIT
-----	Loch Lomond			DIT
Hughes	Hey diddle diddle			CRA

(Hughes)	I have a bonnet trimmed with blue			BOO
-----	I know my love			BOO
-----	I know where I'm going			BOO
-----	I will walk with my love			BOO
-----	Open the door softly	LMH	G-G	ENO
-----	The leprechaun			
-----	The little boats			BOO
-----	The next market day			BOO
Kennedy-Fraser	A fairy's love song			BOO
-----	An Eriskay love lilt			BOO
-----	Land of heart's desire			BOO
-----	Isle of my heart			BOO
Page	The meeting of the waters			DIT
Peel	The early morning			CHA
Vaughn Williams	And all in the morning	L	D-E	GAL
-----	Robin Hood and the pedlar	M	D-E	OXF
-----	Rolling in the dew			OXF
Warlock	Yarmouth Fair	HL	B-E	CFI
Welsh	The ash grove			
Wilson	Come let's be merry			BOO

Miscellaneous Folk Songs (Arr.)

Lyric Soprano

Bartok	Altal mennék én a Tiszán			BOH
-----	Asszonyok, Asszonyok			BOH
-----	Elindultam szép hazámbul			BOH
-----	Feketeföd			BOH
-----	Istenem, Istenem			BOH
-----	Nem mesze van ide kis Margitta			BOH
-----	Töltek a nagy erdö útját			BOH
Brahms	Da unten in Thale			†
-----	In stiller Nacht			†
-----	Mein Maedel hat einen Rosenmund	M	F-F	†
Dvořák	Gypsy songs	LH	D-A	AMP
Falla	Asturiana	HL		AMP
-----	El paño moruno	HL		AMP
-----	Jota	LH		AMP
-----	Nana	HL		AMP
-----	Polo	HL		AMP
-----	Seguidilla murciana	HL		AMP

Ferrari	Il etait un bergere			GSC
-----	Le jardin d'amour	LM	EF-F	GSC
McFeeters	Gentle Mary	H	EF-AF	GSC
Obradors	Chiquitita la novia			
Ravel	Chanson italienne			DUR
-----	Cinq mélodies populaires grecques			CUR
-----	Là-bas vers l'église	MH	GS-E	DUR
-----	Le réveil de la mariée	MH	G-F	DUR
-----	Quel galant!	M	D-F	DUR
-----	Tout gai	MH	EF-F	DUR
Sadero	Stornello pugliese	M	F-F	GSC
Serradell	La golondrina	H	C-A	GSC
Tavares	Bia-ta-ta			
Tiersot	Noël provençal			
-----	Tambourin			
Weckerlin	Aminte	M	C-D	†
-----	Chantons les amours de Jean	H	D-G	GSC
-----	L'amour s'envole	H	E-G	GSC
-----	Maman, dites-moi	M	E-FS	BOS
-----	Mignonette			

Negro Spirituals

Lyric Soprano

Boatner	Oh, what a beautiful city!	HL	D-E	GSC
-----	On mah journey	LH	EF-EF	RIC
Burleigh	De gospel train	HL		RIC
-----	Joshua fit de battle ob Jericho	LH	DS-E	RIC
-----	Little child of Mary	HL		RIC
-----	Little David play on yo harp	HL		RIC
-----	Swing low, sweet chariot	HL		RIC
-----	Weepin' Mary	HL		RIC
-----	Were you there?	HML		RIC
Dett	A man goin' roun'			
-----	I couldn't hear nobody pray			
-----	In dat great gittin' up morning			
-----	Nobody knows de trouble I've seen			
-----	Ride on Jesus	H		JFI
-----	Rise up shepherd an' foller			
-----	Sit down servant			GSC

141

(Dell)	Were you there?			
Johnson	City called Heaven			ROB
-----	Dere's no hidin' place down dere			
-----	Ride on, King Jesus			CFI
Kerby- Forrest	He's got the whole world in His hands	M	G-E	MLS
MacGimsey	Sweet little Jesus boy	ML	D-D	CFI
-----	Workin' workin'			
Price	My soul's been anchored in the Lord			GAM
Ryder	Let us break bread together	LH	D-G	JFI
Wolff	Gimme dat ole time religion			
Work	Wasn't that a mighty day?			

American Songs Employing Agility

Lyric Soprano

Bacon	Four songs	H	DF-G	MUP
Bernstein	La bonne cuisine	H	B-B	GSC
Buzzi-Peccia	Under the greenwood tree	LMH	EF-A	DIT
Charles	Let my song fill your heart	LH	EF-AF	GSC
Clough- Leighter	My lover he comes on the skee	HM	D-F	BOS
Crist	O come hither	HM	B-GS	CFI
Curran	Ho! Mr. Piper	LH	D-G	GSC
Hageman	Miranda	HL		GAL
Hopkinson	O'er the hills	LH	C-G	†
LaForge	Come unto these yellow sands	H	FS-B	GSC
Menotti	Lucy's arietta (The Telephone)			GSC
Nevin	One spring morning	MH	DS-F	BOS
Nordoff	There shall be more joy	M	CS-FS	AMP
Parker	The lark now leaves her watery nest	LH	D-BF	JCH
Speaks	In may time	HL	D-E	JCH

British songs and Arias
Employing Agility

Lyric Soprano

Arne, M.	The lass with the delicate air	MH	D-G	†
Arne, T.	Where by bee sucks	HM		†
Bax	Shieling song	H	CS-A	CHE
Besley	Listening	H	E-AF	CUR
Bishop	Lo! here the gentle lark	H		†
-----	Love has eyes	M		†
-----	Pretty mocking bird Flute	H		†
-----	Should he upbraid	H		†
Bliss	Three jolly gentlemen	H		†
Carey	A pastoral			GSC
Finzi	Let us garlands bring (Shakesperian songs)	M		BOO
German	Charming Chloe	HML		NOV
-----	Waltz song (Tom Jones)	H	B-B	CHA
Green	My lips shall speak the praise	M	E-F	OXF
Handel	From mighty Kings (Judas Maccabaeus)	H	D-A	†
-----	Hallelujah (Esther)	H	E-B	CFI
-----	Let the bright seraphim (Samson) Trumpet	H	E-A	†
-----	Oh! had I Jubal's lyre (Joshua)	H	E-FS	†
-----	Rejoice greatly (The Messiah)	H	E-A	†
-----	So shall the lute and harp awake (Judas Maccabaeus)			†
Hook	Softly waft, ye southern breezes			GSC
Linley	O, bid your faithful Ariel fly			BOO
Morley	It was a lover and his lass	HM		DIT
Purcell	Come unto these yellow sands			AUG
-----	From rosey bow'rs (Don Quixote)			AUG
-----	Hark! the echoing air (The Fairy Queen)			BAF
-----	Nymphs and shepherds (The Libertine)	HM	C-F	†
-----	Strike the viol			BAF

Quilter	Love's philosophy	LMH	D-A	BOO
Scott	Blackbird's song			ELK
Wilson	Come let's be merry			BOO

French Songs and Arias Employing Agility

Lyric Soprano

Bizet	Ouvre ton coeur	MH	DS-GS	†
Campra	Charmant papillon	MH	D-G	GSC
	(Les Fêtes Ve nitiennes)			
Chaminade	L'été	MH	E-A	†
Chausson	Les papillons	M	C-F	GSC
Dalayrac	Jeune fillette	HL	GS-E	DIT
Debussy	Fêtes galantes	LH	CS-A	†
Delibes	Les filles de Cadiz	HM	A-A	†
-----	Passepied	LH	DS-CS	GSC
Dupont	Chanson des noisettes			HEU
Falla	Polo	HL		AMP
Fauré	Mandoline	HL	F-E	†
Ferrari	Le jardin d'amour	LM	EF-F	GSC
Georges	La pluie	HL		INT
Gounod	Air des bijoux (Faust)	H	B-B	†
-----	Je veux vivre	H	F-C	†
	(Roméo et Juliette)			
-----	Mon coeur ne peut changer!			GSC
	(Mireille)			
Grétry	Je ne le dis qu'à vois			LEM
	(La Fausse Magie)			
-----	La fauvette avec ses petits			LEM
	(Zémire et Azor)			
Groulez	Guitares et mandolines			
Massé	Chanson du Tigre			
	(Paul et Virginie)			
Poulenc	Air vif	H	C-AF	ROU
-----	Airs chantés	H	C-AF	ROU
Saint-Saëns	Guitares et mandolines			DUR
Thomas	Je connais un pauvre	H	C-B	†
	enfant (Mignon)			
Vidal	Ariette	LH	F-A	GSC
Weckerlin	L'amour s'envole	H	E-G	GSC

German Songs and Arias Employing Agility

Lyric Soprano

Bach, J.S.	Auch mit gedaempften,			PET

144

(Bach)	schwachen Stimmen (Cantata 36) Violin			
-----	Come visit ye glowing	H		
-----	Hoert, ihr Augen auf zu weinen (Cantata 98) Oboe			PET
-----	Hoert, ihr Voelker (Cantata 76) Violin			BRO
-----	I follow thee (St. John Passion)			†
-----	Jauchzet Gott in allen Landen (Cantata 51)			BRO
-----	Mein glaeubiges Herze (Cantata 68)	HML		†
-----	Mein Seelenschatz (Cantata 18)			BRO
-----	Wie zittern und wanken (Cantata 105)			BRO
Beethoven	Mailied			RIC
Brahms	Botschaft	HL	D-F	†
-----	Das Maedchen spricht	H	E-FS	†
-----	O liebliche Wangen	MLH	E-G	†
Eckert	Swiss echo song	H	A-B	GSC
Haydn	My mother bids me bind my hair	M	E-E	†
-----	The mermaid's song	M	C-F	PRE
Jensen	Am Ufer des Flusses des Manzanares	H	D-FS	GSC
Loewe	Des Glockenthuermers Tochterlein	H	CS-A	SC
-----	Niemand hat's gesehen	LM	DS-FS	†
Mahler	Rheinlegendchen	M	B-FS	†
-----	Wer hat dies Liedlein erdacht?	HL	BF-E	INT
Marx	Und gestern hat er mir Rosen gebracht	H	E-A	AMP
Mendelssohn	Fruehlingslied	H	DS-GS	†
Mozart	Ach, ich liebte (Abduction from Seraglio)			†
-----	Martern aller Arten (Abduction from Seraglio)	H	B-D	†
Nicolai	Now to my aid fun wit and humor (The Merry Wives)			
Schubert	Ballade			
-----	Das Wandern	HLM	E-E	†
-----	Der Hirt auf dem Felsen Clarinet or violoncello	H	BF-B	†
-----	Der Wachtelschlag	H	DS-FS	PET
-----	Mein!	HL		†
-----	Ungeduld	HML		†

Schumann	Auftraege	HL	C-E	†
-----	Fruehlingsnacht	L	CS-E	†
Strauss, J.	Adele's laughing song (Die Fledermaus)	H	D-B	GSC
-----	Blue Danube waltz			GSC
-----	Tales from the Vienna forest	H	EF-C	GSC
-----	Voci di primavera	LMH	EF-C	GSC
Weber	Truebe Augen (Der Freischuetz)			GSC
Wolf	Die Zigeunerin			†

Italian Songs and Arias
Employing Agility

Lyric Soprano

Abbatini	Quanto è bello il mio diletto			PET
Arditi	Il bacio	H	CS-B	†
Ariosti	Vuoi, che parta (Lucio Vero)			PET
Bellini	Ah! non credea mirarti (La Sonnambula)			GSC
-----	Casta diva (Norma)	H	F-C	†
Bononcini	L'esperto (Nocchiero)	HL	B-E	†
Cimara	Canto di primavera		D-G	FRL
Donaudy	Ah mai non cessate			RIC
-----	Spirate pur, spirate			RIC
Donizetti	O luce di quest' anima (Linda di Chamounix)	H	C-E	GSC
-----	Prendi, prendi per mei sei libero (L'Elisir d'Amore)			BRO
-----	Quel guardo (Don Pasquale)			BRO
Gluck	Ah ritorna (Il Trionfo di Clelia)			PET
Handel	Amor commanda (Floridante)	H		†
-----	Ch'io mai vi possa (Siroe)			†
-----	Dira che amor per me (Serse)	H	F-A	CFI
-----	Lusinghe più care (Alessandro)	H	D-G	GSC
-----	Mio caro bene (Rodelinda)			OXF
-----	Qual farfalletta (Partenope)	H	E-A	†
-----	Riportai gloriosa palma (Atalanta)			BOO

146

(Handel)	Sei, mia gioja (Partenope)			CFI
-----	Spietati, io vi giurai (Rodelinda)			BOO
Leoncavallo	Ballatella! (I Pagliacci)	H	CS-AS	†
Lotti	Pur dicesti, o bocca bella	LMH	E-FS	GSC
Mozart	Batti, batti, o bel Masetto (Don Giovanni)	H	C-BF	†
-----	Come scoglio (Così Fan Tutte)			†
-----	Dove sono Le Nozze di Figaro	H	D-A	†
-----	Mi tradi quell' alma ingrata Don Giovanni			†
-----	Misera, dove son			BOO
Paradies	Quel ruscelletto	L	BF-F	CFI
Pergolesi	A Serpina penserete (La Serva Padrona)	HLM	D-F	†
Porpora	Non più fra sassi			PET
Puccini	Ancora un passo (Madama Butterfly)			RIC
Rossini	La danza	MH	E-A	†
-----	La pastorella delle Alpi	H	E-C	CFI
-----	Una voce poco fa (Il Barbiere di Siviglia)	HM	GS-E	GSC
Scarlatti, A.	All acquisto di gloria (Tigrane)	H	C-G	GSC
-----	Già il sole dal Gange	LH	EF-F	GSC
-----	Rugiadose odorose (Il Pirro e Demetrio)	HL	D-E	DIT
-----	Se Florindo è fedele	LM	EF-EF	GSC
Scarlatti, D.	Consolati e spara amante	L	BF-E	GSC
-----	Qual farfalletta			
Sibella	O bimba bimbetta	LMH	D-G	GSC
Stradella	Ragion sempre addita	H	E-G	†
Verdi	Ah fors' è lui (La Traviata)	H	C-DF	†
-----	Ernani involami (Ernani)	H	AF-BF	GSC
-----	Tacea la notte placida (Il Trovatore)	H	D-DF	†
-----	Volta la terrea (Un Ballo in Maschera)	H	D-BF	GSC
Vivaldi	Un certo no so che	HL	DF-EF	†

Miscellaneous Songs and Arias
Employing Agility

Lyric Soprano

Alvarez	La partida	HL	DS-E	GSC
Chopin	My delight	HL		
-----	The maiden's wish	LM	CS-E	GSC
Falla	Nana	HL		AMP
-----	Seguidilla murciana	HL		AMP
Glazounoff	La primavera d'or	H	D-BF	GSC
Granados	El majo discreto	H		INT
Grieg	Solvejg's song	MH	E-G	†
Mignone	Variations for soprano on the popular song Luar do sertao			
Mozart	Et incarnatus est (C Minor Mass)			PET
Mussorgsky	Tiny star where art thou?	LH	DF-F	BOS
Rimsky-Korsakov	Hymn to the sun (Le Coq d'Or)	H	FS-B	GSC

American Songs Employing
Crescendo and Diminuendo

Lyric Soprano

Bacon	Is there such a thing as day?	M	DS-FS	AMP
Barber	Rain has fallen	HM	D-E	GSC
-----	Sleep now	MH	EF-AF	GSC
-----	The daisies	M	C-F	GSC
Beach	Ah, love but a day			ASC
-----	Fairy lullaby			ASC
Cadman	From the land of the sky-blue water			WHI
Campbell-Tipton	A spirit flower	LHM	B-G	GSC
Carpenter	The sleep that flits on baby's eyes	M	B-FS	GSC
-----	When I bring to you colour'd toys	LM	CS-FS	GSC
Duke	Bells in the rain	H	E-GS	CFI
Elwell	In the mountains	M	DF-F	BMI
Engel	Sea shell	M	EF-EF	GSC
Fairchild	A memory			BOS

148

Hopkinson	Beneath a weeping willow's shade	H	D-G	†
-----	My days have been so wondrous free	LH	EF-G	†
La Forge	Hills	HL		RIC
Lubin	The piper	H	C-A	GSC
Manning	White clouds			DIT
Naginski	The pasture	M	BF-EF	GSC
-----	Under the harvest moon	M	D-E	GSC
Niles	I wonder as I wander	HL	BF-D	GSC
Nordoff	Fair Annette's Song			AMP
-----	Serenade	H	CS-FS	AMP
Rogers	At parting	LH	CS-FS	GSC
Thompson	Velvet shoes	M	C-E	ECS
Watts	Wings of night	LH	CS-G	GSC

British Songs and Arias Employing Crescendo and Diminuendo

Lyric Soprano

Balfe	I dream't I dwelt in marble halls (The Bohemian Girl)			†
Bantock	A dream of spring	H	E-G	CHE
Bax	Cradle song			CHA
Benjamin	The wasp			CUR
Bliss	Lovelocks			GOT
Clarke	Shy one	HL	BF-G	BOH
Gibbs	To one who passed whistling through the night	H	F-G	CUR
Handel	Angels ever bright and fair (Theodora)	H	E-F	†
-----	Ask if yon damask rose (Susanna)			†
-----	As when the dove (Acis and Galatea)	H	D-G	†
-----	Let me wander not unseen (L'Allegro)	M	D-G	†
-----	O sleep why dost thou leave me (Semele)	H	DS-GS	†
-----	Sweet bird Flute (L'Allegro)			NOV
-----	What's sweeter than a new-blown rose (Joseph)	H	EF-AF	†
Horn	Cherry ripe	M	D-G	†
-----	I've been roaming	L	B-E	†

149

Ireland	Bed in summer			CUR
Purcell	I attempt from Love's sickness to fly (The Indian Queen)	MH	CS-E	†
Quilter	Dream Valley	H	EF-GF	ROG
-----	To daisies			BOO
Shaw	Song of the Palanquin bearers	LH	E-F	CUR

French Songs and Arias Employing Crescendo and Diminuendo

Lyric Soprano

Auber	Quel Bonheur (Fra Diavolo)			BOO
Auric	Printemps			DUR
Bachelet	Chère nuit	H	DF-BF	GSC
Berlioz	Villanelle	H	E-FS	†
Bizet	Après l'hiver			†
-----	Vielle chanson	H	EF-A	GSC
Chaminade	The silver ring	HM	BF-F	GSC
Charpentier	Depuis le jour (Louise)	MH	D-B	†
Dalayrac	D'un époux chéri			DUR
Dalcroze	Le coeur de ma mie	HML		†
-----	L'oiseau bleu			CFI
David	Charmant oiseau (La Perle du Brésil)	M	D-E	†
Debussy	Air de Lia (L'Enfant Prodigue)	H	E-A	DUR
-----	C'est l'extase	LH	CS-A	†
-----	Crois mon conseil, chere Climène			DUR
-----	En sourdine	M	C-FS	†
-----	Green	H	C-AF	†
-----	La flûte de Pan		B-B	†
-----	Le tombeau des naïades			JOB
-----	Les angélus			HAM
-----	Les cloches	LH	E-GS	†
-----	Les ingénus			DUR
-----	Voici que le printemps	LH	CS-G	BOS
Duparc	Chanson triste	MH	FS-AF	BOS
-----	L'invitation au voyage	HM	E-F	†
-----	Phidylé	MH	EF-AF	BOS
Fauré	Adieu	MH	F-F	†
-----	Au bord de l'eau	HL	C-F	†
-----	Clair de lune	MH	C-G	†

150

(Fauré)	Le secret	LH	F-G	†
-----	Les roses d'Ispahan	HM	D-FS	†
-----	Lydia	MH	G-G	†
-----	Nell	LH	FS-AF	†
-----	Spleen	H	E-FS	MAR
-----	Sylvie	HL	E-F	†
Gounod	Ah, si je redevenais belle (Philémon et Baucis)	H	E-A	GSC
-----	Le jour se lève (Mireille)			CHO
Grétry	Je crains de lui (Richard Coeur de Lion)			LEM
-----	Plus de dépit (Les Deux Avares)			LEM
Hahn	Le rossignol des lilas			
Herold	Air de Nicette (Le Pré aux Clercs)			BRA
Koechlin	L'hiver	H	E-G	†
Lalo	La chanson d'Alouette	H	EF-B	GSC
Liszt	Comment, disaient-ils?	H	C-AF	†
-----	S'il est un charmant gazon	HL		†
Martini	Plaisir d'amour	M	BF-EF	GSC
Massé	Air du rossignol Flute (Les Noces de Jeannette)			
Massenet	Adieu, notre petite table (Manon)			GSC
-----	Gavotte (Manon)			†
-----	Je suis encore tout étourdie (Manon)			HEU
Meyerbeer	Nobles Seigneurs, salut! (Les Huguenots)	LH	C-C	†
Paladilhe	Psyché	HM	BF-F	GSC
Rameau	Dans ces doux asiles (Castor et Pollux)			LEM
-----	La musette			BOS
-----	Le grillon			DUR
Rhené-Baton	Berceuse			DUR
Saint-Saëns	Le bonheur est une chose légère Violin and piano	H	C-A	CHO
Satie	Daphénéo			ROU

German Songs and Arias Employing Crescendo and Diminuendo

Lyric Soprano

Beethoven	Andenken			†

151

(Beethoven)	Mit einem gemalten Band			RIC
-----	O waer' ich schon mit dir vereint (Fidelio)			†
Brahms	Auf dem See	HL	D-F	†
-----	Geheimnis			†
-----	Sandmaennchen	LH	F-G	†
-----	Sonntag	H	D-G	†
-----	Wie Melodien zieht es	HL	A-E	†
Franz	Ach, wenn ich doch ein Immchen war			
-----	Es hat die Rose sich beklagt	LH	DF-F	†
-----	Gute Nacht	HL		†
-----	Stille Sicherheit	M	E-F	†
Haydn	Der erste Kuss			
-----	On might pens uplifted soars (The Creation)	H	E-A	†
Liszt	Kling' leise, mein Lied	HL		†
Mahler	Ich atmet' einen linden Duft	HL		INT
Marx	Wie einst			UNI
Mendelssohn	Das erste Veilchen	M	F-F	†
-----	I will sing of Thy great mercies (Saint Paul)	H	E-F	†
-----	O for the wings of a dove	MLH	D-G	†
Mozart	Durch Zaertlichkeit (Abduction from Seraglio)			RIC
Reger	Des Kindes Gebet	H	F-G	BOT
-----	Mit Rosen bestreut			UNI
-----	Waldeinsamkeit	HML	A-D	BOS
Schubert	An den Mond	HL	F-GF	†
-----	An die Laute	LH	D-F	†
-----	An die Nachtigall	H	C-G	†
-----	Auf dem Wasser zu singen	MH	EF-GF	†
-----	Das Lied im Gruenen			PET
-----	Der Einsame	LH	D-G	†
-----	Der Knabe			PET
-----	Der Musensohn	LH	FS-G	†
-----	Der Schmetterling	LH	E-F	†
-----	Die Taubenpost	HL	D-EF	†
-----	Fruehlingstraum	HL	C-D	†
-----	Geheimes	HL	BF-EF	†
-----	Gott im Fruehling			PET
-----	Gretchen am Spinnrade	H	F-A	†
-----	Hark! hark! the lark	LMH	F-G	†
-----	Im Fruehling	LH	D-FS	†
-----	Lachen und Weinen	HL	C-EF	†
-----	Liebe schwaermt auf allen Wegen			PET

(Schubert)	(Claudine von Villa Bella)			
-----	Liebesbotschaft	H	E-G	†
-----	Sprache der Liebe			PET
-----	Wiegenlied (op. 98)			GSC
Schumann	Der Nussbaum	LMH	D-FS	†
-----	Der Sandmann	HL	AF-DF	†
-----	Die Meerfee			
-----	Fruehlingslust	HL		†
-----	Intermezzo	HL	C-D	†
-----	Lieder der Braut	H	D-A	†
-----	Marienwuermchen	HL	D-D	†
-----	Roeselein, Roeselein			
-----	Schneegloeckchen	HL		†
-----	Volksliedchen	HL		†
Strauss, J.	Ein Maedchen hat es gar nicht gut (The Gypsy Baron)			CRZ
Strauss, R.	All' mein' Gedanken	H	CS-GS	
-----	Die Nacht	HL		†
-----	Schlagende Herzen			†
Wolf	Auch kleine Dinge	HM	D-E	†
-----	Blumengruss	HL	D-E	†
-----	Der Gaertner	HL		†
-----	Der Knabe und das Immlein	L	CS-A	†
-----	Fruehling uebers Jahr			†
-----	Gleich und gleich			†
-----	In dem Schatten meiner Locken	M	C-EF	†
-----	Mausfallen Spruechlein	HL	BF-E	†
-----	Morgentau	HL	D-D	†
-----	Nun wandre, Maria	HL	EF-D	†
-----	Und willst du deinen Liebsten sterben	HL		DIT
-----	Verschwiegene Liebe	LH	DF-FS	†
-----	Wenn du zu den Blumen gehst	HL	B-EF	†

Italian Songs and Arias Employing
Crescendo and Diminuendo

Lyric Soprano

Bononcini	Per la gloria	HL	C-EF	†
-----	Si che fedele			DUR
Caldara	Sebben crudele	HML	E-DS	†
-----	Selve amiche, ombrose piante	HM	E-E	†
De Luca	Non posso disperar	HL	C-E	GSC

153

Donizetti	Chacun le sait (La Fille du Régiment)	H	C-A	RIC
Falconieri	O bellissimi capelli	HL	B-D	†
Handel	Affani del pensier (Ottone)			†
-----	Bel piacere (Agrippina)			†
-----	Caro voi siete all'alma (Serse)	H	E-A	CFI
-----	Ne men con l'ombre (Serse)	H	E-A	CFI
-----	Voi dolce aurette al cor (Tolomeo)			GSC
Monteverdi	Lasciatemi morire (Arianna)	ML	D-D	†
Mozart	L'amero saro costante (Il Re Pastore) Violin or flute	H	D-B	GSC
-----	Venite inginocchiatevi (Le Nozze di Figaro)	H	D-G	†
-----	Zeffiretti lusinghieri (Idomeneo)			†
Pergolesi	Se tu m'ami	LMH	C-G	GSC
Respighi	Bella porta di rubini			RIC
Rosa	Selve, voi che le speranze	MH	D-G	DIT
Scarlatti, A.	La fortuna			BOS
Verdi	Ave Maria (Otello)	H	EF-AF	GSC

Miscellaneous Songs Employing Crescendo and Diminuendo

Lyric Soprano

Arensky	The little fish's song	H	D-A	†
Backer-Gröndahl	In dreaming dance			
Gretchaninoff	My native land	L	C-EF	GSC
Grieg	En fuglevise			
-----	In the boat	LM	D-ES	†
-----	It was a lovely summer evening			
-----	Springtide	M		DIT
Lilljebjorn	When I was seventeen			RIC
Nin	Minué cantado			ESC
Rachmaninoff	Daisies			†
-----	Lilacs	LH	EF-G	†
-----	The island	LH	DF-F	†
Stravinsky	Pastorale			GSC

Lyric Soprano

Burleigh	By the pool at the third roses	H		RIC
Carpenter	Silhouettes	M	C-G	GSC
Charles	When I have sung my songs	HM	BF-EF	GSC
Crist	Evening	H	C-G	GSC
Davis	Nancy Hanks	H	D-G	GAL
De Rose	I heard a forest praying	MH	EF-GF	CHA
Dittenhaver	Hurdy-gurdy playing in the street	H	DF-AF	GAL
Duke	Little elegy	H	FS-A	GSC
-----	The bird			GSC
-----	To Karen, singing	M	CS-G	ELV
Gaines	My heart hath a mind			
Ganz	A memory	HM	B-D	GSC
-----	The angels are stooping	MH	GF-A	GSC
Giannini	Tell me, o blue, blue sky	H		RIC
Griffes	In a myrtle shade	H	FS-A	GSC
-----	Symphony in yellow	M	D-GF	GSC
-----	The dreamy lake	H	BS-GS	GSC
-----	Thy dark eyes to mine	H	EF-AF	GSC
Hageman	Do not go, my love	HL	B-EF	GSC
Huerter	Pirate dreams	HML		DIT
Kingsford	Wallpaper for a little girl's room	M	BF-F	GSC
Kramer	Pleading	LH	D-GF	JFI
-----	Swans	HL		RIC
MacDowell	As the gloaming shadows creep			
-----	Long ago	HL		ASC
-----	The sea	HL	D-D	BRH
MacGimsey	Sweet little Jesus boy	ML	D-D	CFI
Manning	In the Luxembourg gardens	HML	BF-D	GSC
-----	Shoes	M	EF-F	GSC
Nevin	Little boy blue			BOS
-----	Mighty lak' a rose			JCH
Nordoff	Music I heard with you	H	DS-FS	AMP
Schuman	Orpheus with his lute	M	C-FS	GSC
Taylor	A song for lovers	MH	D-F	JFI
Watts	Stresa	H	EF-BF	DIT

British Songs Employing
Piano Singing

Lyric Soprano

Anon	Have you seen but a white lily grow?	H	E-F	GSC
Bainton	The nightingale near the house			CUR
Bax	I heard a piper piping	LH	D-G	CFI
Coleridge-Taylor	She rested by the broken brook	HL		DIT
Delius	The nightingale has a lyre of gold			†
Gibbs	Silver		CS-FS	ROG
Hook	Mary of Allendale			BOO
Hughes	Open the door softly	LMH	G-G	ENO
Ronald	Down in the forest	HML	C-D	ENO
-----	Drift, down drift down			BOO
Scott	Lullaby	MML	BF-DF	GAL
Vaughan Williams	Orpheus with his lute			PRO
-----	Silent noon			GSC

French Songs and Arias Employing
Piano Singing

Lyric Soprano

Aubert	La lettre			DUR
Bizet	Douce mer			GSC
-----	Pastorale	H	C-FS	GSC
Breville	Prieres d'enfant	M	D-F	ROU
Chausson	Dans la forêt	HL		INT
-----	Nocturne	HL		INT
Debussy	Clair de lune	M	CS-FS	JOB
-----	Harmonie du soir			DUR
-----	Il pleure dans mon coeur	LH	CS-GS	†
-----	L'ombre des arbres			†
-----	Le jet d'eau			DUR
-----	Nuits d'etoiles	LH	E-A	MAR
-----	Recueillement			DUR
Duparc	Extase	LMH	FS-A	†
-----	Soupir	HL	CS-F	BOS
Faure	Après un rêve	HM	C-F	†
-----	Dans les ruines d'une abbaye	M	E-FS	†

(Faure)	En sourdine	HL	C-EF	†
-----	Ici-bas!	H	FS-G	†
-----	La lune blanche	HL		†
Ferrari	Le miroir	M	E-F	GSC
Godard	Cachés dans cet asile	MH	DF-F	GSC
	(Jocelyn) Violin or cello			
Gounod	Au rossignol	LMH	D-G	CHO
-----	Sérénade	LMH	D-A	GSC
Grétry	Rose chérie			LEM
	(Zémire et Azor)			
Hahn	A Chloris	H	DS-FS	HEU
-----	Infidélité	M		HEU
-----	L'heure exquise	M	DF-F	†
-----	Offrande	M	D-D	†
-----	Paysage	MH	EF-G	HEU
Koechlin	L'air	M	F-FS	ROU
Leguerney	Je vous envoie	H	C-A	ROU
Liszt	Oh! quand je dors	H	E-A	†
Lully	Au clair de la lune	H	E-D	CFI
Massenet	Crépuscule	M	D-E	GSC
Moret	Le nélumbo	H	E-DF	HEU
Mozart	Oiseaux, si tous les ans	H	C-G	KAL
Poldowski	L'heure exquise	LMH	DF-AF	CHE
Poulenc	C. (J'ai traversé les			ROU
	ponts de C.)			
Rabey	Tes yeux	H	EF-G	DUR
	Violin and piano			
Rameau	Rossignols amoureux			†
	(Hippolyte et Aricie)			
Ravel	D'Anne jouant de	H	CS-GS	GSC
	l'espinette			
-----	D'Anne qui me jecta	HM	CS-FS	GSC
-----	La flûte enchantée	M	DS-FS	DUR
-----	Noël des jouets	M	BS-FS	MAT
-----	Sur l'herbe	MH	C-G	DUR
-----	Trois beaux oiseaux du			DUR
	paradis			
Roussel	Le jardin mouillé	M	C-FS	ROU
Saint-Saëns	Mai	H	G-FS	DUR
Severac	Ma poupée chérie			ROU
Staub	L'heure silencieuse	H	EF-G	DUR
Szulc	Claire de lune	H	E-G	AXE
Weckerlin	Aminte	M	C-D	†
-----	Je connais un berger	M	EF-EF	BOS
	discret			

German Songs and Arias Employing
Piano Singing

Lyric Soprano

Bach, J. S.	Ich nehme mein Leiden (Cantata 75) Oboe d'amore			AUG
-----	Seufzer, Traenen, Kummer, Noth (Cantata 21) Oboe			†
-----	Suesser trost, mein Jesus kommt (Cantata 151) Flute			†
Beethoven	Ich liebe dich	HL	BF-DF	†
Blech	Heimkehr vom Feste			UNI
Brahms	An ein Veilchen	H	DS-GS	†
-----	Eine gute, gute Nacht			†
-----	Es traeumte mir			†
-----	In Waldeseinsamkeit	H	ES-G	†
-----	Lerchengesang	LH	FS-GS	†
-----	Staendchen	HL	BF-E	†
Franz	Ein Stuendlein wohl vor Tag			†
Hindemith	Geburt Marias			AMP
Korngold	Mariettas song (The Dead City)	MH	F-BF	AMP
Mahler	Ich ging mit Lust	HL		INT
-----	Liebst du um Schoenheit	HL		INT
Marx	Marienlied	MH	EF-AF	AMP
-----	Selige Nacht	M	DF-GF	AMP
Mendelssohn	Bei der Wiege	M	DF-EF	GSC
-----	Gruss	M	DS-FS	†
Mozart	Welche Wonne, welche Lust (Abduction from Seraglio)			†
Schubert	Ave Maria	LMH	F-F	†
-----	Danksagung an den Bach	HL	E-F	†
-----	Du bist die Ruh	LMH	EF-AF	†
-----	Erlafsee	H	E-G	†
-----	Im Abendrot	HL	C-D	†
-----	Lob der Thraenen	LM	F-F	†
-----	Nachtviolen			PET
-----	Mondnacht	M	E-FS	†
Strauss, J.	Czardas (Die Fledermaus)			BOO
Strauss, R.	Freundliche Vision	HL	C-F	†
-----	Heimkehr	HL	B-E	†
-----	Ich trage meine minne	M		†
-----	Mein Herz ist stumm	LH	EF-AF	
-----	Meinem Kinde			†
-----	Traum durch die Daemmerung	HML	BF-EF	†

Trunk	In meiner Heimat			
Wolf	Ach, des Knaben Augen	HL		†
-----	Auf ein altes Bild	HL	E-DS	†
-----	Du denkst, mit einem Faedchen			†
-----	Frage und Antwort			PET
-----	Nachtzauber	HL	B-E	INT
-----	Verborgenheit	HL	B-E	†
-----	Wie glaenzt der helle Mond			†

Italian Songs and Arias Employing Piano Singing

Lyric Soprano

Bassani	Posate, dormite (La Serenata)	H	EF-F	GSC
Bononcini	Deh, più a me non v'ascondete	LH	EF-F	†
Cimara	Fiocca la neve	H	G-G	GSC
Faccio	Sortita d'Ofelia (Amleto)			GSC
Gagliano	Dormi, amore (La Flora)	HL	CS-E	DIT
Gluck	O del mio dolce ardor (Paride ed Elena)	LH	D-FS	GSC
Handel	Care selve (Atalanta)	MH	FS-A	†
Jommelli	Chi vuol comprar la bella	H	B-G	GSC
Mozart	Deh vieni non tardar (Le Nozze di Figaro)	H	A-A	†
Pizzetti	I pastori			FRI,
Puccini	O mio babbino caro (Gianni Schicchi)			RIC
Respighi	Notte			BON
Verdi	Addio del passato (La Traviata)			†
-----	Salce, salce (Otello)	H	CS-FS	RIC
-----	Sul fil d'un soffio etesio (Falstaff)	H	DS-A	RIC

Miscellaneous Songs Employing Piano Singing

Lyric Soprano

Alnaes	Lykken mellem to mennesker	M	B-FS	HAN

Arensky	Revery	MH	DS-FS	DIT
-----	Valse	H	DF-GF	GSC
Cui	The statue at Czarskoe-Selo	HM	DF-EF	†
Dvořák	God is my shepherd			AMP
-----	Songs my mother taught me	HM	E-E	†
Gretchaninoff	Hushed the song of the nightingale	MH	E-G	DIT
Grieg	A dream			†
-----	Snegl, Snegl	M	B-F	HAN
Lie	Soft-footed snow	HM		DIT
Mednikoff	The hills of Gruzia	H	DS-A	LAC
Rachmaninoff	Before my window	HM	C-G	†
-----	Here beauty dwells	H	D-B	CFI
-----	In the silence of night	LH	D-A	GSC
-----	Into my open window	HL	B-FS	BOS
Schubert	Ave Maria	LMH	F-F	†
Sinding	Sylvelin	M	E-E	GSC
Tchaikovsky	Cradle song	LH	D-G	†

American Songs Employing Rapid Enunciation

Lyric Soprano

Bacon	Four songs	H	DF-G	MUP
Bernstein	La bonne cuisine	H	B-B	GSC
Boatner	Oh, what a beautiful city!	HL	D-E	GSC
Burleigh	Joshua fit de battle ob Jericho	LH	DS-E	RIC
-----	Little David play on you harp	HL		RIC
Clough-Leighter	My lover he comes on the skee	HM	D-F	BOS
Curran	Ho! Mr. Piper	LH	D-G	GSC
Deis	Come down to Kew			
Griffes	Elves	H	F-AF	GSC
Hadley	My shadow			ASC
Hageman	At the well	LH	EF-AF	GSC
-----	Miranda	HL		GAL
Josten	Cupid's counsel	H	EF-AF	GSC
Kountz	The sleigh	HL	D-FS	GSC
MacDowell	A maid sings light	H	F-G	ASC
Nevin	One spring morning	MH	DS-F	BOS
Sacco	Mexican serenade	HL	D-EF	BOS
Spross	Will o' the wisp			JCH

Warner	Hurdy gurdy	M	D-F	CFI

British Songs Employing
Rapid Enunciation

Lyric Soprano

Bantock	A feast of lanterns	HM	D-F	GAL
Bartlet	Whither runneth my sweetheart			BOO
Bax	Oh dear what can the matter be?	M	D-EF	CHE
Bishop	Love has eyes	M		†
-----	Pretty mocking bird Flute	H		†
Brewer	The fairy pipers	HML		BOH
Dowland	Shall I sue?			STB
German	Charming Chloe	HML		NOV
Gibbs	Five eyes	HL	D-D	BOS
Head	A piper	HL		BOO
Holst	A little music	H		AUG
Hughes	Hey diddle diddle			CRA
Molloy	The Kerry dance	LH	C-G	GSC
Morley	It was a lover and his lass	HM		DIT
Vaughan Williams	The water mill	L	C-D	OXF

French Songs Employing
Rapid Enunciation

Lyric Soprano

Bemberg	Il neige	H	FS-G	GRU
Bizet	Chanson d'avril	H	BF-G	†
Bruneau	Le sabot de frêne			CHO
Chabrier	Les cigales	HML		†
-----	Villanelle des petits canards	HML	B-E	†
Debussy	Chevaux de bois	H	C-G	†
-----	Fantoches	H	D-A	JOB
-----	Fêtes galantes	LH	CS-A	†
-----	Mandoline	HM	BF-F	†
-----	Placet futile			DUR
Delibes	Les filles de Cadix	HM	A-A	†
Dupont	Chanson des noisettes			HEU
Fauré	Mandoline	HL	F-E	†

161

(Fauré)	Notre amour	H	DS-B	†
-----	Poeme d'un jour			HAM
Ferrari	Le jardin d'amour	LM	EF-F	GSC
Fourdrain	Carnaval	M	C-F	RIC
Hahn	Quand je fus pris au pavillon	M		HEU
Hue	A des oiseaux	H	E-G	†
Koechlin	La lune	M	C-F	ROU
Massenet	Première danse	H	E-G	GSC
Monsigny	Il regardait mon bouquet (Le Roi et le Fermier)	H	D-G	GSC
Pierné	Ils étaient trois petits chats blancs			MAR
Poldowski	Cortège	M	D-FS	CHE
Ravel	Manteau de fleurs	H		INT
-----	Nicolette	L	B-FS	ELK
-----	Tout gai	MH	EF-F	DUR
Severac	Chanson pour le petit cheval			ROU
Weckerlin	Chantons les amours de Jean	H	D-G	GSC
-----	Maman, dites-moi	M	E-FS	BOS

German Songs Employing
Rapid Enunciation

Lyric Soprano

Bach, J. S.	Patron, das macht der Wind (Phoebus and Pan)	M	C-G	GSC
Beethoven	Mailied			RIC
-----	Neue Liebe, neues Leben			†
Brahms	Blinde Kuh			†
-----	Das Maedchen spricht	H	E-FS	†
-----	Der Jaeger	HL		†
-----	Dort in den Weiden	LH	A-A	†
-----	Juchhe!			†
-----	O liebliche Wangen	MLH	E-G	†
-----	Vergebliches Staendchen	LHM	E-FS	†
Mendelssohn	Im Gruenen	H	E-BF	AUG
-----	Neue Liebe	H	CS-A	†
Mozart	Warnung	HM	C-D	
Schubert	Das Wandern	HLM	E-E	†
-----	Die Forelle	MLH	EF-GF	†
-----	Die Post	HML	BF-EF	†
-----	Erstarrung	HL	D-F	†
-----	Fruehlingssehnsucht	HL	B-E	†
-----	Mein!	HL		†

162

(Schubert)	Ungeduld	HML		†
-----	Wohin?	HL	B-E	†
Schumann	Auftraege	HL	C-E	†
Wolf	Elfenlied	HL	D-F	†
-----	Ich hab' in Penna	LH		INT
-----	Nixe Binsefuss	H	E-G	†
-----	Waldmaedchen			PET

Italian Songs and Arias Employing Rapid Enunciation

Lyric Soprano

Cavalli	Donzelle fuggite	HL	C-EF	†
Donaudy	Ah mai non cessate			RIC
Falconieri	Non più d'amore	HL	C-D	DIT
-----	Nudo arciero	HL	AF-AF	DIT
Handel	Ch'io mai vi possa (Siroe)			†
-----	Dira che amor per me (Serse)	H	F-A	CFI
Legrenzi	Che fiero costume	HML	C-D	†
Malipiero	Ballata	H		CHE
Mozart	Non so più cosa son (Le Nozze di Figaro)	H	EF-G	†
-----	Voi che sapete (Le Nozze di Figaro)	M	C-F	†
Paisiello	Chi vuol la zingarella	L	C-F	GSC
Paradies	M'ha preso alla sua ragna	M	EF-F	GSC
Pergolesi	A Serpina penserete (La Serva Padrona)	HLM	D-F	†
-----	Stizzoso, mio stizzoso (La Serva Padrona)	H	C-AF	†
Rontani	Or ch'io non segno più	HL	CS-E	DIT
Rossini	La danza	MH	E-A	†
Stradella	Ragion sempre addita	H	E-G	†
Tosti	'A vucchella	LH	F-G	RIC

Miscellaneous Songs Employing Rapid Enunciation

Lyric Soprano

Falla	Seguidilla murciana	HL		AMP
Grieg	My Johann	HL	BF-EF	GSC
-----	The way of the world			
-----	With a water lily			
Mussorgsky	The evening prayer	M	C-E	GSC

163

American Songs Employing
Sustained Singing

Lyric Soprano

Barber	A nun takes the veil	MH	G-G	GSC
-----	Sure on this shining night	MH	D-G	GSC
Bloch	The shelter	MH	CS-GS	GSC
-----	The vagabond	M	E-E	GSC
Burleigh	Sometimes I feel like a motherless child	HML		RIC
-----	Were you there?	HML		RIC
Chadwick	Allah	LH	CS-GS	ASC
Charles	And so, goodbye	LH	EF-AF	GSC
Edwards	By the bend of the river	HML	C-E	GSC
-----	Into the night	HML	C-DF	GSC
Giannini	Be still my heart			ELV
-----	Far above the purple hills	LH	CS-A	RIC
Golde	Love was with me yesterday	LMH	E-A	CFI
Griffes	By a lonely forest pathway	HML	A-EF	GSC
-----	Evening song	H	DS-GS	GSC
-----	The lament of Ian the proud	MH	DS-AS	GSC
-----	The rose of the night	H	CS-A	GSC
Hageman	Music I heard with you	MH	E-A	GAL
Hindemith	The wildflower's song	MH	E-G	AMP
Horsman	In the yellow dusk	MH	FS-A	GSC
-----	The bird of the wilderness	LMH	DB-BF	GSC
Kernochan	We two together	H	EF-AF	GAL
Lang	Irish love song	HML	A-E	ASC
Lieurance	By the waters of Minnetonka			PRE
MacDowell	The swan bent low	LH		ELK
Manning	Sketches of Paris	HL	C-E	GSC
Metcalf	At nightfall	HML	C-DF	ASC
Moore	Sigh no more, ladies			BOO
Nevin	The Rosary	HML	C-D	BOS
Rasbach	Trees	LMH	CS-GS	GSC
Rogers	The star	LH	C-AF	GSC
-----	Wind song	LM	C-G	GSC
Scott	Think on me	HML	D-EF	GAL
Watts	The poet sings	MH	EF-AF	DIT
-----	Transformation	ML	AS-DS	GSC
-----	With the tide	H	DF-A	GSC

British Songs and Arias Employing
Sustained Singing

Lyric Soprano

Arne, T.	Blow, blow thou winter wind	M	C-F	†
-----	In infancy			NOV
-----	Water parted from the sea			GSC
Bantock	Silent strings	MH	F-G	BOO
Bax	The white peace			CHE
Bridge	All things that we clasp	HL		BOS
-----	O that it were so	LMH	D-G	CHA
Britten	The Sally gardens			BOH
Campion	When to her lute Corinna sings			STB
Dowland	Flow, my tears	M	D-E	STB
Dunhill	To the Queen of Heaven	M	C-G	GSC
Grainger	The sprig of thyme	LH	E-FS	GSC
Gurney	Down by the Salley Gardens			OXF
Handel	Come unto Him (The Messiah)	MH	F-G	†
-----	Farewell, ye limpid springs and floods (Jephtha)	H	D-G	†
-----	How beautiful are the feet of them (The Messiah)	H		†
-----	I know that my Redeemer liveth (The Messiah)	MH	E-GS	†
-----	If God be with us, who can be against us (The Messiah)			†
-----	With thee th'unsheltered moor (Solomon)			NOV
Henschel	Morning-hymn	MH	DS-GS	†
Johnson	As I walked forth one summer day			DIT
Purcell	Cease, o my sad soul			POT
-----	If music be the food of love	M	D-G	BOO
-----	Music for a while (Oedipus)	LH		SC
-----	Since from my dear			
Quilter	Come away, come away death			BOO
-----	Go, lovely rose	LMH	F-GF	CHA
Ronald	O, lovely night	HML		BOO
-----	Prelude	HML	B-D	ENO

Scott	The unforeseen	HML		GAL
Stephenson	Love is a sickness	HML	C-D	BOO
Thiman	The silver swan	MH	EF-G	NOV
Thomson	The knight of Bethlehem	LM		NOV
Welsh	The ash grove			

French Songs and Arias Employing
Sustained Singing

Lyric Soprano

Bemberg	Chant hindou	HML	A-EF	†
Berlioz	Autrefois un roi de Thule (La Damnation de Faust)			CST
-----	Le spectre de la rose			CST
-----	Les nuits d'été			AUG
Bizet	Adieu de l'hôtesse arabe	H	BF-G	†
-----	Comme autrefois dans la nuit sombre (Les Pêcheurs des Perles)			CHO
-----	Je dis que rien ne m'épouvante (Carmen)	LH	D-B	†
-----	O dieu Brahma (Les Pêcheurs des Perles)	H	B-D	GSC
Boulanger	Cantique	M	F-F	HAM
Caplet	Les prières			DUR
Chausson	Chanson perpétuelle	H	CS-GS	ROU
-----	L'amour d'Antan	HL		INT
-----	Le colibri	M	F-GF	BOS
-----	Le temps des lilas	MH	D-GS	†
Debussy	Beau soir	LH	C-FS	†
-----	Colloque sentimental			DUR
-----	De fleurs	H	C-AF	†
-----	Romance	HM	C-E	†
Fauré	Aurore	H	D-G	MAR
-----	Le jardin clos	M	C-E	DUR
-----	Le parfum impérissable	LH	GF-GF	
-----	Rencontre	H	EF-AF	†
-----	Vocalise	H		LED
Franck	Nocturne	HL		†
Georges	Hymne au soleil	LH	E-A	HOM
Gluck	Adieu, conservez dans votre âme (Iphigénie en Aulide)			†
-----	Grands dieux (Alceste)	H	E-BF	GSC
-----	Jamais dans ces beaux lieux (Armide)			PET
-----	Non! ce n'est point (Alceste)	H	E-G	†

166

Godard	Florian's song	LMH	D-FS	GSC
Gounod	Plus grand, dans son obscurité (La Reine de Saba)	MH	CS-B	†
Halévy	Il va venir (La Juive)	H	D-CF	†
Honegger	O had I wings like a dove (King David)			CHE
Leguerney	Au sommeil			ROU
Leroux	Le nil Cello or Violin	LH	E-A	†
Lully	Fermez-vous pour jamais (Amadis)			LEM
-----	Plus j'observe ces lieux (Armide)			LEM
Massenet	Charmes des jours passés (Hérodiade)			HEU
-----	Élégie	LM	C-GF	GSC
-----	Il est doux, il est bon (Hérodiade)	MH	EF-BF	GSC
-----	L'amour est une vertu rare (Thaïs)			HEU
Messager	La maison grise (Fortuno)			CHO
Meyerbeer	O beau pays (Les Huguenots)	H	CS-D	GSC
-----	Roberto, o tu che adoro (Robert le Diable)	H	C-C	DEI
Monsigny	Adieu, chère Louise (Le Deserteur)			JOB
Mozart	Dans un bois	H	EF-AF	
Offenbach	Elle a fui, la tourterelle (Tales of Hoffman)	H	D-A	GSC
Poulenc	A sa guitare	M	D-FS	DUR
-----	Air grave			ROU
-----	Bleuet	H	FS-GF	DUR
-----	Fleurs	M	DF-F	ROU
-----	Violon			ROU
Rameau	Tristes apprêts (Castor et Pollux)			CHE
Ravel	Chanson italienne			DUR
-----	Kaddisch	H	C-G	DUR
-----	Là-bas vers l'église	MH	GS-E	DUR
-----	Le paon	M	C-F	DUR
-----	Vocalise en forme de habanera	MH	BF-G	MAR
Roussel	Response d'une épouse sage			DUR
Saint-Saëns	A swan's song Harp or piano and cello	H	D-G	GSC
------	Aimons-nous			DUR

(Saint-Saëns) La cloche   LH   DF-AF   †

German Songs and Arias Employing
Sustained Singing

Lyric Soprano

Bach, C.P.E.	Das Gebet			SIM
-----	Passionslied			SIM
Bach, J. S.	Bist du bei mir	HML	A-EF	†
-----	Bleed and break (St. Matthew Passion)			
-----	Die Armen will der Herr umarmen (Cantata 186) Violin			PET
-----	Die Seele ruht in Jesu Haenden (Cantata 127) 2 Flutes and oboe			AUG
-----	Father what I proffer			
-----	Ruhet hie matte Toene (Cantata 210) Oboe d'amore and violin			AUG
Beethoven	Das Geheimnis			
Brahms	An eine Aeolsharfe	H	EF-AF	†
-----	Daemm'rung senkte sich von oben	LH	BF-G	†
-----	Dein blaues Auge	MH	BF-G	†
-----	Der Tod, das ist die kuehle Nacht	L	AF-F	†
-----	Erinnerung	H	E-G	†
-----	Feldeinsamkeit	HL	C-EF	†
-----	Immer leiser wird mein Schlummer	LH	DF-A	†
-----	Nachtigall	MHL	BF-FS	†
-----	O wuesst' ich doch den Weg zurueck	H	E-FS	†
-----	Ruhe Suessliebchen	HL	BS-E	CFI
-----	Schoen war, das ich dir weihte			†
-----	Wir wandelten	LH	EF-GF	†
-----	Komm, wir wandeln	H	FS-GS	SC
Franz	Dedication	HML	BF-C	†
-----	For music	ML	C-D	†
-----	Im Herbst	HM	A-F	†
-----	Mutter, o sing mich zur Ruh	HL	E-G	†
Haydn	O tuneful voice			
-----	She never told her love	HL	B-D	DIT

(Haydn)	With verdure clad (The Creation)	H	E-BF	†
Hindemith	Pietà from Marienleben			AMP
Lehar	Vilia (The Merry Widow)			CHA
Loewe	Canzonetta	MH	B-A	DIT
Marx	Hat dich die Liebe beruehrt	MH	EF-BF	AMP
-----	Nocturne	H	EF-AF	AMP
-----	Waldseligkeit	H	D-A	UNI
Mendelssohn	Der Mond	HL		†
-----	Hear ye, Israel (Elijah)	H	E-A	†
-----	Jerusalem, thou that killest (Saint Paul)	H	F-F	†
------	Minnelied	H	E-G	AUG
-----	Nachtlied			
-----	On wings of song			JCH
Mozart	Abendempfindung	M	E-F	
-----	Ach, ich fuehl's (Die Zauberfloete)	H	CS-BF	†
-----	Wiegenlied	MH	G-G	†
Reger	Friede	H	EF-G	UNI
Reichardt	In the time of roses			†
Schubert	Am Grabe Anselmos	HL	B-EF	†
-----	An die Musik	HL	A-DS	†
-----	Das Wirtshaus	HL	C-D	†
-----	Der Leiermann	ML	C-D	†
-----	Der Neugierige	HL	CS-EF	†
-----	Der Wegweiser	L	D-EF	†
-----	Des Maedchens Klage	LH	C-E	†
-----	Die Maenner sind mechant			PET
-----	Fruehlingsglaube	M	EF-F	†
-----	Ganymed	LH	EF-G	†
-----	Ihr Bild	HL	C-C	†
-----	Naehe des Geliebten	HL	D-EF	†
-----	Nur wer die Sehnsucht kennt	LH		†
-----	Wanderers Nachtlied 2	LH	F-F	†
-----	Wehmuth	HL	B-D	†
Schumann	An den Sonnenschein	HL	A-D	†
-----	Dein Angesicht	HL	B-EF	†
-----	Der Himmel hat eine Traene geweint			
-----	Die Lotusblume	HLM	BF-F	GSC
-----	Du bist wie eine Blume	HM	F-EF	†
-----	In der Fremde	HL		†
-----	Lied der Suleika			
-----	Mein schoener Stern			
-----	Stille Traenen	HL		†
-----	Wer machte dich so krank?			

Strauss	Ach Lieb, ich muss nun scheiden	H	D-G	
-----	Breit ueber mein Haupt	LH	GF-AF	HSC
-----	Kornblumen	LH	DF-AF	†
-----	Mit deinen blauen Augen	LH	C-GS	†
-----	Morgen	HML	E-F	†
Strauss	Seitdem dein Aug' in meines schaute			SC
Wolf	Anakreons Grab	HL	D-D	†
-----	An eine Aeolsharfe			†
-----	Auf eine Christblume	HL	C-F	†
-----	Bedeckt mich mit Blumen	HL	B-D	†
-----	Das verlassene Maegdlein	HL	D-EF	†
-----	Der Genesene an die Hoffnung	H	BF-AF	PET
-----	Gesang Weylas	HL	DF-F	†
-----	Heb auf dein blondes Haupt	HL	G-DF	†
-----	Herr, was traegt der Boden	HL	B-DS	INT
-----	Im Fruehling	HL	BF-F	†
-----	Lebe wohl	HL	BF-F	†

Italian Songs and Arias Employing Sustained Singing

Lyric Soprano

Boito	Morte di Margherita (L' altra notte) (Mefistofele)	H	D-B	GSC
-----	Angel's serenade Violin	LH	D-G	†
Braga	Angel's serenade Violin	LH	D-G	†
Caccini	Amarilli, mia bella	ML	C-D	†
Caldara	Come raggio di sol	HL	D-F	†
Catalani	Ebben? Ne andrò lontana (La Wally)	H	E-B	RIC
Cesti	Che angoscia, che affanno (Il Pomo d'Oro)	HL	C-DF	DIT
-----	Lasciatemi in pace			
Cilea	Io son l'umile ancella (Adriana Lecouvreur)	H		AMP
-----	Poveri fiori (Adriana Lecouvreur)			SON
Cimarosa	Bel nume che adoro			RIC
Donaudy	O del mio amato ben	M	EF-F	RIC
Durante	Vergin, tutta amor	LM	C-EF	†
Giordano	La mamma morta (Andrea Chenier)	H	CS-B	AMP

170

Gluck	Spiagge amate			†
	(Paride ed Elena)			
Handel	Ombre, piante	H	FS-A	CFI
	(Rodelinda)			
-----	Rendi'l sereno al ciglio	LH	EF-F	†
	(Sosarme)			
-----	V'adoro pupille			BOO
	(Julius Caesar)			
-----	Vieni o figlio caro e mi			†
	consola (Ottone)			
Haydn	Del mio core			GSC
	(Orfeo ed Euridice)			
-----	Pensi a me			
Mascagni	Son pochi fiori			GSC
	(L'Amico Fritz)			
Mozart	Bella mia fiamma, addio			BOO
-----	Ch' io mi scordi di te			BOO
-----	Non mi dir	H	F-B	†
	(Don Giovanni)			
-----	Parto, parto	H		AMP
	(La Clemenza di Tito)			
	B flat clarinet and piano			
-----	Per pietà, ben mio			†
	(Così Fan Tutte)			
-----	Porgi amor	H	D-AF	†
	(Le Nozze di Figaro)			
-----	Ridente la calma			BOS
-----	Se' il padre perdei			RIC
	(Idomeneo)			
Paisiello	Nel cor più non mi sento	HL	C-EF	†
Pergolesi	Nina	HL	CS-D	DIT
Puccini	In quelle trine morbide	H	DF-BF	RIC
	(Manon Lescaut)			
-----	Musetta's waltz	H	EF-BF	RIC
	(La Boeheme)			
-----	Signore, ascolta			RIC
	(Turandot)			
-----	Tu, che di gel sei cinta			RIC
	(Turandot)			
------	Un bel dì vedremo	H	DF-BF	RIC
	(Madama Butterfly)			
-----	Vissi d'arte (Tosca)	MH	EF-BF	RIC
Respighi	Abbandono			BON
-----	Ballata			RIC
-----	Nebbie			†
-----	Nevicata	HM		BON
Sgambati	Separazione	LMH	FS-G	GSC
Sibella	O bocca dolorosa	HM	D-F	GSC
Stradella	Così, amor, mi fai languir	HL	F-G	DIT

171

(Stradella)	Per pietà (Il Floridoro)	HM	D-F	DIT
-----	Pietà, Signore	HM	C-F	GSC
Verdi	Caro nome (Rigoletto)	H	DS-DS	†
-----	D'amor sull'ali rosee (Il Trovatore)	H	C-DF	†
-----	Ecco l'orrido campo (Un Ballo in Maschera)	H	B-C	RIC

Miscellaneous Songs Employing Sustained Singing

Lyric Soprano

Attey	Sweet was the song			BOO
Bach-Gounod	Ave Maria			†
Cherubini	Ave Maria	H	E-A	GSC
Dvořák	Hear my prayer, O Lord			AMP
-----	Lord thou art my refuge and shield			AMP
-----	Turn Thee to me			AMP
Falla	Vivan los que ríen (La Vida Breve)			AMP
Franck	O Lord most Holy	LM	A-FS	BOS
Granados	La maja dolorosa	M		INT
-----	The maja and the nightingale (Goyescas)	H	BS-A	GSC
Gretchaninoff	Over the steppe	LM	C-G	GSC
-----	Wounded birch	HL	B-EF	†
Grieg	I love thee	HML	E-F	†
Kjerulf	Synnove's song	M	C-F	GSC
Rachmaninoff	Oh cease thy singing, maiden fair	H	E-A	CFI
-----	O thou billowy harvest field	HL	CS-E	GSC
-----	The soldier's bride			BOO
-----	To the children	MH	F-G	DIT
-----	Vocalise	LH	CS-A	GSC
Rubinstein	Es blinkt der Thau	LH	EF-GF	GSC
Sibelius	Black roses	M	A-ES	AMP
-----	From the north	H	DS-G	GSC
-----	The first kiss	M		AMP
-----	Was it a dream			BRH
Tchaikovsky	A legend	M	D-E	GSC
-----	All for you			
-----	Complaint of the bride			
-----	None but the lonely heart	HLM	C-F	DIT
-----	Song of the gypsy girl			DIT
-----	Why	HL		†

Lyric Soprano

Alberti	The gypsy			
Bacon	Four songs	H	DF-G	MUP
Barber	I hear an army	LH	D-AF	GSC
Beach	The year's at the spring	MH	AF-AF	ASC
Boatner	Oh, what a beautiful city!	HL	D-E	GSC
Brown	Love is where you find it (The Kissing Bandit)			
Burleigh	Joshua fit de battle ob Jericho	LH	DS-E	RIC
-----	Little David play on you harp	HL		RIC
Buzzi-Peccia	Under the greenwood tree	LMH	EF-A	DIT
Carpenter	If	M	D-E	GSC
-----	Light, my light	M	C-G	GSC
-----	Serenade	LH	CS-A	GSC
Castelnuovo-Tedesco	O mistress mine			CHE
Charles	Let my song fill your heart	LH	EF-AF	GSC
Clough-Leighter	My lover he comes on the skee	HM	D-F	BOS
Crist	O come hither	HM	B-GS	CFI
Curran	Ho! Mr. Piper	LH	D-G	GSC
Deis	Come down to Kew			
Duke	I can't be talkin' of love	H	CS-G	GSC
-----	Just spring			
Elwell	The road not taken	M	B-FS	GSC
Giannini	Sing to my heart a song	H	D-B	ELV
Griffes	Elves	H	F-AF	GSC
-----	Time was, when I in anguish lay	H	E-GS	GSC
Hadley	My shadow			ASC
Hageman	At the well	LH	EF-AF	GSC
-----	Miranda	HL		GAL
Hindemith	The whistling thief	M	F-F	AMP
Hopkinson	O'er the hills	LH	C-G	†
Josten	Cupid's counsel	H	EF-AF	GSC
Kountz	The sleigh	HL	D-FS	GSC
La Forge	Song of the open	MH	EF-AF	DIT
Levitzki	Ah, thou beloved one	H	EF-AF	GSC
MacDowell	A maid sings light	H	F-G	ASC
Mitchell	Love is the wind	MHH	F-A	GAH
Nevin	One spring morning	MH	DS-F	BOS
Nordoff	There shall be more joy	M	CS-FS	AMP

Robyn	A heart that's free	MH	EF-AF	FEI
Rogers	The last song	MLH	E-AF	GSC
Rummel	Ecstasy	LMH	GF-AF	GSC
Saar	The little gray dove	MH	D-BF	GSC
Sacco	Mexican serenade	HL	D-EF	BOS
-----	Rapunzel	MH	FS-BF	GSC
Schneider	Flower rain			SUM
Schuman	Holiday song	M	C-F	GSC
Spross	Will o' the wisp			JCH
Taylor	The rivals	H	E-G	JFI
Warner	Hurdy gurdy	M	D-F	CFI
Warren	White horses of the sea	LH	F-G	GSC
Weaver	Moon-marketing	LMH	E-G	GSC

British Songs and Arias Employing
Spirited Singing

Lyric Soprano

Bantock	A feast of lanterns	HM	D-F	GAL
Bartlet	Whither runneth my sweetheart			BOO
Bax	Oh dear what can the matter be?	M	D-EF	CHE
-----	Shieling song	H	CS-A	CHE
Besley	Listening	H	E-AF	CUR
Bishop	Bid me discourse	H	B-A	†
-----	Lo! here the gentle lark Flute	H		†
-----	Love has eyes	M		†
-----	Should he upbraid	H		†
Bliss	The buckle			CUR
-----	Three jolly gentlemen	H		†
Brewer	The fairy pipers	HML		BOH
Carey	A pastoral			GSC
Dowland	Awake, sweet love	M	E-F	STB
-----	Come again! sweet love	M	D-E	STB
-----	Shall I sue?			STB
Elgar	Be not extreme, O Lord (Light of Life)			NOV
German	Charming Chloe	HML		NOV
-----	Waltz song (Tom Jones)	H	B-B	CHA
Gibbs	Five eyes	HL	D-D	BOS
Handel	From mighty Kings (Judas Maccabaeus)	H	D-A	†
-----	Hallelujah (Esther)	H	E-B	CFI
-----	Love's a dear deceitful jewel	LH	F-F	RBR

174

(Handel)	Rejoice greatly (The Messiah)	H	E-A	†
Head	A piper	HL		BOO
Hook	Softly waft, ye southern breezes			GSC
Jacob	Laughing song	H	D-G	OXF
Lehmann	The cukoo	HH	D-B	BOH
Linley	O, bid your faithful Ariel fly			BOO
Molloy	The Kerry dance	LH	C-G	GSC
Morley	It was a lover and his lass	HM		DIT
Novello	The little damozel	LHM	C-G	BOO
Purcell	Hark! The echoing (The Fairy Queen)			BAF
-----	Nymphs and shepherds (The Libertine)	HM	C-F	†
Quilter	Blow, blow, thou winter wind	HL	C-E	BOO
-----	It was a lover and his lass	HL	CS-E	BOO
-----	Love's philosophy	LMH	D-A	BOO
Ronald	Love, I have won you	HML	EF-EF	ENO
Warlock	Pretty ring time	H	D-G	CFI

French Songs and Arias Employing Spirited Singing

Lyric Soprano

Bizet	Chanson d'avril	H	BF-G	†
-----	Ouvre ton coeur	MH	DS-GS	†
Bruneau	Le sabot de frêne			CHO
Chabrier	Les cigales	HML		†
-----	L'île heureuse	M	B-F	†
-----	Villanelle des petits canards	HML	B-E	†
Chaminade	L'été	MH	E-A	†
Chausson	Les papillons	M	C-F	GSC
Dalcroze	Le petit oiseau			
Debussy	Chevaux de bois	H	C-G	†
-----	De grève	HL		†
-----	De soir	HL		†
-----	Fantoches	H	D-A	JOB
-----	Fêtes galantes	LH	CS-A	†
-----	La mer est plus belle	HL		†
-----	Le balcon			JOB
-----	Le faune			DUR

175

(Debussy)	Mandoline	HM	BF-F	†
-----	Noël des enfants qui n'ont plus de maisons			DUR
Delibes	Myrto	M	A-FS	GSC
Dupont	Mandoline			DUR
Fauré	Mandoline	HL	F-E	†
-----	Noël	LH	EF-AF	GSC
-----	Notre amour	H	DS-B	†
-----	Poème d'un jour			HAM
Fourdrain	Chanson norvégienne	H	E-G	RIC
Georges	La pluie	HL		INT
Gounod	Air des bijoux (Faust)	H	B-B	†
-----	Au printemps	LMH	DF-AF	GSC
-----	Je veux vivre (Roméo et Juliette)	H	F-C	†
-----	Vénise	HL		INT
Grétry	Je ne fais semblant de rein (L'Ami de la Maison)			LEM
-----	La fauvette avec ses petits (Zémire et Azor) Flute			LEM
Hahn	Fêtes galantes			
-----	Le printemps			
-----	Quand je fus pris au pavillon	M		HEU
-----	Si mes vers avaient des ailes	HLM	B-FS	†
Honegger	Les cloches			SEN
Koechlin	La lune	M	C-F	ROU
-----	Le thé	HM	C-E	BOS
-----	Si tu le veux	LH	FS-A	MAR
Laparra	Lettre à une espagnole			ENO
Massenet	Ouvre tes yeux bleus	MH	C-G	†
-----	Première danse	H	E-G	GSC
Pierné	Ils étaient trois petits chats blancs			MAR
-----	Le moulin	ML	C-E	BOS
Poldowski	Cortège	M	D-FS	CHE
Poulenc	Air champêtre			ROU
-----	Air vif	H	C-AF	ROU
Ravel	Manteau de fleurs	H		INT
-----	Nicolette	L	B-FS	ELK
-----	Quel galant!	M	D-F	DUR
-----	Tout gai	MH	EF-F	DUR
Saint-Saëns	Guitares et mandolines			DUR
Severac	Chanson pour le petit cheval			ROU
Thomas	Je connais un pauvre enfant (Mignon)	H	C-B	†

Vidal	Ariette	LH	F-A	GSC
Weckerlin	Chantons les amours de Jean	H	D-G	GSC

German Songs and Arias Employing Spirited Singing

Lyric Soprano

Bach, J. S.	Herr, der Du stark und maechtig bist (Cantata 10)			
-----	I follow Thee also (St. John Passion) Flute			†
-----	Jauchzet Gott in allen Landen (Cantata 51)			BRO
-----	Mein glaeubiges Herze (Cantata 68)	HML		†
-----	Mein Seelenschatz (Cantata 18) Flute and viola			BRO
-----	Patron, das macht der Wind (Phoebus and Pan)	M	C-G	GSC
-----	Wie zittern und wanken (Cantata 105) Oboe			BRO
Beethoven	Busslied			†
-----	Freudvoll und leidvoll	M	DS-E	†
-----	Mailied			RIC
-----	Neue Liebe, neues Leben			†
Brahms	Auf dem Schiffe	LH	GS-A	†
-----	Bei dir sind meine Gedanken	MH	E-FS	†
-----	Blinde Kuh			†
-----	Botschaft	HL	D-F	†
-----	Das Maedchen spricht	H	E-FS	†
-----	Der Gang zur Liebsten	HL		GSC
-----	Der Jaeger	HL		†
-----	Dort in den Weiden	LH	A-A	†
-----	Es liebt sich so lieblich im Lenze	LH	D-GS	†
-----	Juchhe!			†
-----	Mein wundes Herz verlangt			
-----	Meine Lieder	HL	D-DS	†
-----	O liebliche Wangen	MLH	E-G	†
-----	Salome			†
-----	Vergebliches Staendchen	LHM	E-FS	†
Eckert	Swiss echo song	H	A-B	GSC
Franz	Er ist gekommen	HL	EF-F	†
-----	Sonnenuntergang	HL	CS-FS	†

177

Haydn	O how pleasing to the senses (The Seasons)	H		†
-----	The mermaid's song	M	C-F	PRE
Hindemith	The moon	M	DS-EF	AMP
Jensen	Am Ufer des Flusses des Manzanares	H	D-FS	GSC
-----	Murmuring zephyrs	LH	E-AF	GSC
Loewe	Der Zahn			SC
-----	Des Glockenthuermers Tochterlein	H	CS-A	SC
-----	Niemand hat's gesehen	LM	DS-FS	†
Mahler	Das irdische Leben	HL	A-F	INT
-----	Rheinlegendchen	M	B-FS	BOH
-----	Wer hat dies Liedlein erdacht?	HL	BF-E	INT
Marx	Der bescheidene Schaefer			UNI
-----	Und gestern hat er mir Rosen gebracht	H	E-A	AMP
-----	Valse de Chopin	M	CS-GS	AMP
Mendelssohn	Fruehlingslied	H	DS-GS	†
-----	Im Gruenen	H	E-BF	AUG
-----	Neue Liebe	H	CS-A	†
-----	O Jugend	H	E-A	†
-----	Suleika	H	E-GS	†
Mozart	Ach, ich liebte (Abduction from Seraglio)			†
-----	An Chloe	LH	EF-AF	
-----	Die kleine Spinnerin			
-----	Martern aller Arten (Abduction from Seraglio)	H	B-D	†
-----	Sehnsucht nach dem Fruehling			
Nicolai	Now to my aid fun wit and humor (The Merry Wives)			
Schubert	Der Wachtelschlag	H	DS-FS	PET
-----	Die Forelle	MLH	EF-GF	†
-----	Die Post	HML	BF-EF	†
-----	Ellens zweiter Gesang			PET
-----	Erstarrung	HL	D-F	†
-----	Fruehlingssehnsucht	HL	B-E	†
-----	Halt!	HL	E-F	GSC
-----	Heidenroeslein			
-----	Mein!	HL		†
-----	Rastlose Liebe	M	B-F	†
-----	Suleika I	LH	DS-G	†
-----	Suleika II	LH	F-BF	†
-----	Wohin?	HL	B-E	†
Schulze	Staendchen			SIM
Schumann	Auftraege	HL	C-E	†

178

(Schumann)	Er ist's	HL	BF-EF	†
-----	Fruehlingsnacht	L	CS-E	†
-----	Geisternaehe			
-----	Widmung	HL	BF-F	†
Strauss, J.	Adele's laughing song (Die Fledermaus)	H	D-B	GSC
-----	So elend und so treu (The Gypsy Baron)			CRZ
-----	Tales from the Vienna Forest	H	EF-C	GSC
-----	Voci di primavera	LMH	EF-C	GSC
Strauss, R.	Heimliche Aufforderung	HL	B-E	†
-----	Kling			†
-----	Schlechtes Wetter			†
-----	Wie sollten wir geheim sie halten	LH	D-A	
Wolf	Ach, im Maien	HL	C-E	†
-----	Auf einer Wanderung	HL		†
-----	Die Zigeunerin			†
-----	Er ist's	H	D-G	†
-----	Ich hab' in Penna	LH		INT
-----	Liebe mir in Busen zuendet	M	E-F	†
-----	Lied vom Winde			†
-----	Nimmersatte Liebe	LH	CF-AF	†
-----	Nixe Binsefuss	H	E-G	†
-----	Waldmaedchen			PET
-----	Zum neuen Jahr			PET

Italian Songs and Arias Employing Spirited Singing

Lyric Soprano

Arditi	Il bacio	H	CS-B	†
Bellini	Ah! non credea mirarti (La Sonnambula)			GSC
----	Casta diva (Norma)	H	F-C	†
Bononcini	L'esperto nocchiero (Astarte)	HL	B-E	†
Castelnuovo-Tedesco	Recuerdo			
Cavalli	Donzelle fuggite	HL	C-EF	†
Cimara	Canto di primavera		D-G	FRL
D'Astorga	Vo' cercando in queste valli	H	D-G	STB
Donaudy	Ah mai non cessate			RIC
-----	Spirate pur, spirate			RIC

179

Donizetti	Prendi, prendi per mei sei libero (L'Elisir d'Amore)			BRO
Falconieri	Non più d'amore	HL	C-D	DIT
-----	Nudo arciero	HL	AF-AF	DIT
Handel	Amor commanda (Floridante)	H		†
-----	Ch'io mai vi possa (Siroe)			†
-----	Dira che amor per me (Serse)	H	F-A	CFI
-----	Lusinghe più care (Alessandro)	H	D-G	†
-----	Mio caro bene (Rodelinda)			OXF
-----	Qual farfalletta (Partenope)	H	E-A	AUG
-----	Riportai gloriosa palma (Atalanta)			BOO
-----	Sei, mia gioja (Partenope)			CFI
-----	Spietati, io vi giurai (Rodelinda)			BOO
Legranzi	Che fiero costume	HML	C-D	†
Mozart	A questo seno, deh vieni			BOO
-----	Ah lo previdi			PET
-----	Dove sono (Le Nozze di Figaro)	H	D-A	†
-----	Mi tradi quell' alma ingrata (Don Giovanni)			†
-----	Non so più cosa son (Le Nozze di Figaro)	H	EF-G	†
-----	Un moto di gioja (Le Nozze di Figaro)			†
-----	Voi che sapete (Le Nozze di Figaro)	M	C-F	†
Paisiello	Chi vuol la zingarella	L	C-F	GSC
Paradies	M'ha preso alla sua ragna	M	EF-F	GSC
Pergolesi	A Serpina penserete (La Serva Padrona)	HLM	D-F	†
-----	Confusa, smarrita			GSC
------	Stizzoso, mio stizzoso (La Serva Padrona)	H	C-AF	†
Piccini	Se il ciel mi divide (Alessandro di Indie)	M	C-F	†
Porpora	Non più fra sassi			PET
Puccini	Ancora un passo (Madama Butterfly)			RIC
Respighi	Invito alla danza			BON
-----	Pioggia			BON
-----	Scherzo			BON
Rontani	Or ch'io non segno più	HL	CS-E	DIT

180

Rossini	La pastorella delle Alpi	H	E-C	CFI
-----	Una voce poco fa	HM	GS-E	GSC
	(Il Barbiere di Siviglia)			
Scarlatti, A.	All' acquisto di gloria	H	C-G	GSC
	(Tigrane)			
-----	Già il sole dal Gange	LH	EF-F	GSC
-----	Se Florindo è fedele	LM	EF-EF	GSC
Scarlatti, D.	Consolati e spara amante	L	BF-E	GSC
-----	Qual farfalletta			
Verdi	Ernani involami (Ernani)	H	AF-BF	GSC

Miscellaneous Songs Employing
Spirited Singing

Lyric Soprano

Dvořák	The lark			
-----	Tune thy fiddle gypsy			SIM
Falla	El paño moruno	HL		AMP
-----	Seguidilla murciana	HL		AMP
-----	Siete canciones	HL		AMP
Glazounoff	La primavera d'or	H	D-BF	GSC
Granados	El majo discreto	H		INT
Gretchaninoff	The skylark			DIT
Grieg	My Johann	HL	BF-EF	GSC
Mozart	Alleluja	LMH	F-C	†
Mussorgsky	In the corner			INT
Rachmaninoff	Floods of spring	HL		DIT
-----	God took away from me			GSC
-----	Sorrow in spring	H	D-BF	DIT
Rubinstein	The lark	LH	EF-G	DIT
Sandoval	Sin tu amor	H	E-G	GSC
Stravinsky	The cloister (La novice)			DIT
Tchaikovsky	At the ball	MH		GSC
Turina	Cantares			UME
-----	Farruca	M	A-F	UME
-----	Las locas por amor			UME
-----	Madrigal	H	D-BF	UME
-----	Rima	H	A-A	AMP

Songs and Arias Employing Staccato

Lyric Soprano

Arne, M.	The lass with the delicate air	MH	D-G	†
Arne, T.	Polly Willis	H	D-G	†

181

(Arne, T.)	Where the bee sucks	HM		†
Bemberg	Il neige	H	FS-G	GRU
Delibes	Les filles de Cadix	HM	A-A	†
-----	Passepied	LH	DS-CS	GSC
Dupont	Chanson des noisettes			HEU
Fourdrain	Carnaval	M	C-F	RIC
Grieg	Solvejg's song	MH	E-A	†
Handel	Oh! had I jubal's lyre (Joshua)	H	E-FS	†
-----	So shall the lute and harp awake (Judas Maccabaeus)			
Haydn	My mother bids me bind hair	M	E-E	†
Hue	L'âne blanc	H	EF-G	HEU
La Forge	Come unto these yellow sands	H	FS-B	GSC
Liadoff	The musical snuff box	H	CS-D	GSC
Monsigny	Il regardait mon bouquet (Le Roi et le Fermier)	H	D-G	GSC
Mozart	Das Veilchen	LMH	F-G	†
-----	Vedrai carino (Don Giovanni)	H	G-G	†
Saminsky	Queen Estherka's laugh	H	D-A	CFI
Scarlatti, A.	Rugiadose odorose (Il Pirro e Demetrio)	HL	D-E	DIT
Schubert	Der Juengling an der Quelle	LH	E-A	†
Sibella	La Girometta	HML	D-E	GSC
-----	O bimba bimbetta	LMH	D-G	GSC
Strauss, R.	Zerbinetta's aria (Ariadne auf Naxos)			BOO
Verdi	Tacea la notte placida (Il Trovatore)	H	D-DF	†
Watts	The little shepherd's song	H	G-BF	RIC
Weckerlin	Maman, dites-moi	M	E-FS	BOS

American and British Songs of Popular Appeal

Lyric Soprano

Arne, M.	The lass with the delicate air	MH	D-G	†
Balfe	Killarney	H	D-E	GSC
Beach	Ah, love but a day			ASC
Besley	The second minuet	HL		BOO
Bishop	Lo! here the gentle lark Flute	H		†

(Bishop)	Love has eyes	M		†
-----	Pretty mocking bird Flute	H		†
Bliss	The buckle			CUR
Brahe	Bless this house	HML	A-EF	BOO
Buzzi-Peccia	Under the greenwood tree	LMH	EF-A	DIT
Cadman	From the land of the sky-blue water			WHI
-----	Joy	MH	E-A	GSC
Campbell-Tipton	A spirit flower	LHM	B-G	GSC
Carey	A pastoral			GSC
Charles	And so, goodbye	LH	EF-AF	GSC
-----	Let my song fill your heart	LH	EF-AF	GSC
-----	When I have sung my songs	HM	BF-EF	GSC
Clarke	Shy one	HL	BF-G	BOH
Coates	The green hills o' Somerset			
Curran	Dawn	LMH	E-BF	GSC
-----	Ho! Mr. Piper	LH	D-G	GSC
De Rose	I heard a forest praying	MH	EF-GF	CHA
Donaldson	My buddy			REM
Dougherty	Everyone sang			
-----	Love in the dictionary	M	C-G	GSC
-----	Weathers			
Duke	I can't be talkin' of love	H	CS-G	GSC
Edwards	By the bend of the river	HML	C-E	GSC
-----	Into the night	HML	C-DF	GSC
Elgar	Land of hope and glory			BOO
Firestone	You are the song in my heart			
Fox	The hills of home	HML	BF-DF	CFI
Friml	L'amour, toujours l'amour			HAR
Gaynor	May magic			
Goehl	For you alone			SHU
German	Who'll buy my lavender?	HML		BOO
Giannini	Sing to my heart a song	H	D-B	ELV
Griselle and Young	The cuckoo clock	LH	EF-G	GSC
Henschel	Morning-hymn	MH	DS-GS	†
Herbert	Summer serenade			SHU
Kountz	Prayer of the Norwegian child	ML	C-C	GSC
-----	The little French clock	LH	D-G	GAL
-----	The sleigh	HL	D-FS	GSC
La Forge	Song of the open	MH	EF-AF	DIT
Lehmann	The cuckoo	HH	D-B	BOH

183

Levitzki	Ah, thou beloved one	H	EF-AF	GSC
Lieurance	By the waters of Minnetonka			PRE
Malotte	A little song of life	LMH	DS-A	GSC
Manning	In the Luxembourg Gardens	HML	BF-D	GSC
-----	Shoes	M	EF-F	GSC
Mitchell	Love is the wind	MHH	F-A	GAH
Molloy	The Kerry dance	LH	C-G	GSC
Mopper	The lemon-colored dodo	H	F-BF	BOS
Nevin	Little boy blue			BOS
-----	Mighty lak' a rose			JCH
-----	The Rosary	HML	C-D	BOS
Novello	The little damozel	LHM	C-G	BOO
Poldini	Dance of the dolls			CHM
Porter	When love comes your way			HAR
Rasbach	April	LH	EF-G	GSC
-----	Mountains	LH	DF-AF	GSC
-----	Promise	LH	AF-BF	GSC
-----	Trees	LMH	CS-GS	GSC
Rich	American Lullaby	LH	C-F	GSC
Robyn	A heart that's free	MH	EF-AF	FEI
Rogers	At parting	LH	CS-FS	GSC
-----	The star	LH	C-AF	GSC
Ronald	Down in the forest	HML	C-D	ENO
-----	Drift down, drift down			BOO
-----	Love, I have won you	HML	EF-EF	ENO
-----	O, lovely night	HML		BOO
-----	Prelude	HML	B-D	ENO
Russell	Fulfillment	LH	EF-GF	BOS
Rybner	Pierrot	HL		GSC
Saar	The little gray dove	MH	D-BF	GSC
Sandoval	Theme and 3 variations on "Long ago"	H	CS-B	GSC
Schertzinger	March of the grenadiers			FAM
-----	One night of love			ROU
Schneider	Flower rain			SUM
Schuman	Holiday song	M	C-F	GSC
Scott	Blackbird's song			ELK
-----	Think on me	HML	D-EF	GAL
Speaks	In May time	HL	D-E	JCH
Spross	Will o' the wisp			JCH
Strelezki	Dreams	LMH	B-A	GSC
Taylor	A song for lovers	MH	D-F	JFI
Ware	This day is mine	MH	EF-AF	BOS
Warren	Fulfilment	H	D-BF	GAL
Weaver	Moon-marketing	LMH	E-G	GSC
Wilson	My lovely Celia	HL	B-E	BOO
Wolf	Jack in the box			
Wood	A brown bird singing	HLM	FS-G	CHA

| Woodman | Love's in my heart | LH | F-BF | GSC |
| Worth | Midsummer | LM | E-A | GSC |

(See also Humorous Songs, Negro Spirituals,
Folk Songs, Operetta Songs and Opera Arias.)

Miscellaneous Songs of
Popular Appeal

Lyric Soprano

Acqua	Chanson provencale	H	D-BF	GSC
Alvarez	La partida	HL	DS-E	GSC
Arditi	Il bacio	H	CS-B	†
Bach-Gounod	Ave Maria			†
Berger	They all dance the samba	M	A-FS	GSC
Bizet	Agnus Dei	HLM	C-AF	†
-----	Chanson d'avril	H	BF-G	†
-----	Ouvre ton coeur	MH	DS-GS	†
Braga	Angel's serenade Violin	LH	D-G	†
Buzzi-Peccia	Colombetta			RIC
Cavalli	Donzelle fuggite	HL	C-EF	†
Cimara	Canto di primavera		D-G	FRL
Dalcroze	Le coeur de ma mic	HML		†
De Curtis	Torna al Surriento	HM	D-F	CFI
De Mejo	Bela bimba			
Delibes	Les filles de Cadix	HM	A-A	†
-----	Passepied	LH	DS-CS	GSC
Donaudy	O del mio amato ben	M	EF-F	RIC
Dvořák	Songs my mother taught mo	HM	E-E	†
Eckert	Swiss echo song	H	A-B	GSC
Fontenailles	Obstination	MH	EF-GF	DUR
Franz	Dedication	HML	BF-C	†
Freire	Ay, ay, ay	LH		RIC
Glazounoff	La primavera d'or	H	D-BF	GSC
Gounod	Au printemps	LMH	DF-AF	GSC
-----	Sérénade	LMH	D-A	GSC
Grieg	A dream			†
-----	I love thee	HML	E-F	†
-----	My Johann	HL	BF-EF	GSC
-----	Solvejg's song	MH	E-A	†
Hahn	Si mes vers avaient des ailes	HLM	B-FS	†
Hue	A des oiseaux	H	E-G	†
Leroux	Le nil Cello or Violin	LH	E-A	†
Liadoff	The musical snuff box	H	CS-D	GSC
Lilljebjorn	When I was seventeen			RIC
Marx, B.	Senhorinha Brasileira			

Massenet	Elégie	LM	C-GF	GSC
-----	Ouvre tes yeux bleus	MH	C-G	†
Mendelssohn	On wings of song			†
Moret	Le nélumbo	H	E-DF	HEU
Padilla	El relicario			GOL
-----	La violetera			HAR
Pestalozza	Ciribiribin			DIT
Poulenc	Les chemins de l'amour	M		AMP
Rabey	Tes yeux Violin and piano	H	EF-G	DUR
Rachmaninoff	To the children	MH	F-G	DIT
Reichardt	In the time of roses			†
Rimsky-Korsakov	The nightingale and the rose	H	FS-FS	DIT
Rossini	La danza	MH	E-A	†
-----	La pastorella delle Alpi	H	E-C	CFI
Rubinstein	Since first I met thee	H	D-G	DIT
Saint-Saëns	La libellule	H	C-D	DUR
Sandoval	Eres tú			
Schubert	An die Musik	HL	A-DS	†
-----	Ave Maria	LMH	F-F	†
-----	Hark! hark! the lark	LMH	F-G	†
-----	Staendchen			
Schumann	Widmung	HL	BF-F	†
Sibella	La Girometta	HML	D-E	GSC
Strauss, J.	Blue Danube waltz			GSC
-----	Tales from the Vienna forest	H	EF-C	GSC
-----	Voci di primavera	LMH	EF-C	GSC
-----	Wiener Blut			
Tchaikovsky	None but the lonely heart	HLM	C-F	DIT
Tosti	'A vucchella	LH	F-G	RIC
-----	Marechiare	M	D-FS	GSC
Weber	Invitation to the dance	H	FF-EF	GSC
Yradier	La paloma	HL	BF-EF	GSC

(See also Humorous Songs, Negro Spirituals, Folk Songs, Operetta Songs and Opera Arias.)

Arias from British Operas

Lyric Soprano

Arnold	Hist! hist! (Maid of the Mill)	M	D-G	STB
Balfe	I dream't I dwelt in marble halls (The Bohemian Girl)			†

Britten	Church Scene (Peter Grimes)			BOH
-----	Embroidery aria (Peter Grimes)			
Goossens	The fan song (Don Juan de Mahara)			
Handel	Spring is coming (Ottone)	M	D-F	CUR
-----	Trip, blithe streamlet (Serse)			
-----	With artful beguiling (Alessandro)			†
Purcell	Fairest isle (King Arthur)			NOV
-----	From rosy bow'rs (Don Quixote)			AUG
-----	Hark! the echoing air (The Fairy Queen)			BAF
-----	I attempt from love's sickness to fly (The Indian Queen)	MH	CS-E	
-----	Music for a while (Oedipus)	LH		SC
-----	Nymphs and shepherds (The Libertine)	HM	C-F	†
-----	Sweeter than roses (Pausanias)			SC
Vaughn Williams	Greensleeves (Sir John in Love)			OXF

Arias from French Operas

Lyric Soprano

Auber	Quel bonheur (Fra Diavolo)			BOO
Berlioz	Autrefois un roi de Thule (La Damnation de Faust)			CST
Bizet	Comme autrefois dans la nuit sombre (Les Pêcheurs des Perles)			CHO
-----	Je dis que rien ne m'épouvante (Carmen)	LH	D-B	†
-----	O dieu Brahma (Les Pêcheurs des Perles)	H	B-D	GSC
Campra	Charmant papillon (Les Fêtes Venitiennes)	MH	D-G	GSC
Charpentier	Depuis le jour (Louise)	MH	D-B	†

187

David	Charmant oiseau (La Perle du Brésil)	M	D-E	†
Delibes	Pourquoi dans les grands bois (Lakmé)	H	FS-AF	BRO
Dourlen	Je sais attacher des rubans (Le Frère Philippe)			
Gluck	Adieu, conservez dans votre âme (Iphigénie en Aulide)			†
-----	Grands dieux (Alceste)	H	E-BF	GSC
-----	Jamais dans ces beaux lieux (Armide)			PET
-----	L'ai-je bien entendu? (Iphigénie en Aulide)			†
-----	Non! ce n'est point (Alceste)	H	E-G	†
Godard	Cachés dans cet asile (Jocelyn)	MH	DF-F	GSC
Gounod	Ah, si je redevenais belle (Philémon et Baucis)	H	E-A	GSC
-----	Air des bijoux (Faust)	H	B-B	†
-----	Je veux vivre (Roméo et Juliette)	H	F-C	†
-----	Le jour se lève (Mireille)			CHO
-----	Mon coeur ne peut changer! (Mireille)			GSC
-----	Plus grand, dans son obscurité (La Reine de Saba)	MH	CS-B	†
Grétry	Je crains de lui (Richard Coeur de Lion)			LEM
-----	Je ne fais semblant de rein (L'Ami de la Maison)			LEM
-----	Je ne le dis qu'à vous (La Fausse Magie)			LEM
-----	La fauvette avec ses petits (Zémire et Azor) Flute			LEM
-----	Plus de dépit (Les deux Avares)			LEM
-----	Rose chérie (Zémire et Azor)			LEM
-----	Vous etiez, ce que vous n'êtes plus (Le Tableau Parlant)			JOB
Halévy	Il va venir (La Juive)	H	D-CF	†
Lully	Ariette de Cloris (Que soupirer) (Divertissement de Chambord)			
-----	Chant du Vénus (Revenez amours) (Thésée)			LEM

(Lully)	Fermez-vous pour jamais (Amadis)			LEM
-----	Par le secours (Roland)			
-----	Plus j'observe ces lieux (Armide)			LEM
Massé	Air du rossignol (Les Noces de Jeannette) Flute			
-----	Chanson du tigre (Paul et Virginie)			
Massenet	Adieu, notre petite table (Manon)			GSC
-----	Charmes des jours passés (Hérodiade)			HEU
-----	Dis-moi que je suis belle (Thaïs)	H	D-B	HEU
-----	Gavotte (Manon)			†
-----	Il est doux, il est bon (Hérodiade)	MH	EF-BF	GSC
-----	J'ai bien assez de mes tristesses (Don Quichotte)			
-----	Je suis encore tout étourdie (Manon)			HEU
-----	L'amour est une vertu rare (Thaïs)			HEU
-----	Sévillana (Don Cesar da Bazan)			HEU
-----	Tristesse de Dulcinée (Don Quichotte)			HEU
Messager	La maison grise (Fortuno)			CHO
Meyerbeer	Nobles Seigneurs, salut! (Les Huguenots)	LH	C-C	†
-----	O beau pays (Les Huguenots)	H	CS-D	GSC
-----	Roberto, o tu che adoro (Robert le Diable)	H	C-C	DEI
Monsigny	Il regardait mon bouquet (Le Roi et le Fermier)	H	D-G	GSC
-----	La sagesse est un trésor (Rose et Colas)			LEM
Offenbach	Couplets de l'aveu (La Périchole)			
-----	Elle a fui, la tourterelle (Tales of Hoffman)	H	D-A	GSC
Rameau	Air de Vénus (Dardanus)			LEM
-----	Dans ces doux asiles (Castor et Pollux)			LEM
-----	Rossignols amoureux (Hippolyte et Aricie)			†

(Rameau)	Tristes apprêts (Castor et Pollux)			CHE
Ravel	Concepcion's air (Oh la pitoyable adventure (L'Heure espagnole)			
Spontini	Toi que je laisse sur la terre (La Vestale)			
Thomas	Je connais un pauvre enfant H (Mignon)		C-B	†
-----	Me voice dans son boudoir (Mignon)			

Arias from German Operas

Lyric Soprano

Beethoven	O waer' ich schon mit dir vereint (Fidelio)			†
Humperdinck	Ein Maennlein steht im Walde (Haensel und Gretel)	M	C-F	SC
Korngold	Marietta's song (The Dead City)	MH	F-BF	AMP
Mozart	Ach, ich fuehl's (Die Zauberfloete)	H	CS-BF	†
-----	Ach, ich liebte (Abduction from Seraglio)			†
-----	Bester Juengling, mit Entzuecken (Der Schauspieldirector)			RIC
-----	Durch Zaertlichkeit (Abduction from Seraglio)			†
-----	Martern aller Arten (Abduction from Seraglio)	H	B-D	†
-----	Welche Wonne, welche Lust (Abduction from Seraglio)			†
Nicolai	Now to my aid fun wit and humor (The Merry Wives)			
Schubert	Liebe schwaermt auf allen Wegen (Claudine von Villa Bella)			PET
Strauss	Mein Elemer (Arabella)			BOO
-----	Zerbinetta's aria (Ariadne auf Naxos)			BOO
Weber	Truebe Augen (Der Freischuetz)			GSC
-----	Und ob die Wolke (Der Freischuetz)	H	EF-AF	†

Arias From Italian Operas

Lyric Soprano

Bellini	Ah! non credea mirarti (La Sonnambula)			GSC
-----	Casta diva (Norma)	H	F-C	†
Boito	Morte di Margherita (L'altra notte) (Mefistofele)	H	D-B	GSC
Catalani	Dove son (Loreley)	H		RIC
-----	Ebben? Ne andrò lontana (La Wally)	H	E-B	RIC
Cilea	Esser madre è un inferno (L'Arlesiana)			SON
-----	Io son l'umile ancella (Adriana Lecouvreur)	H		AMP
-----	Poveri fiori (Adriana Lecouvreur)			SON
Donizetti	Chacun le sait (La Fille du Régiment)	H	C-A	RIC
-----	Il faut partir (La Fille du Régiment)	H	E-C	GSC
-----	O luce di quest' anima (Linda di Chamounix)	H	C-E	GSC
-----	Prendi, prendi per mei sei libero (L'Elisir d'Amore)			BRO
-----	Quel guardo (Don Pasquale)			BRO
Faccio	Sortita d'Ofelia (Amleto)			GSC
Flotow	Qui sola, vergin rosa (Martha)			BRO
Gagliano	Dormi amore (La Flora)	HL	CS-E	DIT
Giordano	La mamma morta (Andrea Chenier)	H	CS-B	AMP
Gluck	Che fiero momento (Orfeo ed Euridice			HEU
Handel	Dira che amor per me (Serse)	H	F-A	CFI
Leoncavallo	Ballatella! (I Pagliacci)	H	CS-AS	†
Mascagni	Non mi resta che (L'Amico Fritz)			GSC
-----	Son pochi fiori (L'Amico Fritz)			GSC
Monteverdi	Lasciatemi morire (Arianna)	ML	D-D	†
-----	Sento un certo non so che (L'Incoronazione di Poppea)			HEU

191

Mozart	Batti, batti, o bel Masetto (Don Giovanni)	H	C-BF	†
-----	Come scoglio (Così Fan Tutte)			†
-----	Deh vieni non tardar (Le Nozze di Figaro)	H	A-A	†
-----	Dove sono (Le Nozze di Figaro)	H	D-A	†
-----	Geme la tortorella (La Finta Giardiniera)			
-----	L'amero, saro costante (Il Re Pastore) Violin or flute	H	D-B	GSC
-----	Mi tradi quell' alma ingrata (Don Giovanni)			†
-----	Non mi dir (Don Giovanni)	H	F-B	†
-----	Non so più cosa son (Le Nozze di Figaro)	H	EF-G	†
-----	Or sai, chi l'onore (Don Giovanni)			GSC
-----	Parto, parto (La Clemenza di Tito) B flat clarinet and piano	H		AMP
-----	Per pietà, ben mio (Così Fan Tutte)			†
-----	Porgi amor (Le Nozze di Figaro)	H	D-AF	†
-----	Se' il padre perdei (Idomeneo)			RIC
-----	Un moto di gioja (Le Nozze di Figaro)			†
-----	Vedrai carino (Don Giovanni)	H	G-G	†
-----	Venite inginocchiatevi (Le Nozze di Figaro)	H	D-G	†
-----	Voi che sapete (Le Nozze di Figaro)	M	C-F	†
-----	Zeffiretti lusinghieri (Idomeneo)			†
Pergolesi	A Serpina penserete (La Serva Padrona)	HLM	D-F	†
-----	Stizzoso, mio stizzoso (La Serva Padrona)	H	C-AF	†
Pietri	Uno strano senso arcano (Maristella)			
Puccini	Ancora un passo (Madama Butterfly)			RIC

(Puccini)	Chi bel sogno di doretta (La Rondine)	H	C-G	SON
-----	Donde lieta usci (La Boheme)			
-----	In quelle trine morbide (Manon Lescaut)	H	DF-BF	RIC
-----	Musetta's waltz (La Boheme)	H	EF-BF	RIC
-----	O mio babbino caro (Gianni Schicchi)			RIC
-----	Ore dolci e divine (La Rondine)	H	E-A	SON
-----	Senza mamma (Suor Angelica)			RIC
-----	Si, Mi chiamano Mimi (La Boheme)		DF-BF	RIC
-----	Signore, ascolta (Turandot)			RIC
-----	Solo perduta abbandonata (Manon Lescaut)			RIC
-----	Spira sul mare (Madama Butterfly)			RIC
-----	Tu, che di gel sei cinta (Turandot)			RIC
-----	Tu? tu? piccolo Iddio! (Madama Butterfly)			RIC
-----	Un bel di vedremo (Madama Butterfly)	H	DF-BF	RIC
-----	Vissi d'arte (Tosca)	MH	EF-BF	RIC
Rossini	Sombre forêt (Guillaume Tell)			
-----	Una voce poco fa (Il Barbiere di Siviglia)	HM	GS-E	GSC
Verdi	Addio del passato (La Traviata)			†
-----	Ah fors' e lui (La Traviata)	H	C-DF	†
-----	Anch' io dischiuso un giorno (Nabucco)			RIC
-----	Ave Maria (Otello)	H	EF-AF	GSC
-----	Caro Nome (Rigoletto)	H	DS-DS	†
-----	D'amor sull' ali rosee (Il Trovatore)	H	C-DF	†
-----	Ecco l'orrido campo (Un Ballo in Maschera)	H	B-C	RIC
-----	Ernani involami (Ernani)	H	AF-BF	GSC
-----	O madre del cielo (I Lombardi)			
-----	Salce, salce (Otello)	H	CS-FS	RIC

193

(Verdi)	Sul fil d'un soffio	H	DS-A	RIC
	etesio (Falstaff)			
-----	Tacea la notte placida	H	D-DF	†
	(Il Trovatore)			
-----	Volta la terrea	H	D-BF	GSC
	(Un Ballo in Maschera)			
Wolf-Ferrari	Gioia, la nube leggera			BRO
	(Secret of Susanne)			

Miscellaneous Opera Arias

Lyric Soprano

Dvořák	Armida's aria (Armida)			
-----	O lovely moon (Rusalka)			
Falla	Vivan los que ríen			AMP
	(La Vida Breve)			
Gershwin	My man's gone now			CHA
	(Porgy and Bess)			
-----	Summertime			CHA
	(Porgy and Bess)			
Granados	Descúbrase el Pensamiento			GSC
	(Goyescas)			
-----	The maja and the	H	BS-A	GSC
	nightingale (Goyescas)			
Hanson	No witch am I			HAR
	(Merry Mount)			
Janecek	Every now and then			
	(Jenufa)			
Kodaly	I am poor (Hary Janos)			
-----	Two hens of mine			
	(Hary Janos)			
Menotti	Laetitia's aria			RIC
	(Old Maid and the Thief)			
-----	Lucy's arietta			GSC
	(The Telephone)			
-----	Monica's waltz			GSC
	(The Medium)			
-----	To this we've come			
	(The Consul)			
Mussorgsky	Chanson de Parassia	H		CHE
	(The Fair at Sorotchinsk)			
Rimsky-Korsakov	Hymn to the sun	H	FS-B	GSC
	(Le Coq D'Or)			
-----	Little Snow Flake's	H	C-AF	GSC
	arietta (The Snow Maiden)			
-----	Song of India (Sadko)	LH	D-G	GSC

(Rimsky-Korsakov)	Song of the shepherd lehl (Snegourotchka)	LM		DIT
Smetana	Carolina's aria (Two Widows)			
-----	Gladly do I trust you (The Bartered Bride)			BOO
-----	How strange and dead (The Bartered Bride)			BOO
Tchaikovsky	Iolanthe's aria (Iolanthe)			

Arias from Oratorios and Latin Works

Lyric Soprano

Bach, J.S.	For love my Savior now is dying (St. Matthew Passion) Flute			†
-----	Bleed and break (St. Matthew Passion)			†
-----	I follow Thee also (St. John Passion) Flute			†
-----	Seele, deine Specereien (Easter Oratorio) Flute or violin			
Beethoven	O praise Him (Mount of Olives)			
Carissimi	Lamento della figlia de Jephte (Jepthe)			
Dvořák	O grant me in the dust to fall (St. Ludmilla)			
Elgar	Be not extreme, O Lord (Light of Life)			NOV
Fauré	Pie Jesu (The Requiem)			HAM
Gaul	Sun of my soul (Ten Virgins)			
-----	These are they (The Holy City)	H	E-GS	GSC
Handel	Angels ever bright and fair (Theodora)	H	E-F	‖
-----	Ask if you damask rose (Susanna)			†
-----	As when the dove (Acis and Galatea)	H	D-G	†
-----	Beneath the cypress (Susanna)			

195

(Handel)	But o what art can teach (Ode from St. Cecelia's Day)			
-----	Chi sprezzando il somo bene (La Passione)			
-----	Come unto Him (The Messiah)	MH	F-G	†
-----	Farewell, ye limpid springs and floods (Jephtha)	H	D-G	†
-----	From mighty Kings (Judas Maccabaeus)	H	D-A	†
-----	Hallelujah (Esther)	H	E-B	CFI
-----	How beautiful are the feet of them (The Messiah)	H		†
-----	If God be with us, who can be against us (The Messiah)			†
-----	Let me wander not unseen (L'Allegro)	M	D-G	†
-----	Let the bright seraphim (Samson) Trumpet	H	E-A	†
-----	Oh, had I Jubal's lyre (Joshua)	H	E-FS	†
-----	O King of Kings (Esther)	H		CHE
-----	O Liberty, thou choicest treasure (Judas Maccabaeus)			
-----	O sleep, why dost thou leave me (Semele)	H	DS-GS	†
-----	Pious orgies (Judas Maccabaeus)			
-----	Praise the Lord (Esther)	H	E-G	
-----	Rejoice greatly (The Messiah)	H	E-A	†
-----	So shall the lute and harp awake(Judas Maccabaeus)			†
-----	Sweet bird (L'Allegro) Flute			NOV
-----	Thou God most high (Belshazzer)			
-----	What's sweeter than a new-blown rose? (Joseph)	H	EF-AF	†
-----	What though I trace each herb and flower (Solomon)		CS-E	†
-----	With thee th' unsheltered moor (Solomon)			†
Haydn	O how pleasing to the senses (The Seasons)	H		†
-----	On mighty pens uplifted soars (The Creation)	H	E-A	†

196

(Haydn)	With verdure clad	H	E-BF	†
	(The Creation)			
Honegger	O had I wings like a dove			CHE
	(King David)			
Massenet	'Twas even here			
	(Mary Magdeline)			
Mendelssohn	Hear ye, Israel (Elijah)	H	E-A	†
-----	I will sing of Thy great	H	E-F	†
	mercies (Saint Paul)			
-----	Jerusalem, thou that	H	F-F	GSC
	killest (Saint Paul)			
Mozart	Et incarnatus est			PET
	(C Minor Mass)			
Parker	O country bright and fair			
	(Hora Novissima)			
Sullivan	My Redeemer and my Lord			
	(Golden Legend)			

Cantata Arias

Lyric Soprano

Bach, J. S.	Alleluja from (Cantata 51)	BRO
-----	Auch mit gedaempften,	PET
	schwachen Stimmen	
	(Cantata 36) Violin	
-----	Bereite Dir, Jesu	
	(Cantata 147) Violin	
-----	Des Reichtums Glanz auf	
	weiter Erden (Von der	
	Vergnuegsamkeit) Violin	
-----	Die Armen will der Herr	PET
	umarmen (Cantata 186)	
	Violin	
-----	Die Seele ruht in Jesu	AUG
	Haenden (Cantata 127)	
	2 Flutes and oboe	
-----	Eilt, ihr Stunden, kommt	RIC
	herbei (Cantata 30) Violin	
-----	Erfuellet, ihr himmlischen,	NOV
	goettlichen Flammen	
	(Cantata 1) English horn	
-----	Es halt' es mit der blinden	
	Welt (Cantata 94) Oboe d'amore	
-----	Frische Schatten (Cantata 205)	
-----	Genuegsamkeit ist ein Schatz	
	in diesem Leben (Cantata 144)	
	Oboe d'amore	

(Bach, J. S.)	Gerechter Gott, ach rechnest Du Cantata 89 (Oboe)			
-----	Gott versorget alles Leben (Cantata 187) Oboe			
-----	Herr, der Du stark und maechtig bist (Cantata 10)			
-----	Hoechster was ich habe (Cantata 39) Flute			NOV
-----	Hoert doch! der sanften Floeten (Cantata 206) 3 Flutes and continuo			
-----	Hoert, ihr Augen auf zu weinen (Cantata 98) Oboe			PET
-----	Hoert, ihr Voelker (Cantata 76) Violin			BRO
-----	Ich ende behende mein irdisches Leben (Cantata 57) Violin			
-----	Ich nehme mein Leiden (Cantata 75) Oboe d'amore			AUG
-----	Ich will auf den Herren schaun (Cantata 93) Oboe			NOV
-----	Jagen ist die Lust der Goetter (Cantata 208) 2 Waldenhorn			
-----	Jesus soll mein erstes Wort (Cantata 171) Violin			
-----	Liebster Jesu, mein verlangen (Cantata 32) Oboe			
-----	Mein glaeubiges Herze (Cantata 68)	HML		†
-----	Mein Seelenschatz (Cantata 18) Flute and viola			BRO
-----	Meine Seele, sei vergnuegt (Von der Vergnuegsamkeit) Flute			
-----	Meinem Hirten bleib' ich treu (Cantata 92) Oboe d'amore			
-----	Patron, das macht der Wind (Phoebus and Pan)	M	C-G	GSC
-----	Ruhet hie, matte Toene (Cantata 210) Oboe d'amore and violin			AUG
-----	Schweigt ihr Floeten, schweigt ihr Toene (Cantata 210) Flute			
-----	Seufzer, Traenen, Kummer, Noth (Cantata 21) Oboe			†
-----	Sheep may safely graze (Cantata 208) 2 Flutes and continuo	LM	EF-GF	GAL

(Bach, J.S.)	Suesser Trost, mein Jesus kommt (Cantata 151) Flute			
-----	Wie zittern und wanken (Cantata 105) Oboe			BRO
-----	Wirf, mein Herze (Cantata 155) Strings and continuo			
Debussy	Air de Lia (L'Enfant Prodigue)	H	E-A	DUR
Handel	Have mercy, Lord (Te Deum)	HM		†
Rameau	Quand le silence (Air tendre) (Diane et Acteon)			DUR
Scarlatti, D.	Tuo mi chiami (Tinto a Note di Sangue)			OXF

Operetta, Musical Comedy
or Show Songs

Lyric Soprano

Arlen	Over the rainbow (The Wizard of Oz)			FEI
Brown	Love is where you find it (The Kissing Bandit)			
Caryll	By the Saskatchewan (The Pink Lady)			CHA
Christine	Do I love you (Naughty Marietta)			HAR
Coward	I'll follow my secret heart (Conversation Piece)	M	A-FS	CHA
-----	I'll see you again (Bitter Sweet)	M	C-F	HAR
-----	Kiss me (Bitter Sweet)			HAR
-----	Nevermore (Conversation Piece)			CHA
-----	Someday I'll find you (Private Lives)			CHA
-----	Zigeuner (Bitter Sweet)	H	CF-G	HAR
De Koven	Oh promise me (Robin Hood)	HML	C-D	†
Duke	April in Paris (Walk a Little Faster)			HAR
-----	The love I long for (Sadie Thompson)			PAR
Forrest- Grieg	Now (Song of Norway)			CHA
Friml	Donkey serenade (The Firefly)			WIT

(Friml)	Giannina mia (The Firefly)			GSC
-----	Indian love call (Rose Marie)			HAR
-----	Love is like a firefly (The Firefly)	H		GSC
-----	Love me tonight (The Vagabond King)			FAM
-----	Only a rose (The Vagabond King)			GSC
-----	Some day (The Vagabond King)			FAM
German	Waltz song (Tom Jones)	H	B-B	CHA
Gershwin	Bidin' my time (Girl Crazy)			
-----	Love walked in (Goldwyn Follies 1938)			CHA
-----	Somebody loves me (George White's Scandals)			CHA
-----	'S wonderful (Smarty)			CHA
-----	The man I love (Strike up the Band)			BRO
Goetz	So this is love (Little Miss Bluebeard)			HAR
Hahn	Air des adieux (Mozart)			HEU
-----	C'est sa banlieue (Ciboulette)			SAL
-----	Dans une charrette (Ciboulette)			HEU
-----	Etre adoré (Mozart)			HEU
-----	La dernière valse (Une Revue)			HEU
-----	Letter song (Mozart)			HEU
-----	Moi, je m'appelle Ciboulette (Ciboulette)			SAL
Herbert	A kiss in the dark (Orange Blossoms)			WIT
-----	Ah! sweet mystery of life (Naughty Marietta)	LMH	A-A	WIT
-----	Always do as people say you should (The Fortune Teller)			WIT
-----	Cupid tell me why (The Duchess)			WIT
-----	I can't do that sum (Babes in Toyland)			WIT
-----	I'd love to be a lady (Eileen)			WIT

(Herbert)	I list the trill in golden throat (Natoma)			GSC
-----	I'm falling in love with someone (Naughty Marietta)			WIT
-----	Indian Summer (An American Idyll)			HAR
-----	Italian Street song (Naughty Marietta)			WIT
-----	Kiss me again (Mlle. Modiste)	LHM	CS-A	WIT
-----	Make him guess (Princess Pat)			WIT
-----	Moonbeams (The Red Mill)			WIT
-----	Neapolitan love song (Princess Pat)			WIT
-----	'Neath the southern moon (Naughty Marietta)			
-----	Romany life (The Fortune Teller)			WIT
-----	Sweetheart waltz (Sweethearts)			GSC
-----	The commandereress in chief (It Happened in Nordland)			WIT
-----	The knot of blue (It Happened in Nordland)			WIT
-----	The mascot of the troop (Mlle. Modiste)			WIT
-----	Thine alone (Eileen)			WIT
-----	Twilight in Barakeesh (The Rose of Algeria)			WIT
-----	Two laughing Irish eyes (Princess Pat)			WIT
-----	When you're away (The Only Girl)			WIT
Herold	Air de Nicette (Le Pré aux Clercs)			BRA
Kern	All the things you are (Very Warm for May)	M	BF-F	HAR
-----	Dearly beloved (You Were Never Lovlier)			CHA
-----	Don't ever leave me (Sweet Adeline)			CHA
-----	I'm old fashioned (You Were Never Lovelier)			CHA
-----	I've told every little star (Music in the Air)			CHA
-----	Long ago (Cover Girl)			CHA

201

(Kern)	Look for the silver lining (Sally)			CHA
-----	Make Believe (Show Boat)	M	CS-FS	HAR
-----	Our song (When You're in Love)			CHA
-----	Smoke get in your eyes (Roberta)			HAR
-----	The song is you (Music in the Air)	M	C-F	HAR
-----	The touch of your hand (Roberta)			CHA
-----	They didn't believe me (Girl from Utah)			HAR
-----	Why do I love you (Show Boat)	M	C-F	HAR
-----	Why was I born (Sweet Adeline)			HAR
-----	Yesterdays (Roberta)			CHA
-----	You are love (Show Boat)			CHA
Kreisler	Stars in my eyes (The King Steps Out)			CHA
-----	What shall remain (The King Steps Out)			CHA
Lehar	Einer wird kommen (Zarewitsch)			GLO
-----	Ich bin verliebt (Schoen ist die Welt)			GLO
-----	Ich moecht wieder einmal die Heimat sehn (The Land of Smiles)			GLO
-----	Liebe, du Himmel auf Erde (Paganini)			GLO
-----	Lippen Schweigen (The Merry Widow)	LMH	D-A	CHA
-----	Love is like a breeze in May (Paganini)			SAL
-----	Meine Lippen, sie kuessen so heiss (Giuditta)			GLO
-----	My little nest of heavenly blue (Frasquita)	HML		MAR
-----	Vilia (The Merry Widow)			CHA
-----	War einst ein Maedel (Gypsy Love)			BRO
-----	Warum hast du mich aufgewacht gekuesst (Friederike)			SAL

(Lehar)	Wenn du bist das Herz der Welt (Lied)	
Loesser	Lovelier than ever (Where's Charley)	MOR
Luders	Message of the violet (The Prince of Pilsen)	WIT
Messager	Ma foi! pour venir de Provence (Veronique)	CHO
-----	Petite dinde: ah! quel outrage! (Véronique)	CHO
-----	Tu n'est pas beau (La Perichole)	
-----	Valse des cigales (Madame Chrysanthème)	
Milloecker	I give my heart (Mme. Dubarry)	CHA
Monckton	Arcady is ever young (The Arcadians)	CHA
-----	Bring me a rose (The Arcadians)	CHA
Monsigny	Adieu, chère Louise (Le Déserteur)	JOB
Porter	Easy to love (Born to Dance)	CHA
-----	Ev'rytime we say goodbye (Seven Lively Arts)	CHA
-----	I get a kick out of you (Anything Goes)	BRO
-----	Only another boy and girl (Seven Lively Arts)	CHA
-----	So in love (Kiss Me Kate)	CHA
-----	What is this thing called love (Wake Up and Dream)	HAR
Rodgers	Come home (Allegro)	BRO
-----	Falling in love with love (The Boys from Syracuse)	WIL
-----	If I loved you (Carousel)	WIL
-----	I'm in love with a wonderful guy (South Pacific)	CHA
-----	It's a grand night for singing (State Fair)	CHA
-----	Mr. Snow (Carousel)	WIL
-----	My heart stood still (Connecticut Yankee)	HAR
-----	Out of my dreams (Oklahoma)	CHA
-----	What's the use of wond'rin'? (Carousel)	WIL

(Rodgers)	You'll never walk alone (Carousel)			WIL
Romberg	Deep in my heart dear (The Student Prince)			HAR
-----	Lover come back to me (New Moon)	H	D-G	HAR
-----	One kiss (New Moon)			HAR
-----	Romance (The Desert Song)	H	D-BF	HAR
-----	Serenade (The Student Prince)			HAR
-----	Softly as in a morning sunrise (New Moon)			BRO
-----	Something new is in my heart			CHA
Schmidseder	Das ist das Geheimnis von Wien (Der Himmlische Walzer)			
-----	Himmlischer Walzer (Der Himmlische Walzer)			
Schubert	Arietta from Claudine von Villabella			SC
Schwartz	Dancing in the dark (The Band Wagon)			HAR
-----	You and the night and the music (Revenge with Music)			HAR
Strauss, O.	My hero (The Chocolate Soldier)	H	D-G	WIT
Strauss, J.	Adele's laughing song (Die Fledermaus)	H	D-B	GSC
-----	Czardas (Die Fledermaus)			BOO
-----	Ein Maedchen hat es gar nicht gut (The Gypsy Baron)			CRZ
-----	So elend und so treu (The Gypsy Baron)			CRZ
-----	Southern roses (Spitzentuch der Koenigin)			
-----	Spiel' ich die Unschuld vom Lande (Die Fledermaus)			BOO
Tierney	Alice Blue Gown (Irene)			FEI
Wehle	Ein glas Champagner (Anni)			
Weill	September song (Knickerbocker Holiday)			CHA
-----	Somehow I never could believe (Street Scene)			BRO
Youmans	I want to be happy (No, no Nanette)			HAR
Zeller	Sei nicht boes! (Der Obersteiger)			

Song Cycles (Or groups of songs)

Lyric Soprano

Alberti	Four sketches from the Far East	HM	C-F	GSC
Alfano	Three poems by Tagor			
Bacon	Four songs	H	DF-G	MUP
Barber	Hermit songs			GSC
Berg	Siebem frühe Lieder			UNI
Berger	Villanęscas	H	CS-B	GSC
Bergsma	Six songs	H	E-BF	CFI
Berlioz	Les nuits d'été			AUG
Bernstein	I hate music	H	C-A	WIT
-----	La bonne cuisine	H	B-B	GSC
Bliss	Lovelocks			GCT
Brahms	Five songs of Ophelia	HL	B-EF	†
Breville	Prières d'enfant	M	D-F	ROU
Britton	On this island			
Caplet	Les prières			DUR
Chanler	Epitaphs			ARR
-----	The children (9 songs)	M	C-G	GSC
Chausson	La mort de l'amour			
Cornelius	Bridal songs			INT
Crist	Chinese mother goose rhymes	H	C-G	CFI
Debussy	Ariettes oublitées	HL		†
----	Chansons de Bilitis	M	C-FS	†
-----	Fêtes galantes	LH	CS-A	†
-----	Le promenoir des deux amants			DUR
-----	Proses lyriques	HL		JOB
-----	Trots ballades de François Villon			DUR
Dvořák	Gypsy songs	LH	D-A	AMP
Falla	Siète canciones	HL		AMP
Fauré	La bonne chanson	HL		INT
----	Le jardin clos	M	C-E	DUR
-----	Mirages			DUR
-----	Poème d'un jour			HAM
Finzi	Let us garlands bring (Shakesperian songs)	M		BOO
Granados	La maja dolorosa	M		INT
Grieg	Haugtussa	M	B-GF	PET
Gruenberg	Animals and insects	M	A-A	UNI
Head	Over the rim of the moon	LH	C-AF	BOO
Heise	Dyvekes sange			
Holst	Four songs for voice and violin	M	C-G	CHE

205

Honegger	Saluste du Bartas			LEM
-----	Trois chansons			SEN
	String quartet and flute			
-----	Trois poèmes de Claudel			SAL
-----	Three psalms			SAL
Kilpinen	Lieder der Liebe			AMP
Korngold	Songs of farewell	H		AMP
-----	The Eternal			WIT
Leguerney	Je vous envoie	H	C-A	ROU
Manning	Sketches of Paris	HL	C-E	GSC
Martinu	Songs on one page			
Milhaud	Cinq chansons de Paul Vidrac			SAL
-----	Les soirées de Petrograde			DUR
Mussorgsky	The nursery	M	C-G	INT
Osma	Cantares de mi tierra	H	D-G	BOS
Poulenc	Airs chantés	H	C-AF	ROU
-----	Banalités			AMP
-----	Chansons polonaises			ROU
-----	Métamorphoses			SAL
Ravel	Chansons madécasses			DUR
	Flute, cello and piano			
-----	Cinq mèlodies populaires grecques			†
-----	Deux epigrammes de Clément Marot			AMP
-----	Deux mélodies hébraiques (Kaddisch) (Enigme eternelle)			DUR
-----	Histoires naturelles			DUR
-----	Shéhérazade	M	CS-G	DUR
Ronald	Cycle of life			ENO
Rorem	Cycle of holy songs			
Schubert	Songs of Mignon			PET
Schumann	Lieder der Braut	H	D-A	†
-----	Liederkreis			
Slonimsky	Gravestones at Hancock, New Hampshire	H	D-G	AXE
Strauss	Three songs of Ophelia			
Stravinsky	Three Japanese lyrics for Voice, piano, string quartet, 2 flutes, and 2 clarinets			RUM
-----	Trois histoires pour enfants			CHE
Wolf	Geistliche Lieder from Spanisches Liederbuch			PET
Woodford-Finden	Indian love lyrics			⌐OO

Solo Cantatas
Lyric Soprano

Bach, J.S.	Ich bin vergnuegt in meinem Leiden		RIC

(Bach, J.S.)	(Cantata 58) Violin			
-----	Jauchzet Gott in allen			BRO
	Landen (Cantata 51)			
-----	Mein Herze schwimmt			
	im Blut (Unnumbered)			
-----	Non sa che sia dolore			
	(Cantata 209)			
-----	O holder Tag (Cantata 210)			
-----	Weichet nur, betruebte			
	Schatten (Cantata 202) Oboe			
Finzi	Dies natalis			BOO
	(Cantata with orchestra)			
Foss	The song of songs	H		CFI
Handel	Preis der Tonkunst			KSS
Medtner	Sonata-Vocalise			DIT
Mozart	Exsultate jubilate			INT
	2 strings, 2 oboes,			
	2 horns and organ			
Pergolesi	Salve Regina 1			ROM
	2 Violins and cembalo			
-----	Salve Regina 4			ROM
Rameau	Le berger fidèle			DUR
-----	L'Impatience			
Scarlatti, A.	Cantata pastorale (for the			
	Nativity of our Lord			
	Jesus Christ)			
-----	Solitude Ameni apriche			
	Collinette			

See Solo Cantatas of Pergolesi, Handel and
Scarlatti, Kirchenkantaten of Buxtehude and
Symphoniae Sacrae of Schuetz.

Concert Arias

Lyric Soprano

Berg	Der wein (Concert aria)			
Mendelssohn	Infelice (Concert aria,	H	D-BF	GSC
	opus. 94)			
Mozart	A questo seno, deh vieni			BOO
-----	Ah, spiegarti, O Dio			
-----	Ah, lo previdi			PET
-----	Bella mia fiamma, addio			BOO
-----	Ch'io mi scordi di te			BOO
-----	Der Liebe himmlisches			
	Gefuehl			
-----	Misera, dove son			BOO

(Mozart)	Nehmt meinen Dank ihr holden Goenner!			
-----	No, no, che non sei capace			PET
-----	Non temer amato bene			BOO
-----	Popoli di Tessaglia			PET
-----	Schon lacht der holde Fruehling			
-----	Vado, ma dove?			
-----	Voi avete cor fedele			
-----	Vorrei spiegarvi, o Dio			

Christmas Songs

Lyric Soprano

Adam	O Holy Night	LMH		†
Attey	Sweet was the song			BOO
Bacon	Ancient Christmas carol			NEM
Bax	A Christmas carol	H	DF-A	CHE
Benjamin	Before dawn			CUR
Bergsma	Lullee, lullay	H	E-G	CFI
Black	In the sky a wondrous star	H	DF-AF	GRA
Bornschein	Babe of Bethlehem	H	EF-G	CFI
Busser	La salutation angélique	HM		DUR
-----	Le sommeil de l'enfant Jésus			
Carr	As on the night	M	E-FS	GSC
Chaminade	Christmas carol of the birds	MH	D-A	GSC
Clokey	No lullaby need Mary sing			JFI
Cottone	Ninna, nanna	H	FS-A	MCR
De Koven	The white Christ	L	C-D	GSC
Dickinson	The shepherds' story	H		GRA
Dougherty	The first Christmas	H	D-A	GSC
Dunhill	To the Queen of Heaven	M	C-G	GSC
Eakin	What of that midnight long ago	M	D-F	GAL
Fauré	Noël	LH	EF-AF	GSC
Forsyth	The Child Jesus	H	EF-B	GRA
France	A Christmas lullaby	M	DS-F	GAL
Hageman	Christmas eve	HML	BF-EF	GAL
Handel	How beautiful are the feet of them (The Messiah)	H		†
-----	Rejoice greatly (The Messiah)	H	E-A	†
Harker	A child is born in Bethlehem	LH	D-G	GSC

208

(Harker)	There's a song in the air	HL	BF-D	GSC
Harris	The holy infant	H	G-AF	GAL
Head	A slumber song of the Madonna			BOH
-----	Small Christmas tree	H	F-AF	BOO
-----	The little road to Bethlehem	MH	EF-AF	BOO
-----	The robin's carol	H	C-AF	BOH
-----	The three mummers			BOO
Ireland	The Holy Boy	MH	D-G	BOO
Jewell	The vision of the shepherds	HL	A-D	ASC
Kountz	The sleigh	HL	D-FS	GSC
Lynn	The magic night of Christmas	M	D-D	DIT
MacGimsey	Sweet little Jesus boy	ML	D-D	CFI
Martin	The Holy Child	HML	G-G	ENO
McKinney	The Holy Mother sings	MH	AF-AF	JFI
Neidlinger	The birthday of a King	LMH	C-F	GSC
-----	The manger cradle	L	EF-F	GSC
Niles	Our Lovely Lady singing	M	EF-F	GSC
Ohlson	The vigils of Mary	H		GSC
Pinkham	A partridge in a pear tree	H	D-BF	ROW
Ravel	Noël des jouets	M	BS-FS	MAT
Reger	The Virgin's slumber song	MMH	G-G	
Reimann	Joseph tender, Joseph mine	M	F-F	GRA
Sadero	Fa la nana, bambin			
Schubert	Ave Maria	LMH	F-F	†
-----	They sang that night in Bethlehem	LMH	EF-EF	GSC
Sevitzky	Christmas bells			
Strauss	Die heiligen drei Koenige	H	C-G	
Thiman	I saw three ships	L		NOV
Trunk	Mary	HM		AMP
Wagner	Schlaf, holdes Kind			
Warren	Christmas candle	HML	D-E	GSC
Wentzel	Lamkins			GRA
West	It came upon a midnight	MM	E-FS	SUM
Wolf	Die heilige Marie singt			
-----	Fuehr' mich, Kind	H	E-FS	
Yon	Gesù Bambino	HL	B-E	JFI

Easter Songs

Lyric Soprano

Bach, J. S.	Seele, deine Specereien			

(Bach)	(Easter Oratorio) Flute or violin			
Bantock	Easter hymn	M	FS-F	CHE
Barnes	Easter	HM	D-EF	GSC
Burleigh	Were you there?	HML		RIC
Chaffin	Easter message	MH	D-G	FLA
Curran	Crucifixion			
Dennee	Easter song	HM	B-F	ASC
Diack	All in the April evening	LMH	D-G	BOO
Gore	O sing unto the Lord a new song	H		JFI
Guion	At the cry of the first bird	H	D-G	GSC
-----	Mary alone	LH	D-GS	GSC
Hageman	Christ went up into the hills	LH	EF-AF	CFI
Handel	I know that my Redeemer liveth (The Messiah)	MH	E-GS	†
Huhn	Christ is risen	HM	C-E	ASC
Lekberg	A ballad of trees and the Master	H	E-A	GAL
Morris	Alleluja, joyeous Easter hymn			GSC
O'Hara	There is no death	LMH	EF-AF	CHA
Ohlson	The vigils of Mary	H		GSC
Parker	O country bright and fair (Hora Novissima)			
Schubert	Ave Maria	LMH	F-F	GSC
Scott	Angels roll the rock away	MH	E-G	HUN
Stainer	My hope is in the everlasting (The Daughter of Jairus)			
Tchaikovsky	A legend	M	D-E	GSC
Wolf	Herr, was traegt der Boden	HL	B-DS	†
Yon	Christ Triumphant	MH	E-A	JFI
-----	O faithful Cross	HM	C-EF	JFI
-----	Our Paschal Joy	LH	AF-AF	JFI

Patriotic Songs

Lyric Soprano

Alberti	A nation's prayer	H		ELV
Cadman	Glory	H	EF-G	GAL
Dungan	Eternal life	HL		PRE
Elgar	Land of hope and glory			BOO
Foster, F.	The Americans come	MH	F-BF	JFI
Howe	To the unknown soldier	H	D-G	GSC

Lester	Greater love hath no man	LH	B-E	CFI
O'Hara	There is no death	LMH	EF-AF	CHA
Steffe	Battle hymn of the Republic			
Ward				
Stephens	Phantom legions	MHH	EF-BF	CHA

Sacred Songs

Lyric Soprano

Allitsen	The Lord is my light	LMH	D-AF	BOO
Bach, C. P. E.	The last judgement			
Bach, J. S.	Draw near to me	HML		GSC
-----	Father what I proffer			
-----	God my shepherd walks beside me	H		GRA
-----	Sheep may safely graze (Cantata 208) 2 Flutes and continuo	LM	EF-GF	GAL
Beethoven	The worship of God in nature			
Bitgood	The greatest of these is love	M		GRA
Bone and Fenton	Thy word is a lamp	LH	C-F	ROW
Brahms	Ye now are sorrowful	H		GAL
Brown	What are these which are arrayed	HLM	C-F	ASC
Browning	For I am persuaded	LM	DF-G	CFI
-----	The beatitudes	HM	C-F	CFI
Buck	Fear not ye, O Israel	HLM		GSC
Campbell-Tipton	I will give thanks unto the Lord	LMH	DF-AF	GSC
Candlyn	Light at evening time	H	FS-GS	GRA
Chadwick	A ballad of trees and the Master	HML	A-F	DIT
Charles	Incline Thine ear	HL	BF-D	GSC
-----	Love is of God	H	D-G	GSC
Clokey	God is in everything	LH	D-G	JFI
Creston	Psalm 23	MH	F-AF	GSC
Davis	Let not your heart be troubled	HML		WOO
-----	Trust in the Lord	MH	CS-G	GAL
Diack	All in the April evening	LMH	D-G	BOO
Dungan	Eternal life	HL		PRE
Dvořák	God is my shepherd			AMP

211

(Dvořák)	Hear my prayer, O Lord			AMP
-----	Turn Thee to me			AMP
Edmunds	Praise we the Lord	HL	D-D	ROW
Gaul	These are they (The Holy City)	H	E-GS	GSC
Gore	O sing unto the Lord a new song	H		JFI
Gounod	O Divine Redeemer	LMH	C-G	GSC
-----	There is a green hill far away	LMH	E-F	GSC
Guion	Prayer	HL		GSC
Hageman	Christ went up into the hills	LH	EF-AF	CFI
Hamblen	Trust in Him	LH	D-G	GSC
Handel	Have mercy Lord (Te Deum)	HM		†
-----	How beautiful are the feet of them (The Messiah)	H		GSC
-----	I know that my Redeemer liveth (The Messiah)	MH	E-GS	†
-----	Let the bright seraphim (Samson) Trumpet	H	E-A	†
-----	Praise the Lord (Esther)	H	E-G	
-----	Thanks be to Thee	M	CS-E	†
Harker	How beautiful upon the mountains	MLH	EF-G	GSC
Haydn	With verdure clad (The Creation)	H	E-BF	†
Henschel	Morning-hymn	MH	DS-GS	†
Kountz	Lord bless the coming year			
Liddle	How lovely are Thy dwellings	HML		BOS
MacDermid	In my Father's house are many mansions	HML		FRS
MacGimsey	Sweet little Jesus boy	ML	D-D	CFI
Malotte	The beatitudes	LH	E-G	GSC
-----	The Lord's Prayer	MLH	EF-AF	GSC
-----	The twenty third Psalm	HLM	C-F	GSC
McGill	Thine eternal peace	HL	A-CS	GSC
Mendelssohn	Hear ye, Israel (Elijah)	H	E-A	†
Mendelssohn	I will sing of Thy great mercies (Saint Paul)	H	E-F	†
-----	O for the wings of a dove	MLH	D-G	†
Saint-Saëns	Thou, O Lord art my protector	MH	C-A	GSC
Sanderson	Green pastures	HL	BF-EF	BOO
Scott	Angels roll the rock away	MH	E-G	HUN
	Come ye blessed	LMH	EF-AF	GSC

(Scott)	Ride on, ride on	HML		FLA
Sowerby	O God of light	H		GRA
-----	O Jesus, Lord of mercy great	H		GRA
Speaks	The Lord is my light	HML		GSC
-----	Thou wilt keep him in perfect peace	HML		GSC
Stainer	My hope is in the everlasting (The Daugher of Jairus)			
Stevenson	I sought the Lord	HL	D-F	DIT
Stickles	Saith the Lord	LH	D-F	CHA
Thiman	My Master hath a garden	HL		NOV
-----	Thou wilt keep him in perfect peace	H	D-G	GRA
Thompson	My Master hath a garden	M		ECS
Timmings	In the evening it will be light Chimes	H		GRA
Voris	Song of mothers	LH	D-FS	GRA
Weaver	Assurance	H	EF-G	GAL
-----	Praise the Lord, His glories show	H	E-G	GAL
Widor	O Lord most holy			
Wolf	Give praise to Him through whom the world arose			
-----	Prayer (Gebet)			

Wedding Songs
Lyric Soprano

Bach	My heart ever faithful			
Barnby	O perfect love	M	C-G	DIT
Beethoven	Ich liebe dich	HL	BF-DF	†
Bond	I love you truly			BOS
Cough-Leighter	Possession	MH	DF-AF	GSC
De Koven	Oh promise me (Robin Hood)	HML	C-D	†
Dello Joio	How do I love thee?	H	D-G	CFI
Diggle	A wedding prayer	HM	EF-F	GSC
Franck	O Lord most Holy	LM	A-FS	BOS
Geehl	For you alone			SHU
Gounod	Entreat me not to leave thee			GSC
Grieg	I love thee	HML	E-F	†
Lippe	How do I love thee?			BOS
Marx	Hat dich die Liebe beruehrt	MH	EF-BF	AMP
Ronald	Love, I have won you	HML	EF-EF	ENO
Rosa	Wedding song	F	DF-GF	GSC

213

Rowley	Here at Thine altar, Lord			NOV
Schubert	Du bist die Ruh	LMH	EF-AF	†
-----	Ungeduld	HML		†
Schumann	Widmung	HL	BF-F	†
Sowerby	O perfect love	MH	EF-AF	GRA
Strauss	Seitdem dein Aug' in meines schaute			SC
Willan	O perfect love	HM	E-FS	GRA

Songs and Arias With Added Accompanying Instrument

Lyric Soprano

Bach, J.S.	Auch mit gedaempften, schwachen Stimmen (Cantata 36) Violin	PET
-----	For love my Savior now is dying (St. Matthew Passion) Flute	†
-----	Bereite Dir, Jesu (Cantata 147) Violin	
-----	Des Reichtums Glanz auf weiter Erden (Von der Vergnuegsamkeit) Violin	
-----	Die Armen will der Herr umarmen (Cantata 186) Violin	PET
-----	Eilt, ihr Stunden kommt herbei (Cantata 30) Violin	RIC
-----	Erfuellet, ihr himmlischen goettlichen Flammen (Cantata 1) English horn	NOV
-----	Genuegsamkeit ist ein Schatz in diesem Leben (Cantata 144) Oboe d'amore	
-----	Gerechter Gott, ach rechnest Du (Cantata 89) Oboe	
-----	Gott versorget alles Leben (Cantata 187) Oboe	
-----	Hoechster, was ich habe (Cantata 39) Flute	NOV
-----	Hoert doch! der sanften Floeten (Cantata 206) 3 Flutes and continuo	
-----	Hoert, ihr augen, auf zu weinen (Cantata 98) Oboe	PET

214

(Bach)	Hoert, ihr Voelker (Cantata 76) Violin			BRO
-----	Ich bin vergnuegt in meinem Leiden (Cantata 58) Violin			RIC
-----	Ich ende behende mein irdisches Leben (Cantata 57) Violin			
-----	Ich nehme mein Leiden (Cantata 75) Oboe d'amore			AUG
-----	Ich will auf den Herren schaun (Cantata 93) Oboe			NOV
-----	I follow thee also (St. John Passion) Flute			†
-----	Jagen ist die Lust der Goetter (Cantata 208) 2 Waldenhorn			
-----	Jesus soll mein erstes Wort (Cantata 171) Violin			
-----	Liebster Jesu, mein Verlangen (Cantata 32) Oboe			
-----	Meine Seele, sei vergnuegt (Von der Vergnuegsamkeit) Flute			
-----	Meinem Hirten bleib ich treu (Cantata 92) Oboe d'amore			
-----	Ruhet hie, matte Toene (Cantata 210) Oboe d'amore and violin			AUG
-----	Schweigt ihr Floeten, schweigt ihr Toene (Cantata 210) Flute			
-----	Soele, deine Specereien (Easter Oratorio) Flute or violin			
-----	Seufzer, Traenen, Kummer, Noth (Cantata 21) Oboe			†
-----	Suesser Trost, mein Jesus kommt (Cantata 151) Flute			†
-----	Weichet nur, betruebte Schatten (Cantata 202) Oboe			
-----	Wie zittern und wanken (Cantata 105) Oboe			BRO
Bishop	Lo! here the gentle lark Flute	H		†
-----	Pretty mocking bird Flute	H		†
Braga	Angel's serenade Violin	LH	D-G	†
Buxtehude	My Jesus is my lasting joy 2 Violins and organ	H	D-G	GRA
Chausson	Chanson perpétuelle String quartet	H	CS-GS	ROU

215

(Chausson)	Le colibri Violin or cello	M	F-GF	BOS
Couperin	Adolescentalus sum ego Organ, flute and strings			
Forsyth	The Child Jesus Organ	H	EF-B	GRA
-----	The stranger Organ	H	A-B	GRA
Godard	Cachés dans cet asile (Jocelyn) Violin or cello	MH	DF-F	GSC
Gretry	La fauvette avec ses petits (Zemire et Azor) Flute			LEM
Handel	Let the bright seraphim (Samson) Trumpet	H	E-A	†
-----	Nel dolce dell oblio Flute			
-----	Sweet bird (L'Allegro) Flute			NOV
Holst	Four songs for voice and violin	M	C-G	CHE
Honegger	Trois chansons String quartet and flute			SEN
Hue	Soir Païen Flutes			ROU
Kramer	Pleading String quartet	LH	D-GF	JFI
Leroux	Le nil Cello or violin	LH	E-A	†
Massé	Air du rossignol (Les Noces de Jeannette) Flute			
Mozart	Exsultate jubilate 2 Strings, 2 oboes, 2 horns and organ			INT
-----	L'amero, saro costante (Il Re Pastore) Violin or flute	H	D-B	GSC
-----	Parto, parto (La Clemenza di Tito) B Flat clarinet and piano	H		AMP
Pergolesi	Lontananza Cembalo			ROM
-----	Salve Regina 1 2 Violins and cembalo			ROM
Rabey	Tes yeux Violin and piano	H	EF-G	DUR
Ravel	Chansons madécasses Flute, cello and piano			DUR
Saint-Saëns	A swan's song Harp or piano and cello	H	D-G	GSC
-----	Le bonheur est une chose legere Violin and piano	H	C-A	CHO
Schubert	Auf dem Strom Horn or violoncello			PET
-----	Der Hirt auf dem Felsen Clarinet or violoncello	H	BF-B	†

Shepherd	Triptych String quartet	H	GSC
Timmings	In the evening it will be light Chimes	H	GRA
Villa-Lobos	Bachianas Brazileiras, no. 5 8 Celli and bass		AMP
Weinberger	The way to Emmaus Organ		GRA
Wentzel	Lamkins Cello and piano		GRA

American Recital Songs

Dramatic Soprano

Alberti	Oriental serenade	H	CS-A	CFI
-----	White swan of Samarkand			
Barber	A nun takes the veil	MH	G-G	GSC
-----	I hear an army	LH	D-AF	GSC
-----	Monks and raisons	M	DF-E	GSC
-----	Rain has fallen	HM	D-E	GSC
-----	Sure on this shining night	MH	D-G	GSC
-----	The daisies	M	C-F	GSC
Beach	Ah, love but a day			ASC
-----	The year's at the spring	MH	AF-AF	ASC
Bowles	Heavenly grass	ML	B-E	GSC
-----	Letter to Freddy	M	EF-EF	GSC
Braine	Dawn awakes	HML	A-D	ASC
Cadman	Joy	MH	E-A	GSC
Campbell-				
Tipton	A spirit flower	LHM	B-G	GSC
-----	Rhapsodie	LMH	DF-A	GSC
-----	The crying of water	LH	FS-GS	GSC
Carnevali	Come love, with me	LMH	E-A	JFI
Carpenter	Berceuse de guerre	M	C-G	GSC
-----	Don't ceare	M	C-D	GSC
-----	Go, lovely rose	M	DF-EF	GSC
-----	I am like a remnant of a cloud of autumn	L	BF-F	GSC
-----	If	M	D-E	GSC
-----	Light, my light	M	C-G	GSC
-----	On the seashore of endless worlds	M	C-FS	GSC
-----	Serenade	LH	CS-A	GSC
-----	The pools of peace	M	D-F	GSC
-----	The sleep that flits on baby's eyes	M	B-FS	GSC
-----	When I bring to you colour'd toys	LM	CS-FS	GSC
Chadwick	Allah	LH	CS-GS	ASC
Charles	And so, goodbye	LH	EF-AF	GSC
-----	Clouds	HML	C-EF	GSC
-----	Let my song fill your heart	LH	EF-AF	GSC
-----	Night	MH	F-AF	GSC
-----	When I have sung my songs	HM	BF-EF	GSC
Chasins	Dreams			JFI
Clough-				
Leighter	My lover he comes on the skee	HM	D-F	BOS

218

Cowles	The grasshopper			
Crist	Evening	H	C-G	GSC
-----	Knock on the door	H	EF-AF	GSC
-----	Nina, bobo	HL		CFI
-----	O come hither	HM	B-GS	CFI
-----	You will not come again	HML	BF-CS	CFI
Davis	Nancy Hanks	H	D-G	GAL
Deis	Come down to Kew			
Dittenhaver	Lady of the amber wheat	H		GAL
Dougherty	Heaven-haven			
-----	Love in the dictionary	M	C-G	GSC
-----	Madonna of the evening flowers	M		BOO
-----	Sonatina	M	E-FS	GSC
-----	Song for autumn			
Duke	Bells in the rain	H	E-GS	CFI
-----	The bird			GSC
-----	To Karen, singing	M	CS-G	ELV
Edmunds	Billy boy	ML	BF-EF	ROW
-----	Fare you well	MH	F-AF	ROW
Engel	Sea shell	M	EF-EF	GSC
Fairchild	A memory			BOS
Ferrata	Night and the curtains drawn			JFI
Gaines	My heart hath a mind			
Ganz	A memory	HM	B-D	GSC
Gaynor	May magic			
Giannini	Heart cry	H		RIC
-----	If I had known	H		RIC
-----	There were two swans	H	CS-G	ELV
Griffes	Elves	H	F-AF	GSC
-----	Evening song	H	DS-GS	GSC
-----	Sorrow of Mydath	M		GSC
-----	Somphony in yellow	M	D-GF	GSC
-----	The dreamy lake	H	BS-GS	GSC
-----	The lament of Ian the proud	MH	DS-AS	GSC
-----	The rose of the night	H	CS-A	GSC
-----	Thy dark eyes to mine	H	EF-AF	GSC
Guion	Wild geese	M	D-F	CFI
Hadley	My shadow			ASC
-----	The time of parting	HLM	E-G	CFI
Hageman	At the well	LH	EF-AF	GSC
-----	Do not go, my love	HL	B-EF	GSC
-----	Miranda	HL		GAL
-----	Music I heard with you	MH	E-A	GAL
Hindemith	The whistling thief	M	E-F	AMP
Hopkinson	My days have been so wondrous free	LH	EF-G	†

219

Horsman	The bird of the wilderness	LMH	DB-BF	GSC
Howe	Berceuse	HM	EF-F	GSC
Ilgenfritz	Blow, blow thou winter wind			
Josten	Cupid's counsel	H	EF-AF	GSC
Kernochan	We two together	H	EF-AF	GAL
Kingsford	Alas that spring should vanish			
Kramer	Invocation			DIT
-----	Now like a lantern	M		RIC
La Forge	Grieve not, beloved	H	FS-G	RIC
-----	Hills	HL		RIC
-----	Into the light	HL		RIC
-----	Song of love	LH		RIC
Levitzki	Ah, thou beloved one	H	EF-AF	GSC
MacDowell	Midsummer lullaby			AMP
-----	The swan bent low	LH		ELK
Malotte	Upstream	M	C-F	GSC
Manning	In the Luxembourg gardens	HML	BF-D	GSC
McArthur	Night	H	F-AF	GSC
-----	Spring came	HL	D-F	GSC
-----	We have turned again home	LMH	F-G	GSC
McDonald	Daybreak	H		ELV
Mopper	Men	M	D-FS	BOS
Naginski	Look down, fair moon			
-----	The pasture	M	BF-EF	GSC
Nevin	One spring morning	MH	DS-F	BOS
Nordoff	Music I heard with you	H	DS-FS	AMP
-----	Serenade	H	CS-FS	AMP
-----	Tell me, Thyrsis	H	E-G	AMP
-----	There shall be more joy	M	CS-FS	AMP
Olmstead	Thy sweet singing	HL	BF-EF	GSC
Powell	Heartsease	M	DF-G	GSC
Proctor	I light the blessed candles	H	DF-A	GSC
Protheroe	Ah, love but a day	LMH	F-AF	GAM
Rasbach	Mountains	LH	DF-AF	GSC
Rogers	The last song	MLH	E-AF	GSC
-----	Time for making songs	HM	CS-F	DIT
-----	Wind song	LM	C-G	GSC
Rummel	Ecstasy	LMH	GF-AF	GSC
Russell	Fulfillment	LH	EF-GF	BOS
-----	Harbor night	M	D-F	CFI
Rybner	Pierrot	HL		GSC
Sacco	The ragpicker	MH	C-AF	GSC
Sachs	The little worm	LH	CS-FS	FLA
Salter	The cry of Rachel	LH	C-AF	GSC
Sargent	File for future reference	M	CS-E	DIT

Schuman	Holiday Song	M	C-F	GSC
Spross	Will o' the wisp			JCH
Stein	The puffin	M		CFI
Taylor	A song for lovers	MH	D-F	JFI
Thompson	Velvet shoes	M	C-E	ECS
Tyson	Like barley bending	HL	C-EF	GSC
-----	Sea moods	LH	E-AF	GSC
Vene	Age and youth	H	E-A	RIC
Ware	This day is mine	MH	EF-AF	BOS
Warner	Hurdy gurdy	M	D-F	CFI
Warren	We two	LH	E-A	GSC
Watts	Nichavo			
-----	Ponts Vecchio, Florence			DIT
Weaver	A book of verses	H	D-AF	GAL
Wolf	Weather forecast	H	EF-GS	GSC
Worth	Midsummer	LM	E-A	GSC
Zimbalist	Lullaby, oh lullaby			

British Recital Songs

Dramatic Soprano

Arne, T.	Blow, blow thou winter	M	C-F	†
-----	In infancy			NOV
-----	The plague of love			BOO
-----	Where the bee sucks	HM		†
Bainton	Ring out, wild bells	M	C-EF	OXF
Bantock	A feast of lanterns	HM	D-F	GAL
-----	Silent strings	MH	F-G	BOO
Dan	A lullaby			
-----	Cradle song			CHA
-----	O, green grow the rushes	MH	EF-BF	OXF
-----	Rann of exile	H	D-G	CHE
-----	Shieling song	H	CS-A	CHE
Benjamin	Calm sea and mist			CUR
-----	Hedgerow			CUR
-----	The wasp			CUR
Besley	Listening	H	E-AF	CUR
Bishop	Love has eyes	M		†
Bliss	Three jolly gentlemen	H		†
Brewer	The fairy pipers	HML		BOH
Bridge	All things that we clasp	HL		BOS
-----	Love went a-riding	HL		BOS
-----	Mantle of blue	H	D-F	ROG
-----	O that it were so	LMH	D-G	CHA
Clarke	Eight o'clock			ROG
-----	Shy one	HL	BF-G	BOH

221

Coleridge-Taylor	Life and death	HML		ASC
-----	She rested by the broken brook	HL		DIT
Delius	Indian love song	H		†
-----	Love's philosophy			†
Dowland	Come again! sweet love	M	D-E	STB
Dunhill	The cloths of heaven	LM	EF-G	STB
Edmunds	I know my love	HL	BF-EF	ROW
Elgar	Where corals lie	HL		BOO
German	Charming Chloe	HML		NOV
Gibbs	Five eyes	HL	D-D	BOS
-----	Padraic the fidiler			CUR
Green	My lips shall speak the praise	M	E-F	OXF
-----	Salvatiion belongeth unto the Lord	M	F-EF	OXF
Gurney	Under the greenwood tree			ROG
Head	A piper	HL		BOO
-----	Sweet chance that led my steps abroad	LM	C-F	BOH
-----	The happy wanderer			
Hely-Hutchinson	Old mother Hubbard	HL	B-E	CFI
Henschel	Morning-hymn	MH	DS-GS	†
Holst	The heart worships	ML	BF-D	STB
Horn	Cherry ripe	M	D-G	GSC
-----	I've been roaming	L	B-E	†
Hughes	O men from the fields	M	F-F	BOO
Ireland	Bed in summer			CUR
Matthews	All suddenly the wind comes soft	H	C-A	ELV
Moeran	Bright cap			OXF
Morley	It was a lover and his lass	HM		DIT
Purcell	If music be the food of love	M	D-G	BOO
-----	Man is for woman made			
Quilter	Blow, blow thou winter wind	HL	C-E	BOO
-----	It was a lover and his lass	HL	CS-E	BOO
-----	Love's philosophy	LMH	D-A	BOO
-----	Take, o take those lips away			BOO
-----	The fuchsia tree			BOO
-----	Under the greenwood tree			
Ronald	Down in the forest	HML	C-D	ENO
-----	Love, I have won you	HML	EF-EF	ENO

222

Scott	Lullaby	MML	BF-DF	GAL
-----	Night song	ML	BF-EF	ELK
Sharp	My mother did so before me			MEU
-----	Whistle daughter, whistle			DIT
Shaw	Song of the palanquin bearers	LH	E-F	CUR
Stanford	I'll rock you to rest	HML		BOH
Stephenson	Love is a sickness	HML	C-D	BOO
-----	Ships that pass in the night	HML	DF-DF	BOO
Vaughan Williams	Silent noon			GSC

French Recital Songs

Dramatic Soprano

Bachelet	Chère nuit	H	DF-BF	GSC
Bemberg	Chant hindou	HML	A-EF	†
Berlioz	L'absence	H	CS-FS	GSC
-----	Le spectre de la rose			CST
Bernard	Ça fait peur aux oiseaux	H	GS-F	GSC
Bizet	Adieu de l'hôtesse arabe	H	BF-G	†
Chabrier	Espana waltz			ENO
-----	Villanelle des petits canards	HML	B-E	†
Chaminade	The silver ring	HM	BF-F	GSC
Charpentier	Trois sorcieres			
Chausson	Chanson perpétuelle String quartet	H	CS-GS	ROU
-----	La caravane	MH	CS-A	HAM
-----	Le colibri Violin or cello	M	F-GF	BOS
-----	Le temps des lilas	MH	D-GS	†
-----	Les papillons	M	C-F	GSC
Debussy	Beau soir	LH	C-FS	†
-----	C'est l'extase	LH	CS-A	†
-----	Chevaux de bois	H	C-G	†
-----	Colloque sentimental			DUR
-----	De fleurs	H	C-AF	†
-----	Fantoches	H	D-A	JOB
-----	La chevelure	M	CF-FS	†
-----	La flûte de Pan		B-B	†
-----	Mandoline	HM	BF-F	CFI
-----	Romance	HM	C-E	†
-----	Spleen			
Delibes	Le rossignol	M		GSC
Duni	Les temps passés			LEM

223

Duparc	Au pays où se fait la guerre			SAL
-----	Chanson triste	MH	FS-AF	†
-----	Extase	LMH	FS-A	†
-----	La vague et la cloche			ROU
-----	La vie antérieure	HL		†
-----	Lamento	ML	EF-EF	†
-----	La manoir de Rosamunde	HL	B-F	BOS
-----	L'invitation au voyage	HM	E-F	†
-----	Phidylé	MH	EF-AF	BOS
-----	Sérénade florentine	HL		INT
-----	Testament	HL		INT
Fauré	Après un rêve	HM	C-F	†
-----	Automne	MH	D-FS	GSC
-----	Clair de lune	MH	C-G	†
-----	Dans les ruines d'une abbaye	M	E-FS	†
-----	En prière	H	F-F	†
-----	Fleur jetée	HM	BF-FS	†
-----	L'hiver a cessé	HL		INT
-----	Lydia	MH	G-G	†
-----	Mandoline	HL	F-E	†
-----	Prison	LH		†
-----	Rencontre	H	EF-AF	MAR
-----	Soir	LH	D-GS	†
-----	Toujours	LH	F-AF	†
Fourdrain	Carnaval	M	C-F	RIC
-----	Chanson norvégienne	H	E-G	RIC
Franck	La procession	LH	E-GS	†
-----	Nocturne	HL		†
Georges	Hymne au soleil	LH	E-A	HOM
-----	La pluie	HL		INT
Godard	Florian's song	LMH	D-FS	GSC
Gounod	Au printemps	LMH	DF-AF	GSC
-----	Vénise	HL		INT
Hahn	D'une prison	L	BF-EF	HEU
-----	Infidélité	M		HEU
-----	L'enamourée			HEU
-----	L'heure exquise	M	DF-F	†
-----	Offrande	M	D-D	†
-----	Paysage	MH	EF-G	HEU
-----	Si mes vers avaient des ailes	HLM	B-FS	†
Honegger	Les cloches			SEN
Hue	J'ai pleuré en rêve	HL	D-E	BOS
-----	Sonnez les matines	H	FS-G	HEU
Laparra	La maison blanche			
Lenormand	Quelle souffrance	HM	AF-F	HAM
Liszt	Comment, disaient-ils?	H	C-AF	†
-----	Jeanne d'Arc au Bûcher			

(Liszt)	Oh! quand je dors	H	E-A	DIT
Lully	Au clair de la lune	H	E-D	CFI
Martini	Plaisir d'amour	M	BF-EF	GSC
Messiaen	Epouvante			DUR
-----	La maison			DUR
-----	Paysage			DUR
Milhaud	Chant d'amour	M	C-GF	ESC
-----	Chant de Forgeron	M	C-FS	SC
-----	Chant du laboureur	M	B-F	ESC
-----	La tourterelle	M	B-G	DUR
Paladilhe	Lamento provincal	M	CS-FS	HOM
-----	Les trois prières			
-----	Psyché	HM	BF-F	GSC
Parkyns	Le portrait			
Pesse	Chanson rêvée			
Pierné	Ils étaient trois petits chats blancs			MAR
Poldowski	Colombine	H	D-GF	CHE
-----	Dansons la gigue	M	EF-G	MAR
-----	L'heure exquise	LMH	DF-AF	CHE
Poulenc	Air vif	H	C-AF	ROU
-----	Bleuet	H	FS-GF	DUR
-----	Priez pour paix	ML		ROU
-----	Voyage à Paris			AMP
Rameau	Le grillon			DUR
Ravel	Kaddisch	H	C-G	DUR
-----	La flûte enchantée	M	DS-FS	DUR
-----	Tout gai!	MH	EF-F	
-----	Vocalise en forme de habancra	MH	BF-G	MAR
Saint-Saëns	Guitares et mandolines			DUR
-----	L'attente			DUR
-----	La cloche	LH	DF-AF	†
-----	Tristesse			
Satie	Le chapelier			ROU
Severac	Aubade			SAL

German Recital Songs

Dramatic Soprano

Bach, C.P.E.	Passionslied			SIM
Bach, J. S.	Bist du bei mir	HML	A-EF	†
-----	Dir, Dir Jehovah			†
-----	Komm suesser Tod	MH	C-G	†
-----	Willst du dein Herz mir schenken			BRH
Beethoven	Andenken			†

(Beethoven)	Die Ehre Gottes	HL	AF-EF	†
-----	Die Trommel geruehret			†
-----	Fruedvoll und Leidvoll	M	DS-E	†
-----	God is my song			
-----	Ich liebe dich	HL	BF-DF	†
-----	Mit einem gemalten Band			RIC
-----	Neue Liebe, neues Leben			†
-----	Wonne der Wehmut			†
Brahms	Ach, wende diesen Blick			†
-----	Am Sonntag Morgen	L	CS-FS	†
-----	An die Nachtigall	H	DS-G	†
-----	An eine Aeolsharfe	H	EF-AF	†
-----	Auf dem Kirchhofe	HL	BF-EF	†
-----	Auf dem Schiffe	LH	GS-A	†
-----	Auf dem See	HL	D-F	†
-----	Bei dir sind meine Gedanken	MH	E-FS	†
-----	Blinde Kuh			RIC
-----	Botschaft	HL	D-F	†
-----	Daemm' rung senkte sich von oben	LH	BF-G	†
-----	Das Maedchen spricht	H	E-FS	†
-----	Dein blaues Auge	MH	BF-G	†
-----	Der Jaeger	HL		†
-----	Der Kranz			†
-----	Der Schmied	HL	EF-EF	†
-----	Der Tod, das ist die kuehle Nacht	L	AF-F	†
-----	Die Mainacht	HL	BF-FF	†
-----	Dort in den Weiden	LH	A-A	†
-----	Eine gute, gute Nacht			†
-----	Erinnerung	H	E-G	†
-----	Es traeumte mir			†
-----	Feldeinsamkeit	HL	C-EF	†
-----	Fruehlingslied			†
-----	Fruehlingstrost	LH	E-A	†
-----	Geheimnis			†
-----	Gestillte Sehnsucht Viola and piano			†
-----	Immer leiser wird mein Schlummer	LH	DF-A	†
-----	In Waldeseinsamkeit	H	ES-G	†
-----	Juchhe!			†
-----	Klage	LH	FS-FS	†
-----	Lerchengesang	LH	FS-GS	CFI
-----	Liebestreu	ML	C-F	†
-----	Maedchenlied	HL		†
-----	Meine Liebe ist gruen	MLH	ES-A	†
-----	Mondenschein	LH	D-GF	†

226

(Brahms)	Muss es eine Trennung geben?	LH	FS-FS	†
-----	Nachtigall	MHL	BF-FS	†
-----	Nicht mehr zu dir zu gehen			†
-----	O kuehler Wald	MH	A-F	†
-----	O liebliche Wangen	MLH	E-G	†
-----	O wuesst' ich doch den Weg zurueck	H	E-FS	†
-----	Regenlied	HL	CS-F	†
-----	Salamander			†
-----	Salome			†
-----	Sandmaennchen	LH	F-G	†
-----	Schoen war, das ich dir weihte			†
-----	Schwesterlein			†
-----	Sehnsucht	H	EF-AF	†
-----	Sommerabend			†
-----	Sonntag	H	D-G	†
-----	Spanisches Lied			†
-----	Staendchen	HL	BF-E	†
-----	Therese	HL	B-D		
-----	Unbewegte laue Luft			†
-----	Vergebliches Staendchen			†
-----	Von ewiger Liebe	LMH	B-AF	GSC
-----	Wie froh und frisch	HL	B-E	†
-----	Wiegenlied			
-----	Wie Melodien zieht es	HL	A-E	†
-----	Willst du, dass ich geh'?	L	C-G	†
-----	Wir wandelten	LH	EF-GF	†
Franck, J.W.	Auf, auf, zu Gottes Lob			SIM
-----	Sei nur still			
Franz	Dies und das			
-----	Ein Stuendlein wohl vor Tag			†
-----	Er ist gekommen	HL	EF-F	†
-----	For music	ML	C-D	†
-----	Gute Nacht	HL		†
-----	Im Herbst	HM	A-F	†
-----	Mutter, o sing mich zur Ruh	HL	E-G	†
-----	Sonnenuntergang	HL	CS-FS	†
-----	Staendchen	HL		†
-----	Sterne mit den gold' nen Fuesschen	HL	DS-E	†
-----	Weisst du noch	HL		GSC
Handel	Dank sei Dir, Herr (Added to Israel in Egypt)	M	CS-E	†
Haydn	She never told her love	HL	B-D	DIT
-----	The mermaid's song	M	C-F	PRE

Hindemith	Geburt Marias			AMP
Jensen	Am Ufer des Flusses des Manzanares	H	D-FS	GSC
-----	Waldesgespraech			
Konjovic	Lieder meiner Heimat			
Korngold	Love letter			AMP
Liszt	Freudvoll und leidvoll			DUR
Loehnor	O Ewigkeit			SIM
Loewe	Canzonetta	MH	B-A	DIT
-----	Des Glockenthuermers Tochterlein	H	CS-A	SC
-----	Walpurgisnacht	H	G-G	SC
Lohner	O Ewigkeit			
Mahler	Abloesung im Sommer	HL		INT
-----	Das Irdische Leben	HL	A-F	INT
-----	Erinnerung	HL		INT
-----	Fruehlingsmorgen	HL		INT
-----	Hans und Grethe	HL		INT
-----	Ich atmet' einen linden Duft	HL		INT
-----	Ich bin der Welt abbanden gekommen	HL		INT
-----	Ich ging mit Lust	HL		INT
-----	Liebst du um Schoenheit	HL		INT
-----	Nicht wiedersehen	HL		INT
-----	Scheiden und Meiden	HL		INT
-----	Starke Einbildungskraft	HL		INT
-----	Wer hat dies Liedlein erdacht?	HL	BF-E	INT
-----	Wo die schoenen Trompeten blasen	HL	GF-F	INT
Marx	Hat dich die Liebe beruehrt	MH	EF-BF	AMP
-----	Selige Nacht	M	DF-GF	AMP
-----	Und gestern hat er mir Rosen gebracht	H	E-A	AMP
-----	Valse de Chopin	M	CS-GS	AMP
Mendelssohn	An die Entfernte	M	F-F	
-----	And 'res Maienlied			AUG
-----	Bei der Wiege	M	DF-EF	†
-----	Der Mond	HL		†
-----	Die Liebende schreibt	HL		†
-----	Es weiss und raeth es doch keiner	H	D-G	
-----	Frage			†
-----	Gruss	M	DS-FS	†
-----	Im Gruenen	H	E-BF	AUG
-----	Keine von der Erde Schoenen			AUG

228

(Mendelssohn)	Lieblingsplaetzchen	LM	FS-E	†
-----	Morgengruss	M	D-E	AUG
-----	Nachtlied			
-----	Neue Liebe	H	CS-A	†
-----	On wings of song			†
-----	Pagenlied	M	E-E	†
-----	Schilflied	M	F-FS	
-----	Suleika	H	E-GS	†
Mozart	Abendempfindung	M	E-F	
-----	Als Luise die Briefe			GSC
-----	An Chloe	LH	EF-AF	
-----	Die Verschweigung			
-----	Warnung	HM	C-D	
-----	Wiegenlied	MH	G-G	†
Pfitzner	Gretel			BOO
Reger	Mit Rosen bestreut			UNI
-----	Waldeinsamkeit	HML	A-D	BOS
Schoeck	Herbstgefuehl			
-----	Mit einem getmaten Bande			
Schoenberg	Erhebung			GSC
Schubert	Am Feierabend	HL	BF-F	†
-----	Am Grabe Anselmos	HL	B-EF	†
-----	An den Mond	HL	F-GF	†
-----	An die Entfernte			PET
-----	An eine Quelle			PET
-----	An Emma			
-----	Auf dem Flusse	HL	F-E	†
-----	Auf dem Wasser zu singen	MH	EF-GF	†
-----	Aufenthalt	HLM	A-F	†
-----	Aufloesung	LH	D-A	†
-----	Ave Maria	LMH	F-F	†
-----	Das Echo	M	F-F	†
-----	Das Wandern	HLM	E-E	†
-----	Das Wirtshaus	HL	C-D	†
-----	Dass sie hier gewesen!			PET
-----	Dem Unendlichen	L	A-GF	DIT
-----	Der Atlas	HL	BF-F	†
-----	Der Doppelgaenger	HL	G-D	†
-----	Der Erlkoenig	HML	A-E	†
-----	Der Juengling an der Quelle	LH	E-A	†
-----	Der Juengling und der Tod	M	DF-FF	†
-----	Der Leiermann	ML	C-D	†
-----	Der Lindenbaum	HL	A-D	†
-----	Der Musensohn	LH	FS-G	†
-----	Der Neugierige	HL	CS-EF	†
-----	Der Wanderer	HML	FS-D	†
-----	Der Wegweiser	L	D-EF	†

(Schubert)	Des Maedchens Klage	LH	C-E	†
-----	Die Allmacht	HML	G-E	†
-----	Die Forelle	MLH	EF-GF	†
-----	Die junge Nonne	LH	C-GF	†
-----	Die Liebe hat gelogen	LM	G-F	†
-----	Die Maenner sind mechant			PET
-----	Die Nebensonnen	HL	F-D	†
-----	Die Post	HML	BF-EF	†
-----	Die Rose	M	G-FS	PET
-----	Die Unterscheidung	LH	D-G	†
-----	Du bist die Ruh	LMH	EF-AF	†
-----	Du liebst mich nicht	LH	E-FS	†
-----	Ellens zweiter Gesang			PET
-----	Erstarrung	HL	D-F	GSC
-----	Fruehlingsglaube	M	EF-F	†
-----	Fruehlingssehnsucht	HL	B-E	†
-----	Fruehlingstraum	HL	C-D	†
-----	Ganymed	LH	EF-G	†
-----	Gretchen am Spinnrade	H	F-A	†
-----	Gruppe aus dem Tartarus	L	CS-EF	†
-----	Heidenroeslein			
-----	Heimliches Lieben	LH	F-G	†
-----	Ihr Bild	HL	C-C	†
-----	Im Abendrot	HL	C-D	†
-----	Im Fruehling	LH	D-FS	†
-----	In der Ferne	HL		†
-----	Lachen und Weinen	HL	C-EF	†
-----	Letzte Hoffnung	HL		†
-----	Liebesbotschaft	H	E-G	†
-----	Lied der Mignon	HL		†
-----	Lied eines Schiffers an die Dioskuren	HL	A-C	†
-----	Litanei	HLM	C-EF	†
-----	Mein!	HL		†
-----	Mut	HL		†
-----	Nacht und Traeume	HL	C-DF	†
-----	Nur wer die Sehnsucht kennt	LH		†
-----	Schaefers Klagelied	HL	BF-D	†
-----	Schwanengesang			†
-----	Seligkeit			
-----	Staendchen	MH	B-E	†
-----	Traenenregen	HL		GSC
-----	Um Mitternacht	H	F-G	†
-----	Ungeduld	HML		†
-----	Vor meiner Wiege	HL	C-E	†
-----	Wanderers Nachtlied 2	LH	F-F	†
-----	Wiegenlied (Op. 98)			†

(Schubert)	Wohin?	HL	B-E	†
Schumann	Alte Laute	HL	DF-DF	†
-----	Auftraege	HL	C-E	†
-----	Aus den oestlichen Rosen			
-----	Aus den Hebraeischen Gesaengen			
-----	Der Nussbaum	LMH	D-FS	†
-----	Die Lotusblume	HLM	BF-F	†
-----	Die Soldatenbraut	HL	AF-EF	†
-----	Die Tochter Jephthas	HL	A-E	
-----	Du bist wie eine Blume	HM	F-EF	†
-----	Du Ring an meinem Finger	HL	C-F	†
-----	Er, der Herrlichste von Allen	HL	A-EF	†
-----	Er ist's	HL	BF-EF	†
-----	Fruehlingsnacht	L	CS-E	†
-----	Heiss' mich nicht reden			
-----	Hochlaendisches Wiegenlied			†
-----	Ihre Stimme	LH		†
-----	Im Westen	HL		†
-----	Lied der Suleika			
-----	Maerzveilchen	HL	C-C	†
-----	Marienwuermchen	HL	D-D	†
-----	Meine Rose			
-----	Mit Myrthen und Rosen	HL	A-D	†
-----	Mondnacht	M	E-FS	†
-----	O ihr Herren, o ihr Werthen	LH		†
-----	Provenzalisches Lied	LH		†
-----	Requiem			†
-----	Rose, Meer und Sonne			
-----	Schneegloeckchen	HL		†
-----	Seit ich ihn gesehen	HL	DF-DF	†
-----	Sitz' ich allein			
-----	Stille Traenen	HL		†
-----	Talismane			
-----	Volksliedchen	HL		†
-----	Waldesgespraech	HL	A-FS	†
-----	Wer machte dich so krank?			
-----	Widmung	HL	BF-F	†
Strauss	Ach Lieb, ich muss nun scheiden	H	D-G	
-----	Ah, du wolltest mich nicht deinem Mund			
-----	Allerseelen	HL	AS-E	†
-----	Befreit			HSC
-----	Breit ueber mein Haupt	LH	GF-AF	HSC
-----	Caecilie	MH	E-B	GSC
-----	Die Georgine	LH	B-A	†

231

(Strauss, R.)	Die Nacht	HL		†
-----	Du meines Herzens Kroenelein	HL	CS-E	†
-----	Fruendliche Vision	HL	C-F	†
-----	Hat gesagt bleibt s nicht dabei			†
-----	Heimkehr	HL	B-E	†
-----	Heimliche Aufforderung	HL	B-E	†
-----	Ich liebe dich			†
-----	Ich trage meine minne	M		†
-----	Kling			†
-----	Mein Herz ist stumm	LH	EF-AF	
-----	Mit deinen blauen Augen	LH	C-GS	†
-----	Morgen	HML	E-F	†
-----	Ruhe meine Seele			†
-----	Schoen sind doch kalt die Himmelssterne	H	F-BF	
-----	Traum durch die Daemmerung	HML	BF-EF	†
-----	Wiegenliedchen			†
-----	Zueignung	HL	CS-FS	†
Trunk	Der Feind			
-----	Die Nachtigallen			
Wagner	Der Engel	LH	CS-G	†
-----	Im Treibhaus	HL		†
-----	Schmerzen	HL		†
-----	Stehe still!	HL		GSC
-----	Traeume	HL		†
Wolf	Ach, im Maien	HL	C-E	†
-----	Alle gingen, Herz, zu Ruh	HL	C-EF	†
-----	Anakreons Grab	HL	D-D	†
-----	An eine Aeolsharfe			†
-----	Auch kleine Dinge	HM	D-E	†
-----	Auf ein altes Bild	HL	E-DS	†
-----	Bedeckt mich mit Blumen	HL	B-D	†
-----	Blumengruss	HL	D-E	†
-----	Dank des Paria			PET
-----	Das Koehlerweib ist trunken			PET
-----	Das verlassene Maegdlein	HL	D-EF	†
-----	Denk' es, o Seele	LH	EF-F	†
-----	Der Freund	HM	BF-E	PET
-----	Der Gaertner	HL		†
-----	Der Knabe und das Immlein	L	CS-A	†
-----	Der Mond hat eine schwere Klag' erhoben	HL	BF-DF	†
-----	Die Bekehrte			PET
-----	Die ihr schwebet	HL	EF-EF	†

(Wolf)	Die Nacht			†
-----	Die Sproede			†
-----	Du denkst, mit einem Faedchen			†
-----	Elfenlied	HL	D-F	INT
-----	Er ist's	H	D-G	†
-----	Erstes Liebeslied eines Maedchens	H	EF-AF	†
-----	Fussreise	HL	D-E	†
-----	Gebet	HL		†
-----	Geh' Geliebter, geh' jetzt			PET
-----	Gleich und gleich			†
-----	Heimweh (Moerike Lieder)			†
-----	Ich hab' in Penna	LH		†
-----	In dem Schatten meiner Locken	M	C-EF	†
-----	In der Fruehe	HL	C-C	†
-----	Klinge, klinge, mein Pandero	HL	CF-EF	†
-----	Lebe wohl	HL	BF-F	†
-----	Liebe mir in Busen zuendet	M	E-F	†
-----	Lied vom Winde			†
-----	Mausfallen Spruechlein	HL	BF-E	†
-----	Mignon	LH		†
-----	Mir ward gesagt du reisest in die Ferne			†
-----	Morgenstimmung	LH	C-GS	†
-----	Mueh'voll komm' ich und beladen	H	D-G	†
-----	Nachtgruss			†
-----	Neue Liebe	LH	D-AF	†
-----	Nun wandre, Maria	HL	EF-D	†
-----	Peregrina I			†
-----	Sie blasen zum Abmarsch			
-----	Storchenbotschaft			†
-----	Ueber Nacht	LH	D-G	†
-----	Um Mitternacht	HL	G-EF	†
-----	Und willst du deinen Liebsten sterben	HL		†
-----	Verborgenheit	HL	B-E	†
-----	Verschwiegene Liebe	LH	DF-FS	†
-----	Wenn du, mein Liebster	LH	DF-GF	†
-----	Wenn du zu den Blumen gehst	HL	B-EF	†
-----	Wie glaenzt der helle Mond			†
-----	Wie lange schon war immer mein Verlangen			PET
-----	Wiegenlied			

233

(Wolf)	Zitronenfalter im April	HL		†
-----	Zur Ruh', zur Ruh'	HL	A-GF	†
Wolff	Alle Dinge haben Sprache	M	BF-GF	†
-----	Du bist so jung			HMP
-----	Stimme im Dunkeln	M	BF-GF	HMC

Italian Recital Songs

Dramatic Soprano

Bononcini	Deh, lascia			HEU
-----	L'esperto nocchiero (Astarte)	HL	B-E	†
-----	Per la gloria	HL	C-EF	†
Caccini	Amarilli, mia bella	ML	C-D	†
Caldara	Alma del core			GSC
-----	Come raggio di sol	HL	D-F	†
-----	Sebben crudele	HML	E-DS	†
-----	Selve amiche, ombrose piante	HM	E-E	†
Carissimi	Vittoria, mio core	HLM	B-E	†
Casella	Amante sono vaghiccia di voi			RIC
Cavalli	Donzelle fuggite	HL	C-EF	†
Cesti	Intorno all' idol mio (Orontea)	MH	D-F	†
Cimara	Fiocca la neve	H	G-G	GSC
-----	Stornellata marinara	HM		RIC
Cimarosa	Bel nume che adoro			RIC
-----	Nel lasciarti (L'Olympiade)			RIC
D'Astorga	Vo' cercando in queste valli	H	D-G	STB
DeLuca	Non posso disperar	HL	C-E	GSC
Donaudy	O del mio amato ben	M	EF-F	RIC
Durante	Vergin, tutta amor	LM	C-EF	GSC
Falconieri	Non più d'amore	HL	C-D	DIT
-----	Nudo arciero	HL	AF-AF	DIT
-----	O bellissimi capelli	HL	B-D	†
Fasolo	Cangia, cangia tue voglie	H	C-G	GSC
Frescobaldi	Se l'aura spira	HL	C-EF	DIT
Galuppi	La pastorella (Il Filosoto di Campagna)			DUR
Giordani	Caro mio ben	HML	B-D	†
Gluck	Spiagge amate (Paride ed Elena)			†
Handel	Care selve (Atalanta)	MH	FS-A	†

Composer	Title			
(Handel)	Ch'io mai vi possa (Siroe)			†
-----	Lascia ch'io pianga (Rinaldo)			
-----	Ombra mai fu (Serse)	HM	BF-EF	†
-----	Rendi'l sereno al ciglio (Sosarme)	LH	EF-F	†
-----	Sommi Dei (Radimisto)			†
-----	V'adoro pupille (Julius Caesar)			BOO
Haydn	Un tetto umil			
Jommelli	Chi vuol comprar la bella	H	B-G	GSC
Legrenzi	Che fiero costume	HML	C-D	†
Lotti	Pur dicesti, o bocca bella	LMH	E-FS	GSC
Malipiero	Inno a Maria, Nostra Donna	H		CHE
Marcello	Il mio bel foco	LMH	C-G	GSC
-----	Non m' è grave morir per amore	L	C-E	GSC
Paisiello	Chi vuol la zingarella	L	C-F	GSC
Panizza	D'une prison	H	C-G	GSC
Paradies	M'ha preso alla sua ragna	M	EF-F	GSC
Pergolesi	Confusa, smarrita			GSC
-----	Dite ch' ogni momento			BOS
-----	Se tu m'ami	LMH	C-G	GSC
Quagliati	Apra il suo verde seno	HL	E-CS	DIT
Respighi	In alto mare			BON
-----	Mattinata			BON
-----	Nebbie			†
-----	Nevicata	HM		BON
-----	Pioggia			BON
Rontani	Or ch'io non segno più	HL	CS-E	DIT
Rosa	Selve, voi che le speranze	MH	D-G	DIT
Rossini	La danza	MH	E-A	†
Santoliguido	Riflessi			FOR
Scarlatti, A.	La fortuna			BOS
-----	Se Florindo è fedele	LM	EF-EF	GSC
Sibella	La Girometta	HML	D-E	GSC
Stradella	Così, amor, mi fai languir	HL	F-G	DIT
-----	Ragion sempre addita	H	E-G	GSC
-----	Se nel ben			CFI
Torelli	Tu lo sai	HL	BF-F	†
Tosti	Mattinata			RIC
Traetta	Ombra cara, amorosa	HL	B-F	†
Wolf-Ferrari	Un verde praticello			
Zandonai	Ultima rosa	M		RIC

Russian Recital Songs

Dramatic Soprano

Arensky	Autumn	H	CS-FS	GSC
-----	Revery	MH	DS-FS	DIT
Borodin	A dissonance	MH	E-F	†
Cui	The statue at Czarskoe-Selo	HM	DF-EF	†
Dargomijshky	I love you			
-----	The miller			
Gliere	Ah, twine no blossoms	HM	CS-F	DIT
Gretchaninoff	All along the highway			
-----	Hushed the song of the nightingale	MH	E-G	DIT
-----	Lullaby			
-----	Over the steppe	LM	C-G	GSC
-----	Snowflakes			AMP
-----	The snowdrop	HM	BF-F	DIT
Mednikoff	The hills of Gruzia	H	DS-A	LAC
Mussorgsky	Death the commander			
-----	Hopak	HM	CS-FS	GSC
-----	I love you			
-----	Night			GSC
-----	Star, you, will you tell me?			
-----	The miller			
-----	The orphan girl			GSC
-----	Tiny star where art thou	LH	DF-F	BOS
Rachmaninoff	All things depart			BOO
-----	Before my window	HM	C-G	GSC
-----	Daisies			†
-----	Floods of spring	HL		DIT
-----	God took away from me			GSC
-----	How fair this spot	MH		GSC
-----	In the silence of night	LH	D-A	GSC
-----	Lilacs	LH	EF-G	†
-----	Nuit de mai-fragment			
-----	Oh cease thy singing, maiden fair	H	E-A	CFI
-----	O, do not grieve	M	BF-AF	GSC
-----	Oh, no, I pray do not depart	H		DIT
-----	O thou billowy harvest field	HL	CS-E	GSC
-----	The coming of spring	LH	DF-AF	BOS
-----	The island	LH	DF-F	†
-----	The soldier's bride			†
-----	Vocalise	LH	CS-A	GSC
-----	When yesterday we met			BOH

Tchaikovsky	All for you			
-----	Regret			NOV

Scandinavian Recital Songs

Dramatic Soprano

Alnaes	En morgen var din grav	M	CS-D	HAN
-----	Lykken mellem to mennesker	M	B-FS	HAN
-----	Nu brister i alle de kløfter	L	A-F	HAN
-----	Vaarlaengsler			
-----	Ved syrintid			
Grieg	A dream			†
-----	A swan			†
-----	By the brook			GSC
-----	Den Aergjerrige			
-----	Det syng	M	C-GF	HAN
-----	En fuglevise			
-----	Eros	LM	C-F	†
-----	From Monte Pincio			PET
-----	Formål			
-----	Greeting			PET
-----	Gutten			
-----	Heart wounds			
-----	Hope			
-----	I love thee	HML	E-F	†
-----	In the boat	LM	D-ES	†
-----	Prinsessen	HL	B-E	†
-----	Radiant night			
-----	Saint John's eve	L	DF-E	CFI
-----	Simpel sang			
-----	Snegl, Snegl	M	B-F	HAN
-----	Springtide	M		DIT
-----	The wounded heart			PET
-----	To Norway	M	E-F	DIT
-----	Udvandreren	M	EF-F	HAN
-----	Vaer hilset, I Damer	M	D-F	HAN
-----	With a primrose	H	DF-GF	GSC
-----	With a water lily	HM	CS-EF	†
Hakanson	Budbarerskan			
Jonsson	Under haeggarna			
Jordan	Es naht der Herbst			
-----	Og se hun kom			
Kjerulf	Synnove's song	M	C-F	GSC
Lie	Soft-footed snow	HM		DIT
Nielson	Aebleblomsten			HAN

(Nielson)	Sommersang			HAN
Sibelius	Black roses	M	A-ES	AMP
-----	Diamonds on the March snow			
-----	On a balcony by the sea			
Sinding	I hear the gull			JCH
Soderberg	Fågelns visa			
Thrane	Aagots fjeldsang			

Spanish Recital Songs

Dramatic Soprano

Alvarez	La partida	HL	DS-E	GSC
Falla	Siete canciones	HL		AMP
Ginastera	Canción al árbol del olvido			RIC
Ginastera	Triste			RIC
Nin	El amor es como un nino			ESC
-----	El vito			ESC
Obradors	Coplas de curro dulce			
-----	Del cabello mas sutil			RIC
-----	El tumba y le			

Miscellaneous Recital Songs

Dramatic Soprano

Bach-Gounod	Ave Maria			
Bizet	Agnus Dei	HLM	C-AF	
Chajes	Adarim			TRA
Dvořák	Clouds and darkness			
-----	God is my shepherd			AMP
-----	Hear my prayer, O Lord			AMP
-----	I will sing new songs of gladness	HL		†
-----	Lord, Thou art my refuge and shield			AMP
-----	Song my mother taught me	HM	E-E	†
-----	Turn Thee to me			AMP
Fisher	Eili, Eili	LMH	E-G	DIT
Franck	Panis angelicus	LM		
Konjovic	Bosnian song			
-----	Serbian song			
Mozart	Alleluia	LMH	F-C	
Schubert	Ave Maria			
Villa-Lobos	Cançao do carreiro			

British Songs For Opening Recitals

Dramatic Soprano

Green	My lips shall speak the praise	M	E-F	OXF
-----	Salvation belongeth unto the Lord	M	F-EF	OXF
Handel	Have mercy Lord (Te Deum)	HM		†
-----	Let me wander not unseen (L'Allegro)	M	D-G	†
-----	Trip, blithe streamlet (Serse)			
Purcell	If music be the food of love	M	D-G	BOO
-----	Music for a while (Oedipus)	LH		SC
-----	When I am laid in earth (Dido and Aeneas)	LH	C-G	†

German Songs For Opening Recitals

Dramatic Soprano

Bach, J. S.	Bist du bei mir	HML	A-EF	†
Beethoven	Andenken			†
-----	God is my song			
-----	Ich liebe dich	HL	BF-DF	†
Brahms	Nachtigall	MHL	BF-FS	†
Buxtehude	Singet dem Herrn Violin and piano			
Handel	Dank sei Dir, Herr	M	CS-E	†
Mozart	An Chloe	LH	EF-AF	
Schubert	Das Wandern	HLM	E-E	†
-----	Ganymed	LH	EF-G	†
-----	Liebesbotschaft	H	E-G	†
Schumann	Mit Myrthen und Rosen	HL	A-D	†
Wolf	Ueber Nacht	LH	D-G	†
Wolff	Stimme im Dunkeln	M	BF-GF	HMC

Italian Songs and Arias For Opening Recitals

Dramatic Soprano

Beethoven	Ah! Perfido	H		DIT

239

Caccini	Amarilli, mia bella	ML	C-D	†
Caldara	Sebben crudele	HML	E-DS	†
Carissimi	Vittoria, mio core	HLM	B-E	†
Cimara	Stornellata marinara	HM		RIC
Cimarosa	Nel lasciarti (L'Olympiade)			RIC
Durante	Vergin, tutta amor	LM	C-EF	†
Falconieri	O bellissimi capelli	HL	B-D	†
Gluck	Spiagge amate (Paride ed Elena)			†
Handel	Care selve (Atalanta)	MH	FS-A	†
-----	Ch'io mai vi possa (Siroe)			†
-----	Lascia ch'io pianga (Rinaldo)	HM	EF-F	†
-----	Ombra mai fu (Serse)	HM	BF-EF	†
-----	Rendi'l sereno al ciglio (Sosarme)	LH	EF-F	†
-----	V'adoro pupille (Julius Caesar)			BOO
Jommelli	Chi vuol comprar la bella	H	B-G	GSC
Lotti	Pur dicesti, o bocca bella	LMH	E-FS	GSC
Marcello	Il mio bel foco	LMH	C-G	GSC
Mozart	Ch'io mi scordi di te			BOO
-----	Non più di fiori (La Clemenza di Tito)			†
-----	Parto, parto (La Clemenza di Tito) B flat clarinet and piano	H		AMP
Paisiello	Chi vuol la zingarella	L	C-F	GSC
Pergolesi	Se tu m'ami	LMH	C-G	GSC
Stradella	Se nel ben			CFI
Traetta	Ombra cara, amorosa	HL	B-F	†

American Songs For Closing Recitals

Dramatic Soprano

Barber	I hear an army	LH	D-AF	GSC
-----	Sure on this shining night	MH	D-G	GSC
Bassett	Take joy home	LH	EF-BF	GSC
Cadman	Joy	MH	E-A	GSC
Carpenter	Light, my light	M	C-G	GSC
-----	Serenade	LH	CS-A	GSC
Charles	And so, goodbye	LH	EF-AF	GSC
-----	Let my song fill your heart	LH	EF-AF	GSC

(Charles)	Night	MH	F-AF	GSC
-----	When I have sung my songs	HM	BF-EF	GSC
Clough- Leighter	My lover he comes on the skee	HM	D-F	BOS
Crist	Knock on the door	H	EF-AF	GSC
Curran	Life	HM	BF-F	GSC
Dougherty	Everyone sang			
-----	Song for autumn			
Giannini	Sing to my heart a song	H	D-B	ELV
Hageman	At the well	LH	EF-AF	GSC
-----	Miranda	HL		GAL
Horsman	The bird of the wilderness	LMH	DF-BF	GSC
Ilgenfritz	Blow, blow thou winter wind			
Kernochan	We two together	H	EF-AF	GAL
La Forge	Hills	HL		RIC
-----	Into the light	HL		RIC
-----	Song of the open	MH	EF-AF	DIT
Levitzki	Ah, thou beloved one	H	EF-AF	GSC
Malotte	Upstream	M	C-F	GSC
McArthur	Night	H	F-AF	GSC
-----	Spring came	HL	D-F	GSC
McDonald	Daybreak	H		ELV
Nordoff	Tell me, Thyrsis	H	E-G	AMP
Rogers	The last song	MLH	E-AF	GSC
-----	Time for making songs	HM	CS-F	DIT
Rummel	Ecstasy	LMH	GF-AF	GSC
Salter	The cry of Rachel	LH	C-AF	GSC
Schuman	Holiday song	M	C-F	GSC
Speaks	Morning	HML	BF-D	GSC
Tyson	Sea moods	LH	E-AF	GSC
Ware	This day is mine	MH	EF-AF	BOS
Warren	We two	LH	E-A	GSC
Worth	Midsummer	LM	E-A	GSC

(See also Negro Spirituals and Folk Songs.)

Miscellaneous Songs For Closing Recitals

Dramatic Soprano

Besley	Listening	H	E-AF	CUR
Bizet	Adieu de l'hôtesse arabe	H	BF-G	†
Bliss	The buckle			CUR
-----	Three jolly gentlemen	H		†

Brahms	Feinsliebchen, du sollst nicht barfuss geh'n			†
-----	Juchhe!			†
-----	Meine Liebe ist gruen	MLH	ES-A	†
-----	Wie froh und frisch	HL	B-E	†
-----	Willst du, dass ich geh'?	L	C-G	†
Bridge	Love went a-riding	HL		BOS
Dargomijshky	The miller			
Debussy	Chevaux de bois	H	C-G	†
Delius	Love's philosophy			†
Falla	Jota	LH		AMP
Grieg	By the brook			GSC
-----	En fuglevise			
-----	Simpel sang			
-----	Vaer hilset, I Damer	M	D-F	HAN
Head	A piper	HL		BOO
Hely Hutchinson	Old mother Hubbard	HL	B-E	CFI
Henschel	Morning-hymn	MH	DS-GS	DIT
Konjovic	Bosnian song			
Nin	El vito			ESC
Obradors	Coplas de curro dulce			
-----	El tumba y le			
Poulenc	Air vif	H	C-AF	ROU
Quilter	Blow, blow thou winter wind	HL	C-E	BOO
-----	Love's philosophy	LMH	D-A	BOO
Rachmaninoff	Floods of spring	HL		DIT
-----	Oh, no, I pray do not depart	H		DIT
Respighi	Pioggia			BON
Ronald	Love, I have won you	HML	EF-EF	ENO
Schoenberg	Erhebung			GSC
Schubert	Aufloesung	LH	D-A	†
-----	Die Forelle	MLH	EF-GF	†
Schumann	Er ist's	HL	BF-EF	†
Strauss, J.	Blue Danube waltz			GSC
Trunk	Der Feind			
Villa-Lobos	Cançao do carreiro			
Wolf	Er ist's	H	D-G	†
-----	Morgenstimmung	LH	C-GS	†
-----	Wie lange schon war immer mein Verlangen			PET

Atmospheric Songs

Dramatic Soprano

Alnaes	Lykken mellem to mennesker	M	B-FS	HAN
Barber	Rain has fallen	HM	D-E	GSC
Benjamin	Calm sea and mist			CUR
Burleigh	Sometimes I feel like a motherless child	HML		RIC
Carpenter	Go, lovely rose	M	DF-EF	GSC
-----	On the seashore of endless worlds	M	C-FS	GSC
-----	The pools of peace	M	D-F	GSC
-----	When I bring to you colour'd toys	LM	CS-FS	GSC
Chaminade	The silver ring	HM	BF-F	GSC
Charles	Clouds	HML	C-EF	GSC
-----	When I have sung my songs	HM	BF-EF	GSC
Chausson	Les papillons	M	C-F	GSC
Cimara	Fiocca la neve	H	G-G	GSC
Cui	The statue at Czarskoe-Selo	HM	DF-EF	†
Curran	Nocturne Violin	HML	B-DS	GSC
Davis	Nancy Hanks	H	D-G	GAL
Debussy	C'est l'extase	LH	CS-A	†
Duke	Bells in the rain	H	E-GS	CFI
-----	The bird			GSC
Dunhill	The cloths of heaven	LM	EF-G	STB
Duparc	La vie antérieure	HL		†
Eakin	What of that midnight long ago	M	D-F	GAL
Elmore and Reed	Come all ye who weary	L	C-C	JFI
Ferrata	Night and the curtains drawn			JFI
Fourdrain	Chanson norvégienne	H	E-G	RIC
Franz	Sterne mit den gold'nen Fuesschen	HL	DS-E	†
Ganz	A memory	HM	B-D	GSC
Grieg	A dream			†
-----	A swan			†
-----	Det syng	M	C-GF	HAN
-----	In the boat	LM	D-ES	†
-----	Radiant night			
-----	Snegl, Snegl	M	B-F	HAN
-----	Udvandreren	M	EF-F	HAN
Griffes	Symphony in yellow	M	D-GF	GSC
-----	The dreamy lake	H	BS-GS	GSC
Guion	At the cry of the first bird	H	D-G	GSC

Hageman	Do not go, my love	HL	B-EF	GSC
Hahn	D'une prison	L	BF-EF	HEU
-----	L'heure exquise	M	DF-F	†
-----	Paysage	MH	EF-G	HEU
Haydn	She never told her love	HL	B-D	DIT
Holst	The heart worships	ML	BF-D	STB
Hughes	O men from the fields	M	F-F	BOO
Kjerulf	Synnove's song	M	C-F	GSC
Kramer	Now like a lantern	M		RIC
Lie	Soft-footed snow	HM		DIT
Lynn	Gently little Jesus	L	BF-BF	DIT
-----	The magic night of Christmas	M	D-D	DIT
MacGimsey	Sweet little Jesus boy	ML	D-D	CFI
Mahler	Ich ging mit Lust	HL		INT
Marx	Selige Nacht	M	DF-GF	AMP
McArthur	Night	H	F-AF	GSC
Mussorgsky	Tiny star where art thou	LH	DF-F	BOS
Naginski	Look down, fair moon			
Niles	I wonder as I wander	HL	BF-D	GSC
Nordoff	Music I heard with you	H	DS-FS	AMP
Paladilhe	Psyché	HM	BF-F	GSC
Poldowski	L'heure exquise	LMH	DF-AF	CHE
Proctor	I light the blessed candles	H	DF-A	GSC
Rachmaninoff	Lilacs	LH	EF-G	†
Reger	The Virgin's slumber song	MMH	G-G	†
Sacco	The ragpicker	MH	C-AF	GSC
Schubert	Nacht und Traeume	HL	C-DF	†
Schumann	Der Nussbaum	LMH	D-FS	†
Strauss, R.	Die Nacht	HL		†
-----	Traum durch die Daemmerung	HML	BF-EF	†
Tyson	Like barley bending	HL	C-EF	GSC
Vaughan Williams	Silent noon			GSC
Wolf	In dem Schatten meiner Locken	M	C-EF	GSC
-----	Verborgenheit	HL	B-E	†

American Dramatic Songs

Dramatic Soprano

Barber	I hear an army	LH	D-AF	GSC
Beach	Ah, love but a day			ASC
-----	The year's at the spring	MH	AF-AF	ASC

Campbell- Tipton	A spirit flower	LHM	B-G	GSC
-----	The crying of water	LH	FS-GS	GSC
Carpenter	Berceuse de guerre	M	C-G	GSC
-----	I am like a remnant of a cloud of autumn	L	BF-F	GSC
-----	Light, my light	M	C-G	GSC
Crist	You will not come again	HML	BF-CS	CFI
Curran	Life	HM	BF-F	GSC
Giannini	Sing to my heart a song	H	D-B	ELV
Griffes	Evening song	H	DS-GS	GSC
-----	Sorrow of Mydath	M		GSC
-----	The lament of Ian the proud	MH	DS-AS	GSC
-----	The rose of the night	H	CS-A	GSC
-----	Thy dark eyes to mine	H	EF-AF	GSC
Guion	Wild geese	M	D-F	CFI
Hageman	Do not go, my love	HL	B-EF	GSC
-----	Music I heard with you	MH	E-A	GAL
Horsman	The bird of the wilderness	LMH	DF-BF	GSC
Kernochan	We two together	H	EF-AF	GAL
La Forge	Grieve not, beloved	H	FS-G	RIC
-----	Song of the open	MH	EF-AF	DIT
Nordoff	Tell me, Thyrsis	H	E-G	AMP
Protheroe	Ah, love but a day	LMH	F-AF	GAM
Rogers	The last song	MLH	E-AF	GSC
-----	Time for making songs	HM	CS-F	DIT
Salter	The cry of Rachel	LH	C-AF	GSC
Schuman	Holiday song	M	C-F	GSC
Speaks	Morning	HML	BF-D	GSC
Tyson	Sea moods	LH	E-AF	GSC
Vene	Age and youth	H	E-A	RIC
Ware	This day is mine	MH	EF-AF	BOS
Warren	We two	LH	E-A	GSC
Worth	Midsummer	LM	E-A	GSC

British Dramatic Songs and Arias

Dramatic Soprano

Bainton	Ring out, wild bells	M	C-EF	OXF
Bax	Rann of exile	H	D-G	CHE
Besley	Listening	H	E-AF	CUR
Bridge	O that it were so	LMH	D-G	CHA
Clarke	Eight o'clock			ROG
Coleridge- Taylor	Life and death	HML		ASC
Delius	Indian love song	H		†

245

Del Riego	Homing	HML	BF-E	CHA
Elgar	Be not extreme, O Lord			NOV
Henschel	Morning-hymn	MH	DS-GS	†
Purcell	When I am laid in earth (Dido and Aeneas)	LH	C-G	†
Quilter	Blow, blow thou winter wind	HL	C-E	BOO
Ronald	Down in the forest	HML	C-D	ENO
-----	Prelude	HML	B-D	ENO

French Dramatic Songs and Arias

Dramatic Soprano

Berlioz	D'amour l'ardente flamme (La Damnation de Faust)			NOV
-----	Le spectre de la rose			CST
Chausson	Chanson perpétuelle String quartet	H	CS-GS	ROU
-----	La caravane	MH	CS-A	HAM
-----	Poème de l'amour et de la mer	H		INT
Debussy	Air de Lia (L'Enfant Prodigue)	H	E-A	DUR
-----	Chevaux de bois	H	C-G	†
-----	Colloque sentimental			DUR
-----	De fleurs	H	C-AF	†
Duparc	Au pays où se fait la guerre			SAL
-----	La vague et la cloche			ROU
-----	La vie antérieure	HL		†
-----	Le manoir de Rosamunde	HL	B-F	BOS
-----	Phidylé	MH	EF-AF	BOS
-----	Testament	HL		INT
Fauré	Automne	MH	D-FS	GSC
-----	Fleur jetée	HM	BF-FS	†
-----	L'hiver a cessé	HL		INT
-----	Prison	LH		†
-----	Toujours	LH	F-AF	†
Fourdrain	Chanson norvégienne	H	E-G	RIC
Gluck	L'ai-je-bien entendu? (Iphigénie en Aulide)			JOB
-----	Le perfide Renaud me fuit (Armide)			PET
-----	Non! ce n'est point (Alceste)	H	E-G	†
Gounod	Plus grand, dans son obscurité (La Reine de Saba)	MH	CS-B	†

246

Hahn	D'une prison	L	BF-EF	HEU
-----	Offrande	M	D-D	†
Halévy	Il va venir (La Juive)	H	D-CF	†
Honegger	Les cloches			SEN
Hue	J'ai pleuré en rêve	HL	D-E	BOS
Lenormand	Quelle souffrance	HM	AF-F	HAM
Massenet	Charmes des jours passés (Hérodiade)			HEU
-----	Dis-moi que je suis belle (Thaïs)	H	D-B	HEU
-----	Il est doux, il est bon (Hérodiade)	MH	EF-BF	GSC
Meyerbeer	Ah! mon fils (Le Prophète)	M	B-AS	†
Milhaud	Chant du laboureur	M	B-F	ESC
Paladilhe	Lamento provincal	M	CS-FS	HOM
Poldowski	Dansons la gigue	M	EF-G	MAR
-----	L'heure exquise	LMH	DF-AF	CHE
Saint-Saëns	L'attente			DUR
Spontini	Toi que j'implore (La Vestale)			LEM

German Dramatic Songs and Arias

Dramatic Soprano

Beethoven	Abscheulicher, wo eilst du hin? (Fidelio)		B-B	†
Brahms	Ach, wende diesen Blick			†
-----	Am Sonntag Morgen	L	CS-FS	†
-----	Nicht mehr zu dir zu gehen			†
-----	Von ewiger Liebe	LMH	B-AF	†
Bruch	Ave Maria (Das Feuerkreuz)	LH	D-BF	AMP
Franz	Im herbst	HM	A-F	†
Liszt	Freudvoll und Leidvoll			DUR
Loewe	Walpurgisnacht	H	G-G	SC
Mahler	Das Irdische Leben	HL	A-F	INT
-----	Um Mitternacht	HL		INT
Marx	Hat dich die Liebe beruehrt	MH	EF-BF	AMP
-----	Selige Nacht	M	DF-GF	AMP
Mendelssohn	Hear ye, Israel (Elijah)	H	E-A	†
-----	Schilflied	M	F-FS	
Schoenberg	Erhebung			GSC
Schubert	Am Feierabend	HL	BF-F	†
-----	Auf dem Flusse	HL	F-E	†
-----	Aufenthalt	HLM	A-F	†
-----	Dem Unendlichen	L	A-GF	†

(Schubert)	Der Atlas	HL	BF-F	†
-----	Der Doppelgaenger	HL	G-D	†
-----	Der Erlkoenig	HML	A-E	†
-----	Der Lindenbaum	HL	A-D	GSC
-----	Die Allmacht	HML	G-E	†
-----	Die junge Nonne	LH	C-GF	†
-----	Die Liebe hat gelogen	LM	G-F	†
-----	Du liebst mich nicht	LH	E-FS	†
-----	Erstarrung	HL	D-F	†
-----	Fruehlingstraum	HL	C-D	†
-----	Ganymed	LH	EF-G	†
-----	Gruppe aus dem Tartarus	L	CS-EF	†
-----	In der Ferne	HL		†
-----	Mut	HL		†
-----	Schaefers Klagelied	HL	BF-D	†
Schumann	Heiss' mich nicht reden			
-----	Mit Myrthen und Rosen	HL	A-D	†
-----	Talismane			
-----	Waldesgespraech	HL	A-FS	†
Strauss	Caecilie	MH	E-B	†
-----	Kling			†
-----	Ruhe meine Seele			†
-----	Zueignung	HL	CS-FS	†
Trunk	Der Feind			
Wagner	Dich theure Halle	H	DS-A	†
	(Tannhaeuser)			
-----	Du bist der Lenz			†
	(Die Walkuere)			
-----	Schmerzen	HL		†
-----	Senta's ballad			GSC
	(Der Fliegende Hollaender)			
-----	Starke Scheite			GSC
	(Goetterdaemmerung)			
Weber	Bethoerte, die an meine			PET
	Liebe glaubt (Euryanthe)			
-----	Ozean, du Ungeheuer	H	C-C	GSC
	(Oberon)			
Wolf	Alle gingen, herz, zu Ruh	HL	C-EF	†
-----	Das Koehlerweib ist trunken			PET
-----	Denk' es, o Seele	LH	EF-F	†
-----	Der Freund	HM	BF-E	PET
-----	Die ihr schwebet	HL	EF-EF	†
-----	Geh' Geliebter, geh' jetzt			PET
-----	Lebe wohl	HL	BF-F	†
-----	Liebe mir in Busen zuendet	M	E-F	†
-----	Ueber Nacht	LH	D-G	†
-----	Zur Ruh', zur Ruh'	HL	A-GF	†

Dramatic Soprano

Boito	Morte di Margherita (L'altra notte) (Mefistofele)	H	D-B	GSC
Casella	Amante sono vaghiccia di voi			RIC
Catalani	Ebben? Ne andro lontana (La Wally)	H	E-B	RIC
Donizetti	O mio Fernando (La Favorita)	M	B-A	†
Durante	Vergin, tutta amor	LM	C-EF	†
Mascagni	Un di ero piccina (Iris)			RIC
-----	Voi lo sapete (Cavalleria Rusticana)	H	B-A	†
Mozart	Or sai, chi l'onore (Don Giovanni)			†
Pergolesi	Confusa, smarrita			GSC
Ponchielli	Stella del marinar (La Gioconda)	M	B-A	RIC
-----	Suicidio! (La Gioconda)	HM	BF-AF	†
Puccini	In quelle trine morbide (Manon Lescaut)	H	DF-BF	RIC
-----	Tu, che di gel sei cinta (Turandot)			RIC
-----	Un bel di vedremo (Madama Butterfly)	H	DF-BF	RIC
-----	Vissi d'arte (Tosca)	MH	EF-BF	RIC
Respighi	In alto mare			BON
-----	Nebbie			†
Verdi	Ecco l'orrido campo (Un Ballo in Maschera)	H	B-C	RIC
-----	Madre, pietosa Vergine (La Forza del Destino)	H	B-B	RIC
-----	Morrò, ma prima in grazia (Un Ballo in Maschera)			RIC
-----	O don fatale (Don Carlos)	MH	CF-CF	†
-----	Pace, pace mio Dio (La Forza del Destino)	H	CS-BF	†
-----	Ritorna vincitor (Aida)	H	DF-BF	†
-----	Tu che la vanita (Don Carlos)			RIC

Miscellaneous Dramatic Songs and Arias

Dramatic Soprano

Alvarez	La partida	HL	DS-E	GSC

Borodin	A dissonance	MH	E-F	†
Dvořák	Hear my prayer, O Lord			AMP
Gliere	Ah, twine no blossoms	HM	CS-F	DIT
Granados	La maja dolorosa	M		INT
Gretchaninoff	Over the steppe	LM	C-G	GSC
Grieg	A dream			†
-----	A swan			†
-----	Den Aergjerrige			
-----	Eros	LM	C-F	†
-----	In the boat	LM	D-ES	†
-----	Prinsessen	HL	B-E	†
-----	Simpel sang			
-----	Vaer hilset, I Damer	M	D-F	HAN
Mussorgsky	Hopak	HM	CS-FS	GSC
-----	The orphan girl			GSC
Rachmaninoff	Christ is risen	LM	D-F	GAL
-----	Floods of spring	HL		DIT
-----	God took away from me			GSC
-----	O, do not grieve	M	BF-AF	GSC
-----	Oh, no, I pray, do not depart	H		DIT
-----	O thou billowy harvest field	HL	CS-E	GSC
-----	The soldier's bride			†
-----	To the children	MH	F-G	DIT
Sibelius	Black roses	M	A-ES	AMP
Tchaikovsky	Adieu forêts (Jeanne d'Arc)	HM	BF-FS	GSC
-----	All for you			
-----	Letter scene (Eugene Onegin)			GSC
-----	None but the lonely heart	HLM	C-F	DIT

Humorous Songs

Dramatic Soprano

Bax	Oh dear, what can the matter be?	M	D-EF	CHE
Bernstein	I hate music	H	C-A	WIT
Bliss	The buckle			CUR
-----	Three jolly gentlemen	H		†
Brahms	Der Kranz			†
-----	Vergebliches Staendchen	LHM	E-FS	†
Carpenter	Don't ceare	M	C-D	GSC
-----	If	M	D-E	GSC
Chabrier	Villanelle des petits canards	HML	B-E	†

Clarke	Shy one	HL	BF-G	BOH
Crist	Chinese mother goose rhymes	H	C-G	CFI
Dougherty	Love in the dictionary	M	C-G	GSC
Gibbs	Five eyes	HL	D-D	BOS
Grieg	My Johann	HL	BF-EF	GSC
Griselle and Young	The cuckoo clock	LH	EF-G	GSC
Hadley	My shadow			ASC
Hely-Hutchinson	Old Mother Hubbard	HL	B-E	CFI
Hindemith	The whistling thief	M	E-F	AMP
Josten	Cupid's counsel	H	EF-AF	GSC
Lehmann	The cuckoo	HH	D-B	BOH
Loewe	Das Glockenthuermers Tochterlein	H	CS-A	SC
Mahler	Wer hat dies Liedlein erdacht?	HL	BF-E	INT
Mozart	Warnung	HM	C-D	
Nordoff	Serenade	H	CS-FS	AMP
-----	There shall be more joy	M	CS-FS	AMP
Paisiello	Chi vuol la zingarella	L	C-F	GSC
Pierné	Ils etaient trois petits chats blancs			MAR
Reger	Waldeinsamkeit	HMI	A-D	BOS
Rich	American lullaby	LH	C-F	GSC
Rontani	Or ch'io non sengo più	HL	CS-E	DIT
Satie	Le chapelier			ROU
Schubert	Die Maenner sind mechant			PET
-----	Heidenrooslein			
Schuman	Holiday song	M	C-F	GSC
Slonimsky	Gravestones at Hancock, New Hampshire	H	D-G	AXE
Spross	Will o' the wisp			JCH
Stein	The puffin	M		CFI
Wolf	Weather forecast	H	EF-GS	GSC
-----	Der Knabe und das Immlein	L	CS-A	†
-----	Elfenlied	HL	D-F	†
-----	Ich hab' in Penna	LH		
-----	Storchenbotschaft			‡

American Folk Songs (Arr.)

Dramatic Soprano

Brockway	Barbara Allen			GRA
-----	Frog went-a-courting			GRA

251

(Brockway)	The nightingale			GRA
-----	The old maid's song			GRA
Davis	Deaf old woman			GAL
Foster, S.C.	Sweetly she sleeps			
Hughes	Birds' courting song			GSC
Niles	Down in the valley			GSC
-----	I wonder as I wander	HL	BF-D	GSC
-----	The blue Madonna			GSC
Powell	The rich old woman	M		JFI
Siegmeister	He's gone away			

British Folk Songs (Arr.)

Dramatic Soprano

Bax	Oh, dear, what can the matter be?	M	D-EF	CHE
Beethoven	Irish songs			
-----	Scotch songs			
Britten	The Sally gardens			BOH
Gatty	Bendemeer's stream	LMH		BOO
Grainger	The sprig of thyme	LH	E-FS	GSC
Harty	The lowlands of Holland			OXF
Hopekirk	Coming through the rye			DIT
-----	Flow gently, sweet Afton			DIT
-----	Loch Lomond			DIT
Hughes	Down by the Sally gardens			BOO
-----	Hey diddle diddle			CRA
-----	I know my love			BOO
-----	The leprehaun			
Kennedy- Fraser	An Eriskay love lilt			BOO
-----	Land of heart's desire			BOO
-----	The Bens of Jura			BOO
-----	The road to the isles			BOO
Kreisler	Leezie Lindsay			
Page	The foggy dew			
-----	The harp that once through Tara's halls			DIT
Quilter	Ye banks and braes	M	DF-EF	BOH
Vaughan Williams	And all in the morning			STB
-----	Robin Hood and the pedlar	M	D-E	OXF
-----	Rolling in the dew			OXF
Welsh	All through the night			
-----	The ash grove			
Wilson	Come let's be merry			BOO

Miscellaneous Folk Songs (Arr.)

Dramatic Soprano

Brahms	Da unten in Thale			†
-----	Erlaube mir, fein's Maedchen			†
-----	Feinsliebchen, du sollst nicht barfuss geh'n			†
-----	Mein Maedel hat einen Rosenmund	M	F-F	†
Dvořák	Gypsy songs	LH	D-A	AMP
Falla	Jota	LH		AMP
-----	Polo	HL		AMP
Ferrari	Le jardin d'amour	LM	EF-F	GSC
Liddle	An old French carol	LM	F-F	BOO
McFeeters	Gentle Mary	H	EF-AF	GSC
Ravel	Chanson italienne			DUR
-----	Là-bas vers l'église	MH	GS-E	DUR
-----	Tout gai	MH	EF-F	DUR
Weckerlin	Chantons les amours de Jean	H	D-G	GSC

Negro Spirituals

Dramatic Soprano

Boatner	Oh, what a beautiful city!	HL	D-E	GSC
-----	On mah journey	LH	EF-EF	RIC
-----	Trampin' (Tryin' to make Heaven my home)	L	D-F	ELK
Burleigh	De gospel train	HL		RIC
-----	Deep river	HML		RIC
-----	Go down, Moses	HL		RIC
-----	Hard trials	M		RIC
-----	Joshua fit de battle ob Jericho	LH	DS-E	RIC
-----	Little David play on you' harp	HL		RIC
-----	Oh, didn't it rain	LH		RIC
-----	Oh, Peter, go ring a dem bells			RIC
-----	Sometimes I feel like a motherless child	HML		RIC
-----	Swing low, sweet chariot	HL		RIC
-----	Were you there?	HML		RIC
Dett	Sit down servant			GSC
Johnson	City called Heaven			ROB
-----	Dere's no hidin' place down dere			

253

(Johnson)	Hold on			ROB
-----	Honor, honor	HM	C-E	CFI
-----	My good Lord done been here	HM	BF-F	CFI
-----	Witness	HM	D-F	CFI
Kerby-Forrest	He's got the whole world in His hands	M	G-E	MLS
MacGimsey	Sweet little Jesus boy	ML	D-D	CFI
Price	My soul's been anchored in the Lord			GAM
Ryder	Let us break bread together	LH	D-G	JFI
White	Wake up Jacob			PRE

American Songs Employing Agility

Dramatic Soprano

Charles	Let my song fill your heart	LH	EF-AF	GSC
Clough-Leighter	My lover he comes on the skee	HM	D-F	BOS
Crist	O come hither	HM	B-GS	CFI
Curran	Ho! Mr. Piper	LH	D-G	GSC
Gaines	My heart hath a mind			
Hageman	Miranda	HL		GAL
Nevin	One spring morning	MH	DS-F	BOS
Nordoff	There shall be more joy	M	CS-FS	AMP
Speaks	In May time	HL	D-E	JCH

British Songs Employing Agility

Dramatic Soprano

Arne, T.	Where the bee sucks	HM		†
Bax	Shieling song	H	CS-A	CHE
Besley	Listening	H	E-AF	CUR
Bishop	Love has eyes	M		†
Bliss	Three jolly gentlemen	H		†
German	Charming Chloe	HML		NOV
Green	My lips shall speak the praise	M	E-F	OXF
-----	Salvation belongeth unto the Lord	M	F-EF	OXF
Hely-Hutchinson	Old Mother Hubbard	HL	B-E	CFI

254

Moeran	Bright cap			OXF
Morley	It was a lover and his lass	HM		DIT
Purcell	Nymphs and shepherds	HM	C-F	†
	(The Libertine)			
Quilter	Love's philosophy	LMH	D-A	BOO
Scott	Blackbird's song			ELK
Wilson	Come let's be merry			BOO

French Songs Employing Agility

Dramatic Soprano

Bizet	Adieux de l'hôtesse arabe			
-----	Ouvre ton coeur	MH	DS-GS	†
Chausson	Le colibri			
-----	Les papillons	M	C-F	GSC
Delibes	Le rossignol	M		GSC
Fauré	Mandoline	HL	F-E	†
Ferrari	Le jardin d'amour	LM	EF-F	GSC
Georges	La pluie	HL		INT
Meyerbeer	Nobles Seigneurs, salut!			
	(Les Huguenots)			
Poulenc	Air vif	H	C-AF	ROU
Ravel	Kaddisch	H	C-G	DUR
Saint-Saëns	Guitares et mandolines			DUR
Spontini	Toi que j'implore			LEM
	(La Vestale)			

German Songs and Arias Employing Agility

Dramatic Soprano

Bach, J.S.	Mein glaeubiges Herze	HML		†
	(Cantata 68)			
Beethoven	Abscheulicher, wo eilst		B-B	†
	du hin? (Fidelio)			
Brahms	Botschaft	HL	D-F	†
-----	Das Maedchen spricht	H	E-FS	†
-----	O liebliche Wangen	MLH	E-G	†
Franz	Ein Stuendlein wohl vor Tag			†
Haydn	The mermaid's song	M	C-F	PRE
Jensen	Am Ufer des Flusses des	H	D-FS	GSC
	Manzanares			
Keiser	Von dem Landleben			SIM
Loewe	Des Glockenthuermers	H	CS-A	SC
	Tochterlein			
Mahler	Fruehlingsmorgen	HL		INT

255

(Mahler)	Ich bin der Welt abbanden gekommen	HL		INT
-----	Wer hat dies Liedlein erdacht?	HL	BF-E	INT
Marx	Und gestern hat er mir Rosen gebracht	H	E-A	AMP
Schubert	Auf dem Wasser zu singen	MH	EF-GF	†
-----	Das Wandern	HLM	E-E	†
-----	Liebesbotschaft	H	E-G	†
-----	Mein!	HL		†
-----	Ungeduld	HML		†
Schumann	Auftraege	HL	C-E	†
-----	Fruehlingsnacht	L	CS-E	GSC
-----	Mondnacht	M	E-FS	†
-----	Waldesgespraech	HL	A-FS	†
Strauss, J.	Blue Danube waltz			GSC
-----	Czardas (Die Fledermaus)			BOO
Weber	Wie nahte mir der Schlummer (Der Freischuetz)	H	B-B	†

Italian Songs and Arias Employing Agility

Dramatic Soprano

Bellini	Casta diva (Norma)	H	F-C	†
Bononçini	L'esperto nocchiero (Astarte)	HL	B-E	†
Carissimi	Vittoria, mio core	HLM	B-E	†
Cimarosa	Nel lasciarti (L'Olympiade)			RIC
Handel	Ch'io mai vi possa (Siroe)			†
Jommelli	Chi vuol comprar la bella	H	B-G	GSC
Lotti	Pur dicesti, o bocca bella	LMH	E-FS	GSC
Mozart	Come scoglio (Così Fan Tutte)			†
-----	Dove sono (Le Nozze di Figaro)	H	D-A	†
-----	Mi tradi quell' alma ingrata (Don Giovanni)			†
-----	Misera, dove son			BOO
Rossini	Bel raggio lusinghier (Semiramide)	H	CS-A	GSC
-----	La danza	MH	E-A	†
Scarlatti, A.	Se Florindo è fedele	LM	EF-EF	GSC
Stradella	Ragion sempre addita	H	E-G	†
Verdi	Ernani involami (Ernani)	H	AF-BF	GSC
-----	Merce, dilette amiche (I Vespri Siciliani)	MH	A-CS	GSC

Miscellaneous Songs Employing Agility
Dramatic Soprano

Alnaes	En morgen var din grav	M	CS-D	HAN
Alvarez	La partida	HL	DS-E	GSC
Falla	Nana			
-----	Vivan los que rien (La Vida Breve)			AMP
Granados	El majo discreto	H		INT
Mozart	Alleluja	LMH	F-C	†
-----	Et incarnatus est (C Minor Mass)			PET
Mussorgsky	Tiny star where art thou	LH	DF-F	BOS
Sibelius	From the north	H	DS-G	GSC
Stravinsky	Pastorale			GSC
Turina	Cantilena	M	C-EF	UME

American Songs Employing Crescendo and Diminuendo

Dramatic Soprano

Barber	Rain has fallen	HM	D-E	GSC
-----	The daisies	M	C-F	GSC
Beach	Ah, love but a day			ASC
Campbell-Tipton	A spirit flower	LHM	B-G	GSC
-----	The crying of water	LH	FS-GS	GSC
Carpenter	Go, lovely rose	M	DF-EF	GSC
-----	The pools of peace	M	D-F	GSC
-----	The sleep that flits on baby's eyes	M	B-FS	GSC
-----	When I bring to you colour'd toys	LM	CS-FS	GSC
Charles	Clouds	HML	C-EF	GSC
Duke	Bells in the rain	H	E-GS	CFI
Engel	Sea shell	M	EF-EF	GSC
Fairchild	A memory			BOS
Hopkinson	My days have been so wondrous free	LH	EF-G	†
Howe	Berceuse	HM	EF-F	GSC
La Forge	Hills	HL		RIC
Naginski	The pasture	M	BF-EF	GSC
Niles	I wonder as I wander	HL	DF-D	GSC
Nordoff	Serenade	H	CS-FS	AMP
Rogers	At parting	LH	CS-FS	GSC
Thompson	Velvet shoes	M	C-E	ECS

British Songs and Arias Employing
Crescendo and Diminuendo

Dramatic Soprano

Arne, T.	The plague of love			BOO
Bax	A lullaby			
-----	Cradle song			CHA
Benjamin	Calm sea and mist			CUR
-----	The wasp			CUR
Clarke	Shy one	HL	BF-G	BOH
Delius	Indian love song	H		†
Gurney	Under the greenwood tree			ROG
Handel	Angels ever bright and fair (Theodora)	H	E-F	†
-----	Let me wander not unseen (L'Allegro)	M	D-G	†
Horn	Cherry ripe	M	D-G	†
-----	I've been roaming	L	B-E	†
Ireland	Bed in summer			CUR
Purcell	I attempt from love's sickness to fly (The Indian Queen)	MH	CS-E	†
Quilter	The fuchsia tree			BOO
Scott	Night song	ML	BF-EF	ELK
Shaw	Song of the palanquin bearers	LH	E-F	CUR

French Songs and Arias Employing
Crescendo and Diminuendo

Dramatic Soprano

Bachelet	Chère nuit	H	DF-BF	GSC
Bernard	Ça fait peur aux oiseaux	H	GS-F	GSC
Chaminade	The silver ring	HM	BF-F	GSC
David	Charmant oiseau (La Perle du Brésil)	M	D-E	†
Debussy	Air de Lia (L'Enfant Prodigue)			DUR
-----	C'est l'extase	LH	CS-A	†
-----	La flûte de Pan		B-B	†
Duparc	Chanson triste	MH	FS-AF	†
-----	L'invitation au voyage	HM	E-F	†
-----	Phidylé	MH	EF-AF	BOS
-----	Sérénade florentine	HL		INT
Fauré	Clair de lune	MH	C-G	†
-----	En prière	H	F-F	†
-----	Lydia	MH	G-G	†

258

Liszt	Comment, disaient-ils?	H	C-AF	†
Martini	Plaisir d'amour	M	BF-EF	GSC
Meyerbeer	Nobles Seigneurs, salut!	LH	C-C	†
	(Les Huguenots)			
Paladilhe	Psyché	HM	BF-F	GSC
Rameau	Le grillon			DUR

German Songs Employing
Crescendo and Diminuendo

Dramatic Soprano

Beethoven	Andenken			†
-----	Mit einem gemalten Band			RIC
Brahms	Auf dem See	HL	D-F	†
-----	Geheimnis			†
-----	Sandmaennchen	LH	F-G	†
-----	Sonntag	H	D-G	†
-----	Spanisches Lied			†
-----	Therese	HL	B-D	†
-----	Wie Melodien zieht es	HL	A-E	†
Franz	Gute Nacht	HL		†
-----	Sterne mit den gold' nen	HL	DS-E	†
	Fuesschen			
Mahler	Fruehlingsmorgen	HL		INT
-----	Ich atmet einen linden	HL		INT
	Duft			
Mendelssohn	Lieblingsplaetzchen	LM	FS-E	†
-----	Pagenlied	M	E-E	†
Reger	Mit Rosen bestreut			UNI
-----	Waldeinsamkeit	HML	A-D	BOS
Schubert	An den Mond	HL	F-GF	†
-----	Auf dem Wasser zu singen	MH	EF-GF	†
-----	Der Musensohn	LH	FS-G	†
-----	Der Wanderer	HML	FS-D	†
-----	Fruehlingstraum	HL	C-D	GSC
-----	Gretchen am Spinnrade	H	F-A	†
-----	Im Fruehling	LH	D-FS	†
-----	Lachen und Weinen	HL	C-EF	†
-----	Liebesbotschaft	H	E-G	†
-----	Nacht und Traeume	HL	C-DF	†
-----	Wiegenlied (Op. 98)			†
Schumann	Aus den oestlichen Rosen			
-----	Der Nussbaum	LMH	D-FS	†
-----	Die Soldatenbraut	HL	AF-EF	†
-----	Maerzveilchen	HL	C-C	†
-----	Marienwuermchen	HL	D-D	†
-----	Provenzalisches Lied	LH		†

(Schumann)	Schneegloeckchen	HL		†
-----	Volksliedchen	HL		†
Strauss	Die Nacht	HL		†
Wolf	Auch kleine Dinge	HM	D-E	†
-----	Blumengruss	HL	D-E	†
-----	Der Gaertner	HL		†
-----	Der Knabe und das Immlein	L	CS-A	†
-----	Gleich und gleich			†
-----	In dem Schatten meiner Locken	M	C-EF	†
-----	Mausfallen Spruechlein	HL	BF-E	†
-----	Nun wandre, Maria	HL	EF-D	†
-----	Und willst du deinen Liebsten sterben	HL		†
-----	Verschwiegene Liebe	LH	DF-FS	GSC
-----	Wenn du zu den Blumen gehst	HL	B-EF	†

Italian Songs and Arias Employing Crescendo and Diminuendo

Dramatic Soprano

Bononcini	Per la gloria	HL	C-EF	†
Caldara	Alma del core			GSC
-----	Sebben crudele	HML	E-DS	†
-----	Selve amiche, ombrose piante	HM	E-E	†
Cesti	Intorno all'idol mio (Orontea)	MH	D-F	†
De Luca	Non posso disperar	HL	C-E	GSC
Falconieri	O bellissimi capelli	HL	B-D	†
Fasolo	Cangia, cangia tue voglie	H	C-G	GSC
Frescobaldi	Se l'aura spira	HL	C-EF	DIT
Handel	Ombra mai fu (Serse)	HM	BF-EF	†
Marcello	Non m'è grave morir per amore	L	C-E	GSC
Monteverdi	Lasciatemi morire (Arianna)	ML	D-D	†
Pergolesi	Se tu m'ami	LMH	C-G	GSC
Respighi	Mattinata			BON
Rosa	Selve, voi che le speranze	MH	D-G	DIT
Scarlatti, A.	La fortuna			BOS
Verdi	Ave Maria (Otello)	H	EF-AF	GSC

Miscellaneous Songs Employing
Crescendo and Diminuendo

Dramatic Soprano

Backer- Groendahl	In dreaming dance			
Gretchaninoff	The snowdrop	HM	BF-F	DIT
Grieg	En fuglevise			
-----	In the boat	LM	D-ES	†
-----	It was a lovely summer evening			
-----	Springtide	M		DIT
-----	With a water lily	HM	CS-EF	†
Rachmaninoff	Daisies			†
-----	Lilacs	LH	EF-G	†
-----	The island	LH	DF-F	†
Turina	Cantilena	M	C-EF	UME

American Songs Employing Piano Singing

Dramatic Soprano

Barber	Rain has fallen	HM	D-E	GSC
Campbell- Tipton	A spirit flower	LHM	B-G	GSC
-----	The crying of water	LH	FS-GS	GSC
Carpenter	Go, lovely rose	M	DF-EF	GSC
-----	On the seashore of endless worlds	M	C-FS	GSC
-----	The pools of peace	M	D-F	GSC
-----	The sleep that flits on baby's eyes	M	B-FS	GSC
-----	When I bring to you colour'd toys	LM	CS-FS	GSC
Charles	Clouds	HML	C-EF	GSC
-----	When I have sung my songs	HM	BF-EF	GSC
Crist	Evening	H	C-G	GSC
Davis	Nancy Hanks	H	D-G	GAL
Duke	Bells in the rain	H	E-GS	CFI
-----	The bird			GSC
-----	To Karen, singing	M	CS-G	ELV
Engel	Sea shell	M	EF-EF	GSC
Fairchild	A memory			BOS
Gaines	My heart hath a mind			
Ganz	A memory	HM	B-D	GSC
Griffes	Symphony in yellow	M	D-GF	GSC

(Griffes)	The dreamy lake	H	BS–GS	GSC
-----	Thy dark eyes to mine	H	EF–AF	GSC
Hageman	Do not go, my love	HL	B–EF	GSC
Howe	Berceuse	HM	EF–F	GSC
MacGimsey	Sweet little Jesus Boy	ML	D–D	CFI
Manning	In the Luxembourg gardens	HML	BF–D	GSC
Naginski	The pasture	M	BF–EF	GSC
Niles	I wonder as I wander	HL	BF–D	GSC
Nordoff	Music I heard with you	H	DS–FS	AMP
-----	Serenade	H	CS–FS	AMP
Taylor	A song for lovers	MH	D–F	JFI
Thompson	Velvet shoes	M	C–E	ECS

British Songs Employing Piano Singing

Dramatic Soprano

Bax	Cradle song			CHA
Benjamin	Calm sea and mist			CUR
Clarke	Shy one	HL	BF–G	BOH

Coleridge-
  Taylor
	She rested by the broken
	  brook
		HL		DIT

Dunhill	The cloths of Heaven	LM	EF–G	STB
Handel	Let me wander not unseen (L'Allegro)	M	D–G	†
Ronald	Down in the forest	HML	C–D	ENO
Scott	Lullaby	MML	BF–DF	GAL
Vaughan Williams	Silent noon			GSC

French Songs Employing Piano Singing

Dramatic Soprano

Bernard	Ça fait peur aux oiseaux	H	GS–F	GSC
Chaminade	The silver ring	HM	BF–F	GSC
Debussy	La flûte de Pan		B–B	†
Duparc	Extase	LMH	FS–A	†
Fauré	Après un rêve	HM	C–F	†
-----	Clair de lune	MH	C–G	†
-----	Dans les ruines d'une abbaye	M	E–FS	†
-----	En prière	H	F–F	†
-----	Lydia	MH	G–G	†
Hahn	D'une prison	L	BF–EF	HEU
-----	Infidélité	M		HEU

262

(Hahn)	L'heure exquise	M	DF-F	†
-----	Offrande	M	D-D	†
-----	Paysage	MH	EF-G	HEU
Liszt	Comment, disaient-ils?	H	C-AF	†
-----	Oh! quand je dors	H	E-A	†
Lully	Au clair de la lune	H	E-D	CFI
-----	Bois épais (Amadis)	ML	C-EF	†
Paladilhe	Psyché	HM	BF-F	GSC
Poldowski	L'heure exquise	LMH	DF-AF	CHE
Ravel	La flûte enchantée	M	DS-FS	DUR

German Songs and Arias Employing
Piano Singing

Dramatic Soprano

Beethoven	Ich liebe dich	HL	BF-DF	†
Brahms	Eine gute, gute Nacht			†
-----	Es traeumte mir			†
-----	Geheimnis			†
-----	In Waldeseinsamkeit	H	ES-G	†
-----	Lerchengesang	LH	FS-GS	†
-----	Sandmaennchen	LH	F-G	†
-----	Spanisches Lied			†
-----	Staendchen	HL	BF-E	†
Bruch	Ave Maria (Das Feuerkreuz)	LH	D-BF	AMP
Franz	Ein Stuendlein wohl vor Tag			†
-----	Gute Nacht	HL		†
-----	Sterne mit den gold' nen Fuesschen	HL	DS-E	†
Hindemith	Geburt Marias			AMP
Korngold	Marietta's song (The Dead City)	MH	F-BF	AMP
Mahler	Erinnerung	HL		INT
-----	Fruehlingsmorgen	HL		INT
-----	Ich atmet' einen linden Duft	HL		INT
-----	Ich bin der Welt abbanden gekommen	HL		INT
-----	Ich ging mit Lust	HL		INT
-----	Liebst du um Schoenheit	HL		INT
-----	Wo die schoenen Trompeten blasen	HL	GF-F	INT
Marx	Selige Nacht	M	DF-GF	AMP
Mendelssohn	Bei der Wiege	M	DF-EF	†
-----	Gruss	M	DS-FS	†
-----	Lieblingsplaetzchen	LM	FS-E	†

(Mendelssohn)	Pagenlied	M	E-E	†
Schubert	Auf dem Wasser zu singen	MH	EF-GF	†
-----	Ave Maria	LMH	F-F	†
-----	Du bist die Ruh	LMH	EF-AF	†
-----	Fruehlingstraum	HL	C-D	†
-----	Im Abendrot	HL	C-D	†
-----	Im Fruehling	LH	D-FS	†
-----	Lachen und Weinen	HL	C-EF	†
-----	Liebesbotschaft	H	E-G	†
-----	Nacht und Traeume	HL	C-DF	†
-----	Wiegenlied (Op. 98)			†
Schumann	Der Nussbaum	LMH	D-FS	†
-----	Marienwuermchen	HL	D-D	†
-----	Mondnacht	M	E-FS	†
-----	Requiem			†
-----	Volksliedchen	HL		†
Strauss, J.	Czardas (Die Fledermaus)			BOO
Strauss, R.	Allerseelen	HL	AS-E	†
-----	Die Nacht	HL		†
-----	Freundliche Vision	HL	C-F	†
-----	Heimkehr	HL	B-E	†
-----	Ich trage meine Minne	M		UNI
-----	Mein Herz ist stumm	LH	EF-AF	
-----	Traum durch die Daemmerung	HML	BF-EF	†
-----	Wiegenliedchen			†
Wagner	Der Engel	LH	CS-G	†
-----	Euch Lueften die mein Klagen (Lohengrin)			†
-----	Im Treibhaus	HL		†
Wolf	Auf ein altes Bild	HL	E-DS	†
-----	Der Gaertner	HL		†
-----	Du denkst, mit einem Faedchen			†
-----	Gleich und gleich			†
-----	In dem Schatten meiner Locken	M	C-EF	†
-----	Mausfallen Spruechlein	HL	BF-E	†
-----	Schlafendes Jesuskind	HL	AS-F	†
-----	Verborgenheit	HL	B-E	†
-----	Verschwiegene Liebe	LH	DF-FS	†
-----	Wie glaenzt der helle Mond			†

Italian Songs and Arias Employing Piano Singing

Dramatic Soprano

Bononcini	Deh più a me non v'ascondete

Cimara	Fiocca la neve	H	G–G	GSC
D'Astorga	Vo' cercando in queste valli			
Frescobaldi	Se l'aura spira	HL	C–EF	DIT
Gagliano	Dormi amore			DIT
Handel	Care selve (Atalanta)	MH	FS–A	†
Jommelli	Chi vuol comprar la bella	H	B–G	GSC
Monteverdi	Lasciatemi morire (Arianna)	ML	D–D	†
Respighi	Notte			BON
Verdi	Ave Maria (Otello)	H	EF–AF	GSC
-----	O cieli azzuri (Aida)	H	B–C	†
-----	Salce, salce (Otello)	H	CS–FS	RIC

Miscellaneous Songs Employing
Piano Singing

Dramatic Soprano

Alnaes	En morgen var din grav	M	CS–D	HAN
-----	Lykken mellem to mennesker	M	B–FS	HAN
Arensky	Revery	MH	DS–FS	DIT
Cui	The statue at Czarskoc-Selo	HM	DF–EF	†
Dvořák	God is my shepherd			AMP
-----	Songs my mother taught me	HM	E–E	†
Gretchaninoff	Hushed the song of the nightingale	MH	E–G	DIT
Grieg	A dream			†
-----	A swan			†
-----	In the boat	LM	D–ES	†
-----	Radiant night			
-----	Snegl, Snegl	M	B–F	HAN
Lie	Soft-footed snow	HM		DIT
Mednikoff	The hills of Gruzia	H	DS–A	LAC
Rachmaninoff	Before my window	HM	C–G	†
-----	In the silence of night	LH	D–A	GSC

American Songs Employing
Rapid Enunciation

Dramatic Soprano

Boatner	Oh, what a beautiful city!	HL	D–E	GSC

Burleigh	Joshua fit de battle ob Jericho	LH	DS-E	RIC
-----	Little David play on yo harp	HL		RIC
Carpenter	Don't ceare	M	C-D	GSC
Clough-Leighter	My lover he comes on the skee	HM	D-F	BOS
Curran	Ho! Mr. Piper	LH	D-G	GSC
Deis	Come down to Kew			
Griffes	Elves	H	F-AF	GSC
Hadley	My shadow			ASC
Hageman	At the well	LH	EF-AF	GSC
-----	Miranda	HL		GAL
Josten	Cupid's counsel	H	EF-AF	GSC
Kountz	The sleigh	HL	D-FS	GSC
Nevin	One spring morning	MH	DS-F	BOS
Spross	Will o' the wisp			JCH
Warner	Hurdy-gurdy	M	D-F	CFI

British Songs Employing
Rapid Enunciation

Dramatic Soprano

Bantock	A feast of lanterns	HM	D-F	GAL
Bax	Oh dear, what can the matter be?	M	D-EF	CHE
Bishop	Love has eyes	M		†
Brewer	The fairy pipers	HML		BOH
German	Charming Chloe	HML		NOV
Gibbs	Five eyes	HL	D-D	BOS
Head	A piper	HL		BOO
Hughes	Hey diddle diddle			CRA
Morley	It was a lover and his lass	HM		DIT

French Songs Employing
Rapid Enunciation

Dramatic Soprano

Bernard	Ça fait peur aux oiseaux	H	GS-F	GSC
Chabrier	Villanelle des petits canards	HML	B-E	†
Debussy	Chevaux de bois	H	C-G	†
-----	Fantoches	H	D-A	JOB
-----	La flûte de Pan		B-B	†

266

(Debussy)	Mandoline	HM	BF-F	†
Fauré	Dans les ruines d'une abbaye	M	E-FS	†
-----	Mandoline	H	F-E	†
-----	Toujours	LH	F-AF	†
Ferrari	Le jardin d'amour	LM	EF-F	GSC
Fourdrain	Carnaval	M	C-F	RIC
Milhaud	La tourterelle	M	B-G	DUR
Pierné	Ils étaient trois petits chats blancs			MAR
Poldowski	Dansons la gigue	M	EF-G	MAR
Ravel	Tout gai	MH	EF-F	DUR
Saint-Saëns	L'attente			DUR
Weckerlin	Chantons les amours de Jean	H	D-G	GSC

German Songs Employing
Rapid Enunciation

Dramatic Soprano

Beethoven	Neue Liebe, neues Leben			†
Brahms	Blinde Kuh			†
-----	Das Maedchen spricht	H	E-FS	†
-----	Der Jaeger	HL		†
-----	Dort in den Weiden	LH	A-A	†
-----	Juchhe!			†
-----	Meine Liebe ist gruen	MLH	ES-A	†
-----	O liebliche Wangen	MLH	E-G	†
-----	Staendchen	HL	BF-E	†
-----	Vergebliches Staendchen	LHM	E-FS	†
Loewe	Walpurgisnacht	H	G-G	SC
Mendelssohn	An die Entfernte	M	F-F	
-----	Im Gruenen	H	E-BF	AUG
-----	Neue Liebe	H	CS-A	†
Mozart	Warnung	HM	C-D	
Schubert	Am Feierabend	HL	BF-F	†
-----	Das Wandern	HLM	E-E	†
-----	Die Forelle	MLH	EF-GF	†
-----	Die Post	HML	BF-EF	†
-----	Erstarrung	HL	D-F	†
-----	Fruehlingssehnsucht	HL	B-E	†
-----	Mein!	HL		†
-----	Ungeduld	HML		†
-----	Wohin?	HL	B-E	DIT
Schumann	Auftraege	HL	C-E	†
-----	Volksliedchen	HL		†
Wolf	Elfenlied	HL	D-F	†

(Wolf)   Ich hab, in Penna   LH   †

Italian Songs and Arias Employing
Rapid Enuncation

Dramatic Soprano

Carissimi	Vittoria, mio core	HLM	B-E	†
Cavalli	Donzelle fuggite	HL	C-EF	†
Falconieri	Non più d'amore	HL	C-D	DIT
-----	Nudo arciero	HL	AF-AF	DIT
Handel	Ch'io mai vi possa (Siroe)			†
Legrenzi	Che fiero costume	HML	C-D	†
Mozart	Non so più cosa son (Le Nozze di Figaro)	H	EF-G	†
-----	Voi che sapete (Le Nozze di Figaro)	M	C-F	†
Paisiello	Chi vuol la zingarella	L	C-F	GSC
Paradies	M'ha preso alla sua ragna	M	EF-F	GSC
Rontani	Or ch'io non segno più	HL	CS-E	DIT
Rossini	La danza	MH	E-A	†
Stradella	Ragion sempre addita	H	E-G	†

Miscellaneous Songs Employing
Rapid Enunciation

Dramatic Soprano

Falla	Seguidilla murciana	HL		AMP
Grieg	In the boat	LM	D-ES	†
-----	My Johann	HL	BF-EF	GSC
-----	Simpel sang			
-----	The way of the world			DIT
-----	Til min dreng			
-----	With a waterlily			
Mussorgsky	The evening prayer	M	C-E	GSC
-----	The magpie and the gypsy dancer			GSC

American Songs Employing
Sustained Singing

Dramatic Soprano

Barber	A nun takes the veil	MH	G-G	GSC
-----	Sure on this shining night	MH	D-G	GSC

Burleigh	Deep river	HML		RIC
-----	Sometime I feel like a motherless child	HML		RIC
-----	Were you there?	HML		RIC
Chadwick	Allah	LH	CS-GS	ASC
Charles	And so, goodbye	LH	EF-AF	GSC
Curran	Nocturne Violin	HML	B-DS	GSC
Edwards	By the bend of the river	HML	C-E	GSC
-----	Into the night	HML	C-DF	GSC
Foster, S.C.	Sweetly she sleeps			
Griffes	Evening song	H	DS-GS	GSC
-----	The lament of Ian the proud	MH	DS-AS	GSC
-----	The rose of the night	H	CS-A	GSC
Hageman	Music I heard with you	MH	E-A	GAL
Horsman	The bird of the wilderness	LMH	DF-BF	GSC
Kernochan	We two together	H	EF-AF	GAL
Lieurance	By the waters of Minnetonka			PRE
MacDowell	The swan bent low	LH		ELK
McDonald	Daybreak	H		ELV
Metcalf	At nightfall	HML	C-DF	ASC
Powell	Heartsease	M	DF-G	GSC
Rogers	Wind song	LM	C-G	GSC
Scott	Think on me	HML	D-EF	GAL

British Songs and Arias Employing Sustained Singing

Dramatic Soprano

Arne, T.	Blow, blow thou winter wind	M	C-F	†
-----	In infancy			NOV
Bantock	Silent strings	MH	F-G	BOO
Bridge	All things that we clasp	HL		BOS
-----	O that it were so	LMH	D-G	CHA
Britten	The Sally gardens			BOH
Clarke	Eight o'clock			ROG
Coleridge-Taylor	Life and death	HML		ASC
Del Riego	Homing	HML	BF-F	CHA
Dunhill	To the Queen of Heaven	M	C-G	GSC
Grainger	The sprig of thyme	LH	E-FS	GSC
Handel	Come unto Him (The Messiah)	MH	F-G	†
-----	How beautiful are the feet of them (The Messiah)	H		†
-----	I know that my Redeemer liveth (The Messiah)	MH	E-GS	†

269

Henschel	Morning-hymn	MH	DS-GS	†
Holst	The heart worships	ML	BF-D	STB
Purcell	If music be the food of love	M	D-G	BOO
-----	Music for a while (Oedipus)	LH		SC
-----	When I am laid in earth (Dido and Aeneas)	LH	C-G	†
Ronald	O, lovely night	HML		BOO
-----	Prelude	HML	B-D	ENO
Stephenson	Love is a sickness	HML	C-D	BOO
Welsh	All through the night			
-----	The ash grove			

French Songs and Arias Employing Sustained Singing

Dramatic Soprano

Bemberg	Chant hindou	HML	A-EF	†
Berlioz	D'amour l'ardente flamme (La Damnation de Faust)			NOV
-----	Le spectre de la rose			CST
Bizet	Adieu de l'hôtesse arabe	H	BF-G	†
Chausson	Chanson perpétuelle	H	CS-GS	ROU
-----	Le colibri Violin or cello	M	F-GF	BOS
-----	Le temps des lilas	MH	D-GS	†
Debussy	Beau soir	LH	C-FS	†
-----	Chansons de Bilitis	M	C-FS	†
-----	Colloque sentimental			DUR
-----	De fleurs	H	C-AF	†
-----	La chevelure	M	CF-FS	†
-----	Romance	HM	C-E	†
Duparc	Au pays où se fait la guerre			SAL
-----	La vie antérieure	HL		†
-----	Lamento	ML	EF-EF	†
Fauré	Automne	MH	D-FS	GSC
-----	Le jardin clos	M	C-E	DUR
-----	Prison	LH		†
-----	Rencontre	H	EF-AF	†
-----	Soir	LH	D-GS	†
Franck	Nocturne	HL		INT
Georges	Hymne au soleil	LH	E-A	HOM
Gluck	Adieu, conservez dans votre âme (Iphigenie en Aulide)			†
-----	Divinités du Styx (Alceste)	MH	DF-AF	†
-----	Grands dieux (Alceste)	H	E-BF	GSC

270

(Gluck)	Non! ce n'est point (Alceste)	H	E-G	†
Godard	Florian's song	LMH	D-FS	GSC
Gossec	Ah! faut-il me venger (Thésée)			LEM
Gounod	Plus grand, dans son obscurité (La Reine de Saba)	MH	CS-B	†
Halévy	Il va venir (La Juive)	H	D-CF	†
Hue	J'ai pleuré en rêve	HL	D-E	BOS
Lenormand	Quelle souffrance	HM	AF-F	HAM
Massenet	Charmes des jours passés (Hérodiade)			HEU
-----	Elégie	LM	C-GF	GSC
-----	Il est doux, il est bon (Hérodiade)	MH	EF-BF	GSC
Meyerbeer	Ah! mon fils (Le Prophète)	M	B-AS	†
-----	O beau pays (Les Huguenots)	H	CS-D	GSC
Offenbach	Elle a fui, la tourterelle (Tales of Hoffman)	H	D-A	GSC
Paladilhe	Lamento provincal	M	CS-FS	HOM
Poulenc	Bleuet	H	FS-GF	DUR
Ravel	Chanson italienne			DUR
-----	Kaddisch	H	C-G	DUR
-----	Là-bas vers l'église	MH	GS-E	DUR
-----	Vocalise en forme de habanera	MH	BF-G	MAR
Saint-Saëns	La cloche	LH	DF-AF	†

German Songs and Arias Employing Sustained Singing

Dramatic Soprano

Bach, C.P.E.	Passionslied			SIM
Bach, J.S.	Bist du bei mir	HML	A-EF	†
-----	Willst du dein Herz mir schenken			BRH
Beethoven	Die Ehre Gottes	HL	AF-EF	†
-----	Wonne der Wehmut			†
Bohm	Calm as the night	HML	A-EF	†
Brahms	An die Nachtigall	H	DS-G	†
-----	An eine Aeolsharfe	H	EF-AF	†
-----	Auf dem Kirchhofe	HL	BF-EF	†
-----	Daemm'rung senkte sich von oben	LH	BF-G	†
-----	Dein blaues Auge	MH	BF-G	†

271

(Brahms)	Der Tod, das ist die kuehle Nacht	L	AF-F	†
-----	Die Mainacht	HL	BF-FF	†
-----	Erinnerung	H	E-G	†
-----	Feldeinsamkeit	HL	C-EF	†
-----	Immer leiser wird mein Schlummer	LH	DF-A	†
-----	Liebestreu	ML	C-F	†
-----	Mondenschein	LH	D-GF	†
-----	Muss es eine Trennung geben?	LH	FS-FS	†
-----	Nachtigall	MHL	BF-FS	†
-----	O kuehler Wald	MH	A-F	†
-----	O wuesst' ich doch den Weg zurueck	H	E-FS	†
-----	Schoen war, das ich dir weihte			†
-----	Sommerabend			RIC
-----	Wir wandelten	LH	EF-GF	†
Franz	Dedication	HML	BF-C	†
-----	For music	ML	C-D	†
-----	Im Herbst	HM	A-F	†
-----	Mutter, o sing mich zur Ruh	HL	E-G	†
Haydn	She never told her love	HL	B-D	DIT
Korngold	Love letter			AMP
Lehar	Vilia (The Merry Widow)			CHA
Liszt	Freudvoll und leidvoll			DUR
Loewe	Canzonetta	MH	B-A	DIT
Lohner	O Ewigkeit			
Mahler	Um Mitternacht	HL		INT
Marx	Hat dich die Liebe beruehrt	MH	EF-BF	AMP
Mendelssohn	Der Mond	HL		†
-----	Hear ye, Israel (Elijah)	H	E-A	†
-----	Jerusalem, thou that killest (Saint Paul)	H	F-F	†
-----	Nachtlied			
-----	On wings of song			†
Mozart	Abendempfindung	M	E-F	
-----	Die ihr des unermesslichen Weltalls			
-----	Wiegenlied	MH	G-G	†
Schoenberg	Erhebung			GSC
Schubert	Am Grabe Anselmos	HL	B-EF	†
-----	An die Musik	HL	A-DS	†
-----	Auf dem Flusse	HL	F-E	†
-----	Das Wirtshaus	HL	C-D	†
-----	Der Doppelgaenger	HL	G-D	†

(Schubert)	Der Leiermann	ML	C-D	†
-----	Der Lindenbaum	HL	A-D	†
-----	Der Neugierige	HL	CS-EF	†
-----	Der Wegweiser	L	D-EF	†
-----	Des Maedchens Klage	LH	C-E	†
-----	Die Allmacht	HML	G-E	†
-----	Die Liebe hat gelogen	LM	G-F	†
-----	Die Maenner sind mechant			PET
-----	Die Nebensonnen	HL	F-D	†
-----	Du liebst mich nicht	LH	E-FS	†
-----	Fruehlingsglaube	M	EF-F	†
-----	Ganymed	LH	EF-G	†
-----	Ihr Bild	HL	C-C	†
-----	In der Ferne	HL		†
-----	Lied eines Schiffers an die Dioskuren	HL	A-C	†
-----	Litanei	HLM	C-EF	†
-----	Nur wer die Sehnsucht kennt	LH		†
-----	Schaefers Klagelied	HL	BF-D	†
-----	Staendchen	MH	B-E	†
-----	Wanderers Nachtlied 2	LH	F-F	GSC
Schumann	Aus den Hebraeischen Gesaengen			
-----	Die Lotusblume	HLM	BF-F	†
-----	Du bist wie eine Blume	HM	F-EF	†
-----	Du Ring an meine Finger	HL	C-F	†
-----	Ihre Stimme	LH		†
-----	Im Westen	HL		†
-----	Lied der Suleika			
-----	Mit Myrthen und Rosen	HL	A-D	†
-----	Seit ich ihn gesehen	HL	DF-DF	†
-----	Stille Traenen	HL		†
-----	Wer machte dich so krank?			
Strauss	Ach Lieb, ich muss nun scheiden	H	D-G	
-----	Befreit			HSC
-----	Breit ueber mein Haupt	LH	GF-AF	HSC
-----	Mit deinen blauen Augen	LH	C-GS	†
-----	Morgen	HML	E-F	†
-----	Ruhe meine Seele			†
Wagner	Elizabeth's prayer (Tannhaeuser)	LMH	DF-GF	†
-----	Elsa's dream (Lohengrin)	MH	EF-AF	†
-----	Five Wesendonck songs			GSC
-----	Mild und leise (Tristan und Isolde)	H	E-A	GSC
-----	Schmerzen	HL		†

(Wagner)	Senta's ballad			GSC
	(Der Fliegende Hollaender)			
-----	Traeume	HL		†
-----	War es so schmaehlich			†
	(Die Walkuere)			
Weber	Und ob die Wolke	H	EF-AF	†
	(Der Freischuetz)			
Wolf	Alle gingen, herz, zu Ruh	HL	C-EF	†
-----	Anakreons Grab	HL	D-D	†
-----	An eine Aeolsharfe			†
-----	Bedeckt mich mit Blumen	HL	B-D	†
-----	Das verlassene Maegdlein	HL	D-EF	†
-----	Denk' es, o Seele	LH	EF-F	†
-----	Der Mond hat eine schwere	HL	BF-DF	†
	Klag' erhoben			
-----	Gebet	HL		†
-----	Herr, was traegt der	HL	B-DS	†
	Boden			
-----	In der Fruehe	HL	C-C	†
-----	Lebe wohl	HL	BF-F	†
-----	Morgenstimmung	LH	C-GS	†
-----	Mueh'voll komm' ich und	H	D-G	†
	beladen			
-----	Neue Liebe	LH	D-AF	†
-----	Um Mitternacht	HL	G-EF	†
-----	Zur Ruh', zur Ruh'	HL	A-GF	†
Wolff	Alle Dinge haben Sprache	M	BF-GF	†
-----	Du bist so jung			HMP

Italian Songs and Arias Employing Sustained Singing

Dramatic Soprano

Beethoven	Ah! perfido	H		DIT
Boito	Morte di Margherita	H	D-B	GSC
	(L'altra notte) (Mefistofele)			
Bononcini	Deh, lascia			HEU
Caccini	Amarilli, mia bella	ML	C-D	†
Caldara	Come raggio di sol	HL	D-F	†
Catalani	Ebben? Ne andrò lontana	H	E-B	RIC
	(La Wally)			
Cimara	Stornellata marinara	HM		RIC
Cimarosa	Bel nume che adoro			RIC
Donaudy	O del mio amato ben	M	EF-F	RIC
Donizetti	O mio Fernando	M	B-A	†
	(La Favorita)			
Durante	Vergin, tutta amor	LM	C-EF	†

274

Gluck	Spiagge amate			†
	(Paride ed Elena)			
Handel	Lascia ch'io pianga	HM	EF-F	†
	(Rinaldo)			
-----	Rendi 'l sereno al ciglio	LH	EF-F	†
	(Sosarme)			
-----	V'adoro pupille			BOO
	(Julius Caesar)			
Mascagni	Un di ero piccina (Iris)			RIC
-----	Voi lo sapete	H	B-A	†
	(Cavalleria Rusticana)			
Mozart	Ch'io mi scordi di te			BOO
-----	Deh, se piacer mi vuoi			RIC
	(La Clemenza di Tito)			
-----	Non mi dir	H	F-B	†
	(Don Giovanni)			
-----	Non più di fiori			†
	(La Clemenza di Tito)			
-----	Parto, parto (La Clemenza	H		AMP
	di Tito) B flat clarinet			
	and piano			
-----	Per pietà, ben mio			†
	(Cosi Fan Tutte)			
-----	Porgi amor (Le Nozze	H	D-AF	†
	di Figaro)			
Pergolesi	Dite ch'ogni momento			BOS
Ponchielli	Suicidio! (La Gioconda)	HM	BF-AF	†
Puccini	In quelle trine morbide	H	DF-BF	RIC
	(Manon Lescaut)			
-----	Tu, che di gel sei cinta			RIC
	(Turandot)			
-----	Un bel di vedremo	H	DF-BF	RIC
	(Madama Butterfly)			
-----	Vissi d'arte (Tosca)	MH	EF-BF	RIC
Respighi	Nebbie			†
-----	Nevicata	HM		BON
Stradella	Così, amor, mi fai languir	HL	F-G	DIT
-----	Se nel ben			CFI
Torelli	Tu lo sai	HL	BF-F	†
Verdi	D'amor sull'ali rosee	H	C-DF	†
	(Il Trovatore)			
-----	Ecco l'orrido campo	H	B-C	RIC
	(Un Ballo in Maschera)			
-----	Madre, pietosa Vergine	H	B-B	RIC
	(La Forza del Destino)			
-----	Morrò, ma prima in grazia			RIC
	(Un Ballo in Maschera)			
-----	Tu che la vanita			RIC
	(Don Carlos)			

275

Dramatic Soprano

Arensky	Autumn	H	CS-FS	GSC
Bach-				
Gounod	Ave Maria			†
Borodin	A dissonance	MH	EF	†
Dvořák	Hear my prayer, O Lord			AMP
-----	Lord thou art my refuge and shield			AMP
-----	Turn Thee to me			AMP
Falla	Vivan los que ríen (La Vida Breve)			AMP
Gliere	Ah, twine no blossoms	HM	CS-F	DIT
Granados	La maja dolorosa	M		INT
Gretchaninoff	Over the steppe	LM	C-G	GSC
Grieg	I love thee	HML	E-F	†
-----	To Norway	M	E-F	DIT
Kjerulf	Synnove's song	M	C-F	GSC
Rachmaninoff	Christ is risen	LM	D-F	GAL
-----	Oh cease thy singing, maiden fair	H	E-A	CFI
-----	O, do not grieve	M	BF-AF	GSC
-----	O thou billowy harvest field	HL	CS-E	GSC
-----	The soldier's bride			†
-----	To the children	MH	F-G	DIT
-----	Vocalise	LH	CS-A	GSC
Sibelius	Black roses	M	A-ES	AMP
Sinding	I hear the gull			JCH
Tchaikovsky	Adieu forêts (Jeanne d'Arc)	HM	BF-FS	GSC
-----	All for you			
-----	None but the lonely heart	HLM	C-F	DIT

American Songs Employing Spirited Singing

Dramatic Soprano

Barber	I hear an army	LH	D-AF	GSC
Bassett	Take joy home	LH	EF-BF	GSC
Beach	The year's at the spring	MH	AF-AF	ASC
Boatner	Oh, what a beautiful city!	HL	D-E	GSC
Burleigh	Joshua fit de battle ob Jericho	LH	DS-E	RIC

(Burleigh)	Little David play on yo harp	HL		RIC
Carpenter	Don't ceare	M	C-D	GSC
-----	If	M	D-E	GSC
-----	Light, my light	M	C-G	GSC
-----	Serenade	LH	CS-A	GSC
Charles	Let my song fill your heart	LH	EF-AF	GSC
Clough- Leighter	My lover he comes on the skee	HM	D-F	BOS
Crist	O come hither	HM	B-GS	CFI
Curran	Ho! Mr. Piper	LH	D-G	GSC
-----	Life	HM	BF-F	GSC
Deis	Come down to Kew			
Giannini	Sing to my heart a song	H	D-B	ELV
Griffes	Elves	H	F-AF	GSC
Guion	Wild geese	M	D-F	CFI
Hadley	My shadow			ASC
Hageman	At the well	LH	EF-AF	GSC
-----	Miranda	HL		GAL
Hindemith	The whistling thief	M	E-F	AMP
Josten	Cupid's counsel	H	EF-AF	GSC
Kountz	The sleigh	HL	D-FS	GSC
LaForge	Song of the open	MH	EF-AF	DIT
Levitzki	Ah, thou beloved one	H	EF-AF	GSC
Mitchell	Love is the wind	MHH	F-A	GAH
Nevin	One spring morning	MH	DS-F	BOS
Nordoff	There shall be more joy	M	CS-FS	AMP
Rogers	The last song	MLH	E-AF	GSC
Rummel	Ecstasy	LMH	GF-AF	GSC
Saar	The little gray dove	MH	D-BF	GSC
Salter	The cry of Rachel	LH	C-AF	GSC
Schuman	Holiday song	M	C-F	GSC
Speaks	Morning	HML	BF-D	GSC
Spross	Will o' the wisp			JCH
Warner	Hurdy gurdy	M	D-F	CFI

British Songs and Arias Employing
Spirited Singing

Dramatic Soprano

Bantock	A feast of lanterns	HM	D-F	GAL
Bax	Oh dear what can the matter be?	M	D-EF	CHE
-----	Shieling song	H	CS-A	CHE
Benjamin	Hedgerow			CUR
Besley	Listening	H	E-AF	CUR

Bishop	Love has eyes	M		†
Bliss	The buckle			CUR
-----	Three jolly gentlemen	H		†
Brewer	The fairy pipers	HML		BOH
Bridge	Love went a-riding	HL		BOS
Dowland	Come again! sweet love	M	D-E	STB
Elgar	Be not extreme, O Lord (Light of Life)			NOV
German	Charming Chloe	HML		NOV
Gibbs	Five eyes	HL	D-D	BOS
-----	Padraic the fidiler			CUR
Head	A piper	HL		BOO
Lehmann	The cuckoo	HH	D-B	BOH
Moeran	Bright cap			OXF
Morley	It was a lover and his lass	HM		DIT
Purcell	Nymphs and shepherds (The Libertine)	HM	C-F	†
Quilter	Blow, blow, thou winter wind	HL	C-E	BOO
-----	It was a lover and his lass	HL	CS-E	BOO
-----	Love's philosophy	LMH	D-A	BOO
Ronald	Love, I have won you	HML	EF-EF	ENO

French Songs Employing Spirited Singing

Dramatic Soprano

Bizet	Ouvre ton coeur	MH	DS-GS	†
Chabrier	Villanelle des petits canards	HML	B-E	†
Chausson	La caravane	MH	CS-A	HAM
-----	Les papillons	M	C-F	GSC
Debussy	Chevaux de bois	H	C-G	†
-----	Fantoches	H	D-A	JOB
-----	Mandoline	HM	BF-F	†
Duni	Les temps passés			LEM
Duparc	Le manoir de Rosamunde	HL	B-F	BOS
-----	Testament	HL		INT
Fauré	Fleur jetée	HM	BF-FS	†
-----	L'hiver a cessé	HL		INT
-----	Mandoline	HL	F-E	†
-----	Toujours	LH	F-AF	†
Fourdrain	Chanson norvégienne	H	E-G	RIC
Georges	La pluie	HL		INT
Gounod	Au printemps	LMH	DF-AF	GSC
-----	Vénise	HL		INT
Hahn	Si mes vers avaient des ailes	HLM	B-FS	†

278

Honegger	Les cloches			SEN
Massenet	Ouvre tes yeux bleus	MH	C-G	†
Milhaud	Chant d'amour	M	C-GF	ESC
-----	Chant du laboureur	M	B-F	ESC
-----	La tourterelle	M	B-G	DUR
Pierné	Ils étaient trois petits chats blancs			MAR
Poldowski	Colombine	H	D-GF	CHE
-----	Dansons la gigue	M	EF-G	MAR
Poulenc	Air vif	H	C-AF	ROU
Ravel	Tout gai	MH	EF-F	DUR
Saint-Saëns	Guitares et mandolines			DUR
-----	L'attente			DUR
Weckerlin	Chantons les amours de Jean	H	D-G	GSC

German Songs and Arias Employing
Spirited Singing

Dramatic Soprano

Bach, J.S.	Herr der Du stark und maechtig bist (Cantata 10)			
-----	Mein glaeubiges Herze (Cantata 68)	HML		†
Beethoven	Die Trommel geruehret			†
-----	Freudvoll und leidvoll	M	DS-E	†
-----	Neue Liebe, neues Leben			†
Brahms	Auf dem Schiffe	LH	GS-A	†
-----	Bei dir sind meine Gedanken	MH	E-FS	†
-----	Blinde Kuh			†
-----	Botschaft	HL	D-F	†
-----	Das Maedchen spricht	H	E-FS	†
-----	Der Gang zur Liebsten	HL		†
-----	Der Jaeger	HL		†
-----	Der Schmied	HL	EF-EF	†
-----	Dort in den Weiden	LH	A-A	†
-----	Juchhe!			†
-----	Klage	LH	FS-FS	†
-----	Meine Liebe ist gruen	MLH	ES-A	†
-----	O liebliche Wangen	MLH	E-G	†
-----	Salome			†
-----	Sehnsucht	H	EF-AF	†
-----	Vergebliches Staendchen	LHM	E-FS	GSC
-----	Wie froh und frisch	HL	B-E	†
Franz	Er ist gekommen	HL	EF-F	†
-----	Sonnenuntergang	HL	CS-FS	†

Haydn	The mermaid's song	M	C-F	PRE
Jensen	Am Ufer des Flusses des Manzanares	H	D-FS	GSC
Loewe	Des Glockenthuermers Tochterlein	H	CS-A	SC
-----	Walpurgisnacht	H	G-G	SC
Mahler	Das Irdische Leben	HL	A-F	INT
-----	Hans und Grethe	HL		INT
-----	Wer hat dies Liedlein erdacht?	HL	BF-E	INT
Marx	Und gestern hat er mir Rosen gebracht	H	E-A	AMP
-----	Valse de Chopin	M	CS-GS	AMP
Mendelssohn	An die Entfernte	M	F-F	
-----	Im Gruenen	H	E-BF	AUG
-----	Neue Liebe	H	CS-A	†
-----	Suleika	H	E-GS	†
Mozart	An Chloe	LH	EF-AF	
Schubert	Am Feierabend	HL	BF-F	†
-----	Aufenthalt	HLM	A-F	†
-----	Die Forelle	MLH	EF-GF	†
-----	Die Post	HML	BF-EF	†
-----	Ellens zweiter Gesang			PET
-----	Erstarrung	HL	D-F	†
-----	Fruehlingssehnsucht	HL	B-E	†
-----	Heidenroeslein			
-----	Mein!	HL		†
-----	Mut	HL		†
-----	Wohin?	HL	B-E	†
Schumann	Auftraege	HL	C-E	†
-----	Er, der Herrlichste von Allen	HL	A-EF	†
-----	Er ist's	HL	BF-EF	†
-----	Fruehlingsnacht	L	CS-E	†
-----	Waldesgespraech	HL	A-FS	†
-----	Widmung	HL	BF-F	†
Strauss	Caecilie	MH	E-B	†
-----	Heimliche Aufforderung	HL	B-E	†
-----	Kling			†
-----	Zuegnung	HL	CS-FS	†
Wagner	Dich theure Halle (Tannhaeuser)	H	DS-A	†
-----	Du bist der Lenz (Die Walkuere)			†
-----	Ho-jo-to-ho! (Die Walkuere)	H	DS-C	†
-----	Stehe still!	HL		†
Weber	Bethoerte, die an meine Liebe glaubt (Euryanthe)			PET

(Weber)	Wie nahte mir der Schlummer (Der Freischuetz)	H	B-B	†
Wolf	Ach, im Maien	HL	C-E	†
-----	Das Koehlerweib ist trunken			PET
-----	Die ihr schwebet	HL	EF-EF	†
-----	Er ist's	H	D-G	†
-----	Erstes Liebeslied eines Maedchens	H	EF-AF	DIT
-----	Fussreise	HL	D-E	†
-----	Geh' Geliebter, geh' jetzt			PET
-----	Ich hab' in Penna	LH		†
-----	Klinge, klinge, mein Pandero	HL	CF-EF	†
-----	Liebe mir in Busen zuendet	M	E-F	†
-----	Lied vom Winde			†

Italian Songs and Arias Employing Spirited Singing

Dramatic Soprano

Bellini	Casta diva (Norma)	H	F-C	†
Bononcini	L'esperto nocchiero (Astarte)	HL	B-E	†
Carissimi	Vittoria, mio core	HLM	B-E	†
Casella	Amante sono vaghiccia di voi			RIC
Cavalli	Donzelle fuggite	HL	C-EF	†
D'Astorga	Vo' cercando in queste valli	H	D-G	STB
Falconieri	Non più d'amore	HL	C-D	DIT
-----	Nudo arciero	HL	AF-AF	DIT
Handel	Ch'io mai vi possa (Siroe)			†
Legrenzi	Che fiero costume	HML	C-D	†
Marcello	Il mio bel foço	LMH	C-G	†
Mozart	Dove sono (Le Nozze di Figaro)	H	D-A	†
-----	Mi tradi quell' alma ingrata (Don Giovanni)			†
-----	Non so più cosa son (Le Nozze di Figaro)	H	EF-G	†
-----	Voi che sapete (Le Nozze di Figaro)	M	C-F	†
Paisiello	Chi vuol la zingarella	L	C-F	GSC
Paradies	M'ha preso alla sua ragna	M	EF-F	GSC
Pergolesi	Confusa, smarrita			GSC
Piccini	Se il ciel mi divide	M	C-F	†

281

(Piccini)	(Alessandro di Indie)			
Ponchielli	Stella del marinar (La Gioconda)	M	B-A	RIC
Respighi	In alto mare			BON
-----	Pioggia			BON
Rontani	Or ch'io non segno più	HL	CS-E	DIT
Rossini	Bel raggio lusinghier (Semiramide)	H	CS-A	GSC
Scarlatti, A.	Se Florindo è fedele	LM	EF-EF	GSC
Verdi	Ernani involami (Ernani)	H	AF-BF	GSC
-----	Merce, dilette amiche (I Vespri Siciliani)	MH	A-CS	GSC
-----	Pace, pace mio Dio (La Forza del Destino)	H	CS-BF	†

Miscellaneous Songs Employing Spirited Singing

Dramatic Soprano

Alnaes	Nu brister I alle de kløfter	L	A-F	HAN
Dvořák	I will sing new songs of gladness	HL		†
Falla	Siete canciones	HL		AMP
Grieg	My Johann	HL	BF-EF	GSC
-----	Simpel sang			
-----	Vaer hilset, I Damer	M	D-F	HAN
-----	With a water lily			
Mussorgsky	Hopak	HM	CS-FS	GSC
Rachmaninoff	Floods of spring	HL		DIT
-----	God took away from me			GSC
-----	Oh, no, I pray do not depart	H		DIT

Songs and Arias Employing Staccato

Dramatic Soprano

Arne, T.	Where the bee sucks	HM		†
Fourdrain	Carnaval	M	C-F	RIC
Handel	Oh! had I Jubal's lyre (Joshua)	H	E-FS	†
Mozart	Das Veilchen	LMH	F-G	GSC
-----	Vedrai carino (Don Giovanni)	H	G-G	†
Saminsky	Queen Estherka's laugh	H	D-A	CFI

282

Scarlatti, A.	Rugiadose odorose	HL	D-E	DIT
Schubert	Der Juengling an der Quelle	LH	E-A	†
Sibella	La Girometta	HML	D-E	GSC
Verdi	Tacea la notte placida (Il Trovatore)	H	D-DF	†

American and British Songs of Popular Appeal

Dramatic Soprano

Balfe	Killarney	H	D-E	GSC
Bassett	Take joy home	LH	EF-BF	GSC
Beach	Ah, love but a day			ASC
Bishop	Love has eyes	M		†
Bliss	The buckle			CUR
Brahe	Bless this house	HML	A-EF	BOO
Cadman	Joy	MH	E-A	GSC
Campbell- Tipton	A spirit flower	LHM	B-G	GSC
Carnevali	Come love, with me	LMH	E-A	JFI
Charles	And so, goodbye	LH	EF-AF	GSC
-----	Let my song fill your heart	LH	EF-AF	GSC
-----	When I have sung my songs	HM	BF-EF	GSC
Clarke ,	Shy one	HL	BF-G	BOH
Curran	Ho! Mr. Piper	LH	D-G	GSC
-----	Life	HM	BF-F	GSC
Del Riego	Homing	HML	BF-E	CHA
Dougherty	Everyone sang			
-----	Love in the dictionary	M	C-G	GSC
Edwards	By the bend of the river	HML	C-E	GSC
-----	Into the night	HML	C-DF	GSC
Elgar	Land of hope and glory			BOO
Fenner	Night song	L	BF-EF	FEN
Fox	The hills of home	HML	BF-DF	CFI
Gaynor	May magic			
German	Who'll buy my lavender?	HML		BOO
Giannini	Sing to my heart a song	H	D-B	ELV
Griselle and Clock	The cuckoo clock	LH	EF-G	GSC
Hely- Hutchinson	Old mother Hubbard	HL	B-E	CFI
Henschel	Morning-hymn	MH	DS-GS	†
La Forge	Song of love	LH		RIC
-----	Song of the open	MH	EF-AF	DIT
Lehmann	The cuckoo	HH	D-B	BOH
Levitzki	Ah, thou beloved one	H	EF-AF	GSC

283

Lieurance	By the waters of Minnetonka			PRE
Manning	In the Luxembourg gardens	HML	BF-D	GSC
Mitchell	Love is the wind	MHH	F-A	GAH
Rasbach	Mountains	LH	DF-AF	GSC
Rich	American Lullaby	LH	C-F	GSC
Rogers	At parting	LH	CS-FS	GSC
Ronald	Down in the forest	HML	C-D	ENO
-----	Love, I have won you	HML	EF-EF	ENO
-----	O, lovely night	HML		BOO
-----	Prelude	HML	B-D	ENO
Russell	Fulfillment	LH	EF-GF	BOS
Rybner	Pierrot	HL		GSC
Saar	The little gray dove	MH	D-BF	GSC
Sachs	The little worm	LH	CS-FS	FLA
Schuman	Holiday song	M	C-F	GSC
Scott	Blackbird's song	M	C-F	GSC
Scott	Think on me	HML	D-EF	GAL
Speaks	In may time	HL	D-E	JCH
-----	Morning	HML	BF-D	GSC
Spross	Will o' the wisp			JCH
Strelezki	Dreams	LMH	B-A	GSC
Taylor	A song for lovers	MH	D-F	JFI
Ware	This day is mine	MH	EF-AF	BOS
Wilson	My lovely Celia	HL	B-E	BOO
Worth	Midsummer	LM	E-A	GSC

(See also Humorous Songs, Negro Spirituals,
Folk songs, Operetta Songs and Opera Arias.)

Miscellaneous Songs Of Popular Appeal

Dramatic Soprano

Alvarez	La partida	HL	DS-E	GSC
Bach-Gounod	Ave Maria			†
Bizet	Agnus Dei	HLM	C-AF	†
-----	Ouvre ton coeur	MH	DS-GS	†
Bohm	Calm as the night	HML	A-EF	†
Cavalli	Donzelle fuggite	HL	C-EF	†
Donaudy	O del mio amato ben	M	EF-F	RIC
Dvořák	Songs my mother taught me	HM	E-E	†
Franz	Dedication	HML	BF-C	†
Gounod	Au printemps	LMH	DF-AF	GSC
Grieg	A dream			†
-----	I love thee	HML	E-F	†
-----	My Johann	HL	BF-EF	GSC

284

Hahn	Si mes vers avaient des ailes	HLM	B-FS	†
Massenet	Elégie	LM	C-GF	GSC
-----	Ouvre tes yeux bleus	MH	C-G	†
Mendelssohn	On wings of song			†
Mozart	Alleluja	LMH	F-C	†
Ponce	Estrellita	LH		†
Rachmaninoff	To the children	MH	F-G	DIT
Reichardt	In the time of roses			†
Rossini	La danza	MH	E-A	GSC
Schubert	An die Musik	HL	A-DS	†
-----	Ave Maria	LMH	F-F	GSC
-----	Staendchen			
Schumann	Widmung	HL	BF-F	†
Sibella	La Girometta	HML	D-E	GSC
Sieczynski	Vienna, city of my dreams			HAR
Stolz	Im Prater blueh'n die Baeume			
Strauss, J.	Blue Danube waltz			GSC
Strauss, R.	Zueignung	HL	CS-FS	†
Tchaikovsky	None by the lonely heart	HLM	C-F	DIT

(See also Humorous Songs, Negro Spirituals,
Folk Songs, Operetta Songs and Opera Arias.)

Arias From British Operas

Dramatic Soprano

Britten	Church scene (Peter Grimes)			
-----	Embroidery aria (Peter Grimes)			
Handel	Trip, blithe streamlet (Serse)			
Purcell	I attempt from love's sickness to fly (The Indian Queen)	MH	CS-E	†
-----	Music for a while (Oedipus)	LH		SC
-----	Nymphs and shepherds (The Libertine)	HM	C-F	†
-----	The Plaint (The Fairy Queen)			
-----	When I am laid in earth (Dido and Aeneas)	LH	C-G	†

Arias From French Operas

Dramatic Soprano

Berlioz	D'amour l'ardente flamme (La Damnation de Faust)			NOV
David	Charmant oiseau (La Perle du Brésil)	M	D-E	†
Gaveaux	Dieu d'Israel (L'Enfant Prodigue)			
Gluck	Adieu, conservez dans votre âme (Iphigénie en Aulide)			†
-----	Ah, malgré moi (Alceste)			†
-----	Divinités du Styx (Alceste)	MH	DF-AF	†
-----	Grands dieux (Alceste)	H	E-BF	GSC
-----	L'ai-je bien entendu? (Iphigenie en Aulide)			†
-----	Le perfide Renaud me fuit (Armide)			PET
-----	Non! ce n'est point (Alceste)	H	E-G	†
Gossec	Ah! faut-il me venger (Thésée)			LEM
Gounod	Plus grand, dans son obscurité (La Reine de Saba)	MH	CS-B	†
Halévy	Il va venir (La Juive)	H	D-CF	†
Lully	Bois épais (Amadis)	ML	C-EF	†
-----	Chant du Vénus (Revenez amours) (Thésée)			LEM
Massenet	Charmes des jours passés (Hérodiade)			HEU
-----	Dis-moi que je suis belle (Thaïs)	H	D-B	HEU
-----	Il est doux, il est bon (Hérodiade)	MH	EF-BF	GSC
-----	Pleurez, mes yeux (Le Cid)			HEU
-----	Plus de tourments (Le Cid)	H	F-BF	HEU
Meyerbeer	Ah! mon fils (Le Prophète)	M	B-AS	†
-----	Nobles Seigneurs, salut! (Les Huguenots)	LH	C-C	†
-----	O beau pays (Les Huguenots)	H	CS-D	GSC
Offenbach	Couplets de l'aveu (La Périchole)			
-----	Elle a fui, la tourterelle (Tales of Hoffman)	H	D-A	GSC
Reyer	O palais radieux (Sigurd)			HEU

(Reyer)	Salut, splendeur du jour (Sigurd)			HEU
Spontini	O nume tutelar (La Vestale)			
-----	Toi que je laisse sur la terre (La Vestale)			LEM
-----	Toi que j'implore (La Vestale)			LEM

Arias From German Operas

Dramatic Soprano

Beethoven	Abscheulicher, wo eilst du hin? (Fidelio)		B-B	†
Korngold	Marietta's song (The Dead City)	MH	F-BF	AMP
Strauss	Composer's song (Ariadne auf Naxos)			BOO
-----	Da geht er hin (Der Rosenkavalier)			BOO
-----	Es gibt ein Reich (Ariadne auf Naxos)			BOO
Wagner	Dich theure Halle (Tannhaeuser)	H	DS-A	†
-----	Du bist der Lenz (Die Walkuere)			†
-----	Elizabeth's prayer (Tannhaeuser)	LMH	DF-GF	†
-----	Elsa's dream (Lohengrin)	MH	EF-AF	†
-----	Euch Lueften die mein Klagen (Lohengrin)			†
-----	Ho-jo-to-ho! (Die Walkuere)	H	DS-C	†
-----	Mild und leise (Tristan und Isolde)	H	E-A	†
-----	O Sachs! mein Freund! (Die Meistersinger)			GSC
-----	Senta's ballad (Der Fliegende Hollaender)			GSC
-----	Starke Scheite (Goetterdaemmerung)			†
-----	War es so schmaehlich (Die Walkuere)			†
Weber	Bethoerte die an meine Liebe glaubt (Euryanthe)			DIT
-----	Ozean, du Ungeheur (Oberon)	H	C-C	GSC

| (Weber) | Und ob die Wolke (Der Freischuetz) | H | EF-AF | † |
| ----- | Wie nahte mir der Schlummer (Der Freischuetz) | H | B-B | † |

Arias From Italian Operas

Dramatic Soprano

Bellini	Casta diva (Norma)	H	F-C	†
Boito	Morte di Margherita (L'Altra notte) (Mefistofele)	H	D-B	GSC
Catalani	Dove son (Loreley)			SON
-----	Ebben? Ne andrò lontana (La Wally)	H	E-B	RIC
Donizetti	O mio Fernando (La Favorita)	M	B-A	†
Mascagni	Un di ero piccina (Iris)			RIC
-----	Voi lo sapete (Cavalleria Rusticana)	H	B-A	†
Monteverdi	Lasciatemi morire (Arianna)	ML	D-D	†
Mozart	Al desio di chi t'adora (Appendix, Nozze di Figaro)			
-----	Come scoglio (Così Fan Tutte)			†
-----	Deh, se piacer mi vuoi (La Clemenza di Tito)			RIC
-----	Dove sono (Le Nozze di Figaro)	H	D-A	†
-----	Mi tradi quell' alma ingrata (Don Giovanni)			†
-----	Non mi dir (Don Giovanni)	H	F-B	†
-----	Non più di fiori (La Clemenza di Tito)			†
-----	Non so più cosa son (Le Nozze di Figaro)	H	EF-G	†
-----	Or sai, chi l'onore (Don Giovanni)			GSC
-----	Parto, parto (La Clemenza di Tito) B flat clarinet and piano	H		AMP
-----	Per pietà, ben mio (Cosi Fan Tutte)			†
-----	Porgi amor (Le Nozze di Figaro)	H	D-AF	†
-----	Vedrai carino (Don Giovanni)	H	G-B	†

288

(Mozart)	Voi che sapete (Le Nozze di Figaro)	M	C-F	†
Ponchielli	Stella del marinar (La Gioconda)	M	B-A	RIC
-----	Suicidio! (La Gioconda)	HM	BF-AF	†
Puccini	Donde lieta uscì (La Boheme)			
-----	In quelle trine morbide (Manon Lescaut)	H	DF-BF	RIC
-----	Laggiù nel soledad (La Fanciulla del West)			RIC
-----	Non la sospiri (Tosca)			RIC
-----	Tu, che di gel sei cinta (Turandot)			RIC
-----	Un bel dì vedremo (Madama Butterfly)	H	DF-BF	RIC
-----	Vissi d'arte (Tosca)	MH	EF-BF	RIC
Rossini	Bel raggio lusinghier (Semiramide)	H	CS-A	GSC
Verdi	Ave Maria (Otello)	H	EF-AF	GSC
-----	D'amor sull'ali rosee (Il Trovatore)	H	C-DF	†
-----	Ecco l'orrido campo (Un Ballo in Maschera)	H	B-C	RIC
-----	Ernani involami (Ernani)	H	AF-BF	GSC
-----	Madre, pietosa Vergine (La Forza del Destino)	H	B-B	RIC
-----	Merce, dilette amiche (I Vespri Siciliani)	MH	A-CS	GSC
-----	Morrò, ma prima in grazia (Un Ballo in Maschera)			RIC
-----	O cieli azzuri (Aida)	H	B-C	†
-----	O don fatale (Don Carlos)	MH	CF-CF	†
-----	Oh patria mia (Aida)	H	B-C	GSC
-----	Pace, pace mio Dio (La Forza del Destino)	H	CS-BF	†
-----	Ritorna vincitor (Aida)	H	DF-BF	†
-----	Salce, salce (Otello)	H	CS-FS	RIC
-----	Tu che la vanita (Don Carlos)			RIC
-----	Un macchia è qui tuttora (Macbeth)			

Miscellaneous Opera Arias

Dramatic Soprano

Borodin	Arioso of Jaroslavna (Prince Igor)		BOO

Falla	Vivan los que ríen (La Vida Breve)			AMP
Menotti	To this we've come (The Consul)			
Rimsky- Korsakov	Song of the shepherd lehl (Snegourotchka)	LM		DIT
Tchaikovsky	Adieu forêts	HM	BF-FS	GSC
-----	Letter scene (Eugene Onegin)			GSC

Arias From Oratorios and Latin Works

Dramatic Soprano

Elgar	Be not extreme, O Lord (Light of Life)			NOV
Gaul	These are they (The Holy City)	H	E-GS	GSC
Handel	Angels ever bright and fair (Theodora)	H	E-F	†
-----	Come unto Him (The Messiah)	MH	F-G	†
-----	How beautiful are the feet of them (The Messiah)	H		†
-----	I know that my Redeemer liveth (The Messiah)	MH	E-GS	†
-----	Let me wander not unseen (L'Allegro)	M	D-G	†
-----	Recitative and aria of Nitocris (Belshazzer)			BOO
Mendelssohn	Hear ye, Israel (Elijah)	H	E-A	†
-----	I will sing of Thy great mercies (Saint Paul)	H	E-F	†
-----	Jerusalem, thou that killest (Saint Paul)	H	F-F	†
Mozart	Et incarnatus est (C Minor Mass)			PET

Cantata Arias

Dramatic Soprano

| Bach, J.S. | Herr, der Du stark und
maechtig bist (Cantata 10) | | | |

290

(Bach)	Mein glaeubiges Herze (Cantata 68)	HML		†
-----	Sheep may safely graze (Cantata 208) 2 Flutes and continuo	LM	EF-GF	GAL
Bruch	Ave Maria (Das Feuerkreuz)	LH	D-BF	AMP
Debussy	Air de Lia (L'Enfant Prodigue)	H	E-A	DUR
Handel	Have mercy Lord (Te Deum)	HM		†
Tchaikovsky	Prayer (Moscow Cantata)	M	A-GF	GAL

Operetta, Musical Comedy or Show Songs

Dramatic Soprano

De Koven	Oh promise me (Robin Hood)	HML	C-D	†
-----	Ah! sweet mystery of life (Naughty Marietta)	LMH	A-A	WIT
-----	I can't do that sum (Babes in Toyland)			WIT
-----	Kiss me again (Mlle. Modiste)	LHM	CS-A	WIT
-----	'Neath the southern moon (Naughty Marietta)			
Kern	All the things you are (Very Warm for May)	M	BF-F	HAR
-----	My Bill (Show Boat)			BRO
-----	The song is you (Music in the Air)	M	C-F	HAR
-----	You are love (Show Boat)			CHA
Lehar	Lippen Schweigen (The Merry Widow)	LMH	D-A	CHA
-----	Vilia (The Merry Widow)			CHA
Porter	Begin the Beguine (Jubilee)	L	BF-F	HAR
-----	Night and day (Gay Divorcee)	M	BF-EF	HAR
Rodgers	Out of my dreams (Oklahoma)			CHA
Romberg	Lover come back to me (New Moon)	H	D-G	HAR
Strauss, J.	Love's roundelay (A Waltz Dream)			MAR
-----	Czardas (Die Fledermaus)			BOO

Youmans	Through the years (Through the Years)	HML	A-F	MLR

Song Cycles (Or groups of songs)
Dramatic Soprano

Bax	Celtic song cycle	MH	BF-A	CHE
Beethoven	Irish songs Piano, violin and cello			
-----	Scotch songs Piano, violin and cello			
-----	Sechs geistliche Lieder			
Bernstein	I hate music	H	C-A	WIT
Brahms	Five songs of Ophelia	HL	B-EF	†
-----	Two songs for alto, viola and piano			
Carpenter	Gitanjali	M	B-G	GSC
Chanler	The children (9 songs)	M	C-G	GSC
Chausson	Poème de l'amour et de la mer	H		INT
Cornelius	Bridal songs			INT
-----	Six Christmas songs	HL		BOS
Crist	Chinese mother goose rhymes	H	C-G	CFI
Debussy	Chansons de Bilitis	M	C-FS	†
Dvořák	Gypsy songs	LH	D-A	AMP
Falla	Siete canciones	HL		AMP
Fauré	Le jardin clos	M	C-E	DUR
Granados	La maja dolorosa	M		INT
Grieg	Haugtussa	M	B-GF	PET
Holst	Four songs for voice and violin	M	C-G	CHE
——Mussorgsky	The nursery	M	C-G	INT
Poulenc	Tel jour, telle nuit	M	B-A	DUR
Ravel	Shéhérazade	M	CS-G	DUR
Schubert	Die schoene Muellerin	HL		†
-----	Die Winterreise			GSC
-----	Songs of Mignon			PET
Schumann	Frauenliebe und Leben	HL		†
-----	Lieder der Braut	H	D-A	†
-----	Liederkreis			
Slonimsky	Gravestones at Hancock, New Hampshire	H	D-G	AXE
Strauss	Four last songs			
Wagner	Five Wesendonck songs			GSC
Woodford-Finden	Indian love lyrics			BOO

Solo Cantatas

Dramatic Soprano

Foss	The song of songs	H		CFI
Pergolesi	Salve Regina 5			

(See Solo Cantatas of Pergolesi, Handel and
Scarlatti, Kirchenkantaten of Buxtehude and
Symphoniae Sacrae of Schuetz)

Concert Arias

Dramatic Soprano

Beethoven	Ah! Perfido	H		DIT
Mendelssohn	Infelice (concert aria, opus 94)	H	D-BF	GSC
Mozart	Ch'io mi scordi di te			BOO
-----	Misera, dove son			BOO
Schubert	Auf dem Strom			

Christmas Songs

Dramatic Soprano

Adam	O holy night	LMH		†
Bax	A Christmas carol	H	DF-A	CHE
Bergsma	Lulee, lullay	H	E-G	CFI
Brahms	Geistliches Wiegenlied Piano and viola			†
Branscombe	Hail ye time of holidays			
Carr	As on the night	M	E-FS	GSC
Clokey	No lullaby need Mary sing			JFI
Dunhill	To the Queen of Heaven	M	C-G	GSC
Eakin	What of that midnight long ago	M	D-F	GAL
Elmore and Reed	Come all ye who weary	L	C-C	JFI
France	A Christmas lullaby	M	DS-F	GAL
Hageman	Christmas eve	HML	BF-EF	GAL
Handel	How beautiful are the feet of them (The Messiah)	H		†
Harker	A child is born in Bethlehem	LH	D-G	GSC
-----	There's a song in the air	HL	DF-D	GSC
Head	A slumber song of the Madonna			BOH

(Head)	The little road to Bethlehem	MH	EF-AF	BOO
-----	The three mummers			BOO
Ireland	The Holy Boy	MH	D-G	BOO
Kountz	The sleigh	HL	D-FS	GSC
Lehmann	No candle was there and no fire	MH	EF-G	CHA
Lynn	Gently little Jesus	L	BF-BF	DIT
-----	The magic night of Christmas	M	D-D	DIT
Martin	The Holy Child	HML	G-G	ENO
McKinney	The Holy Mother sings	MH	AF-AF	JFI
Niles	Our lovely Lady singing	M	EF-F	GSC
Reger	The Virgin's slumber song	MMH	G-G	†
Schubert	Ave Maria	LMH	F-F	†
Strauss	Die heiligen drei Koenige	H	C-G	
Thiman	I saw three ships	L		NOV
Thorp	Come, Mary, take courage	M	DS-FS	GAL
Trunk	The Christ child in the manger	HM		AMP
Warren	Christmas candle	HML	D-E	GSC
Wentzel	Lamkins Cello and piano			GRA
Wolf	Schlafendes Jesuskind	HL	AS-F	†
Wright	A Babe lies in His cradle warm	MD	D-D	GSC
Yon	Gesu Bambino	HL	B-E	JFI

Easter Songs

Dramatic Soprano

Bantock	Easter hymn	M	FS-F	CHE
Barnes	Easter	HM	D-EF	GSC
Chaffin	Easter message	MH	D-G	FLA
Curran	Crucifixion			
Davis	Christ is risen today	M		GAL
Diack	All in the April evening	LMH	D-G	BOO
Granier	Hosanna	HH	F-BF	DIT
Guion	At the cry of the first bird	H	D-G	GSC
Hageman	Christ went up into the hills	LH	EF-AF	CFI
Handel	I know that my Redeemer liveth (The Messiah)	MH	E-GS	†
Huhn	Christ is risen	HM	C-E	ASC
LaForge	Before the Crucifix	HML	BF-EF	GSC
Lekberg	A ballad of tree and the Master	H	E-A	GAL

Mahler	Um Mitternacht	HL		INT
O'Connor	Alleluia	ML	D-D	BOO
O'Hara	There is no death	LMH	EF-AF	CHA
Rachmaninoff	Christ is risen	LM	D-F	GAL
Schubert	Ave Maria	LMH	F-F	†
Scott	Angels roll the rock away	MH	E-G	HUN
-----	The first Easter morn	LH	F-G	GSC
Wolf	Herr, was traegt der Boden	HL	B-DS	†
Yon	Christ triumphant	MH	E-A	JFI
-----	O faithful Cross	HM	C-EF	JFI
-----	Our Paschal Joy	LH	AF-AF	JFI

Patriotic Songs

Dramatic Soprano

Alberti	A nation's prayer	H		ELV
Cadman	Glory	H	EF-G	GAL
Dungan	Eternal life	HL		PRE
Elgar	Land of hope and glory			BOO
Foster, F.	The Americans come	MH	F-BF	JFI
Howe	To the unknown soldier	H	D-G	GSC
Lester	Greater love hath no man	LH	B-E	CFI
O'Hara	There is no death	LMH	EF-AF	CHA
Steffe	Battle hymn of the Republic			
Ward				
Stephens	Phantom legions	MHH	EF-BF	CHA

Sacred Songs

Dramatic Soprano

Allitsen	The Lord is my light	LMH	D-AF	BOO
Bach, J.S.	Draw near to me	HML		GSC
-----	Sheep may safely graze (Cantata 208) 2 Flutes and continuo	LM	EF-GF	GAL
Beethoven	The worship of God in nature			
Bitgood	Be still and know that I am God	ML		GRA
-----	The greatest of these is love	M		GRA
Bizet	O Lord be merciful	HL		GSC
Bone and Fenton	Thy word is a lamp	LH	C-F	ROW
Buck	Fear not ye, O Israel	HLM		GSC

295

Campbell-Tipton	I will give thanks unto the Lord	LMH	DF-AF	GSC
Chadwick	A ballad of trees and the Master	HML	A-F	DIT
Charles	Love is of God	H	D-G	GSC
Clokey	God is in everything	LH	D-G	JFI
Creston	Psalm 23	MH	F-AF	GSC
Davis	Let not your heart be troubled	HML		WOO
-----	Trust in the Lord	MH	CS-G	GAL
Dvořák	God is my shepherd			AMP
-----	Hear my prayer, O Lord			AMP
-----	Turn Thee to me			AMP
Edmunds	Praise we the Lord	HL	D-D	ROW
Gaul	These are they (The Holy City)	H	E-GS	GSC
Goodhall	The mountain	M	D-E	GAL
Gounod	O Divine Redeemer	LMH	C-G	GSC
Guion	Prayer	HL		GSC
Handel	Have mercy Lord (Te Deum)	HM		†
-----	How beautiful are the feet of them (The Messiah)	H		†
-----	I know that my Redeemer liveth (The Messiah)	MH	E-GS	†
-----	Thanks be to Thee	M	CS-E	†
Harker	How beautiful upon the mountains	MLH	EF-G	GSC
Henschel	Morning-hymn	MH	DS-GS	†
Holst	The heart worships	ML	BF-D	STB
Liddle	How lovely are Thy dwellings	HML		BOS
MacDermid	In my Father's house are many mansions	HML		FRS
Malotte	The Lord's Prayer			GSC
-----	The twenty-third Psalm	HLM	C-F	GSC
Mendelssohn	Hear ye, Israel (Elijah)	H	E-A	†
-----	I will sing of Thy great mercies (Saint Paul)	H	E-F	†
Schubert	The Omnipotent			
Scott	Come ye blessed	LMH	EF-AF	GSC
-----	Ride on, ride on	HML		FLA
Sowerby	Thou art my strength	H	E-G	GRA
Speaks	The Lord is my light	HML		GSC
-----	Thou wilt keep him in perfect peace	HML		GSC
Stevenson	Praise	M	F-F	CFI
Stickles	Saith the Lord	LH	D-F	CHA

Tchaikovsky	Lord, Almighty God (Moscow Cantata)	M		GRA
Thiman	Thou wilt keep him in perfect peace	H	D–G	GRA
Thompson	My Master hath a garden	M		ECS
Ware	The greatest of these	LH	EF–AF	BOS
Weaver	Assurance	H	EF–G	GAL
-----	Build thee more stately mansions	M	C–E	GAL
-----	Praise the Lord his glories show	H	E–G	GAL
Wolf	Morning prayer (Morgenstimme)			
-----	Prayer (Gebet)			

Wedding Songs

Dramatic Soprano

Barnby	O perfect love	M	C–G	DIT
Beethoven	Ich liebe dich	HL	BF–DF	†
Cough-Leighter	Possession	MH	DF–AF	GSC
DeKoven	Oh promise me (Robin Hood)	HML	C–D	†
Dello Joio	How do I love thee?	H	D–G	CFI
Franck	O Lord most Holy	LM	A–FS	BOS
Grieg	I love thee	HML	E–F	†
Lippe	How do I love thee?			BOS
Manney	Consecration	MHH	E–A	DIT
Marx	Hat dich die Liebe beruehrt	MH	EF–BF	AMP
Ronald	Love, I have won you	HML	EF–EF	ENO
Rowley	Here at thine altar, Lord			NOV
Sacco	With this ring	M	F–F	BVC
Saxe	Wedded souls			
Schubert	Du bist die Ruh	LMH	EF–AF	†
-----	Ungeduld	HML		†
Schumann	Du Ring an meinem Finger	HL	C–F	†
-----	Widmung	HL	BF–F	†
Sowerby	O perfect love	MH	EF–AF	GRA
Strauss	Ich liebe dich			†
Thiman	The God of love my shepherd is	ML	A–D	NOV
Willan	O perfect love	HM	E–FS	GRA

Songs and Arias With Added
Accompanying Instrument

Dramatic Soprano

Beethoven	Irish songs Piano, violin and cello			
-----	Scotch songs Piano, violin and cello			
Brahms	Geistliches Wiegenlied Piano and viola			†
-----	Gestillte Sehnsucht Viola and piano			†
Buxtehude	Singet dem Herrn Violin and piano			
Chausson	Chanson perpétuelle String quartet	H	CS-GS	ROU
-----	Le colibri Violin or cello	M	F-GF	BOS
Curran	Nocturne Violin	HML	B-DS	GSC
Holst	Four songs for voice and violin	M	C-G	CHE
Mozart	Parto, parto (La Clemenza di Tito) B flat clarient and piano	H		AMP
Thomson	Stabat mater aria String quartet	H	D-BF	COS
Wentzel	Lamkins Cello and piano			GRA

Coloratura, Lyric or Dramatic Soprano

Anon	Have you seen but a white lily grow	H	E-F	GSC
Balfe	Killarney	H	D-E	GSC
Barber	A Nun takes the veil	MH	G-G	GSC
-----	Monks and raisons	M	DF-E	GSC
-----	Rain has fallen	HM	D-E	GSC
Bax	Oh dear what can the matter be	M	D-EF	CHE
Bloch	The vagabond	M	E-E	GSC
Boatner	Oh what a beautiful city	HL	D-E	GSC
-----	On mah journey	LH	EF-EF	RIC
Bowles	Cabin	ML	CS-CS	GSC
-----	Letter to Freddy	M	EF-EF	GSC
Burleigh	Joshua fit de battle ob Jericho	LH	DS-E	RIC
Carpenter	If	M	D-E	GSC
Chanler	The lamb	M	C-D	AMP
Cowles	The fragrance of a song	HM	E-F	GSC
De Koven	Oh promise me (Robin Hood)	HML	C-D	GSC
Dowland	Awake sweet love	M	E-F	STB
-----	Come again, sweet love	M	D-E	STB
-----	Flow, my tears	M	D-E	STB
Ganz	The angels are stooping	MH	GF-A	GSC
Gibbs	Five eyes	HL	D-D	BOS
Grainger	The sprig of thyme	LH	E-FS	GSC
Green	My lips shall speak the praise	M	E-F	OXF
Hadley	My shadow	M	D-E	AEC
Handel	Angels ever bright and fair (Theodora)	H	E-F	GSC
-----	Come unto Him (The Messiah)	MH	F-G	GSC
-----	Love's a dear deceitful jewel	LH	F-F	RBR
Hindemith	The whistling thief	M	E-F	AMP
Hopkinson	My love is gone to sea	HL	D-E	ASC
Howe	Berceuse	HM	FF-F	GSC
Hughes	Open the door softly	LMH	G-G	ENO
Johnson	His name so sweet	H	D-D	CFI
Kagen	All day I hear	H	F-FS	WTR
-----	Let it be forgotten	M	F-F	WTR
MacDowell	The Sea	HL	D-D	BRH
MacGimsey	Sweet little Jesus Boy	ML	D-D	CFI
Manning	Shoes	M	EF-F	GSC

Metcalf	At nightfall	HML	C-DF	ASC
Milford	So sweet love seemed	HL	D-D	GRA
-----	Love on my heart	H	FS-FS	NOV
Naginski	Under the harvest moon	M	D-E	GSC
Ronald	Down in the forest	HML	C-D	ENO
-----	Love I have won you	HML	EF-EF	ENO
Rosseter	When Laura smiles	LM	D-E	STB
Sacco	Mexican serenade	HL	D-EF	BOS
Sargent	Three a. m.	M	DF-E	GSC
Scott	Think on me	HML	D-EF	GAL
Shaw	Song of the palanquin bearers	LH	E-F	CUR
Speaks	In May time	HL	D-E	JCH
Stephenson	Love is a sickness	HML	C-D	BOO
-----	Ships that pass in the night	HML	DF-DF	BOO
Taylor Vaughan Williams	O can ye sew cushions	H	G-G	OXF
Williams	Robin Hood and the pedlar	M	D-E	OXF
Warren	Wander shoes	LH	F-G	FLA
-----	White horses of the sea	LH	F-G	GSC

French Songs of Limited Range

Coloratura, Lyric or Dramatic Soprano

David	Charmant oiseau (La Perle du Bresil)	M	D-E	GSC
Duparc	L'invitation au voyage	HM	E-F	BOS
Fauré	Adieu	MH	F-F	MAR
-----	En prière	H	F-F	MAR
-----	Ici-bas!	H	FS-G	GSC
-----	La fée aux chansons	LH	F-F	HAM
-----	La parfum imperissable	LH	GF-GF	†
-----	Mandoline	HL	F-E	GSC
-----	Serenade Toscane	MH	G-AF	HAM
-----	Spleen	H	E-FS	MAR
-----	Sylvie	HL	E-F	INT
Ferrari	Le jardin d'amour	LM	EF-F	GSC
Franck	Le mariage des roses	M	E-FS	BOS
-----	Lied	LH	FS-FS	†
Hue	J'ai pleuré en rêve	HL	D-E	BOS
-----	Sonnez les matines	H	FS-G	HEU
Koechlin	L'air	M	F-FS	ROU
Lully	Au clair de la lune	M	E-D	CFI
Massenet	Crepuscule	M	D-E	GSC
Poldowski	Effet de neige	M	EF-F	CHE
Poulenc	Bleuet	H	FS-GF	DUR

Saint Saens	Mai	H	G–FS	DUR
Weckerlin	Aminte	M	C–D	GSC

German Songs of Limited Range

Coloratura, Lyric or Dramatic Soprano

Brahms	Bei dir sind meine Gedanken	MH	E–FS	GSC
-----	Das Maedchen spricht	H	E–FS	CFI
-----	Dort in den Weiden	LH	A–A	CFI
-----	Klage	LH	FS–FS	CFI
-----	Mein Maedel hat einen Rosenmund	M	F–F	GSC
-----	Mit vierzig Jahren	HL	FS–D	CFI
-----	O wuesst ich doch dem Weg zurueck	H	E–FS	CFI
Franz	Er ist gekommen	HL	EF–F	DIT
-----	For Music	ML	C–D	DIT
Haydn	My mother bids me bind my hair	M	E–E	GSC
-----	She never told her love	M	D–EF	
Hindemith	The moon	M	DS–EF	AMP
Loewe	Walpurgisnacht	H	G–G	SC
Mendelssohn	Bei der Wiege	M	DF–EF	GSC
-----	Das erste Veilchen	M	F–F	AUG
-----	I will sing of Thy great mercies (Saint Paul)	H	E–F	GSC
-----	Jerusalem, Thou that killest (Saint Paul)	H	F–F	GSC
-----	Morgengruss	M	D–E	AUG
Mozart	Abendempfindung	M	E–F	
-----	Warnung	HM	C–D	
-----	Wiegenlied	MH	G–G	GSC
Reger	Des kindes Gebet	H	F–G	BOT
Schubert	An den Mond	HL	F–GF	GSC
-----	Das Echo	M	F–F	GSC
-----	Der Musensohn	LH	FS–G	DIT
-----	Der Schmetterling	LH	E–F	DIT
-----	Halt	HL	E–F	GSC
-----	Heimliches Lieben	LH	F–G	DIT
-----	Im Abendrot	HL	C–D	GSC
-----	Nacht und Traeume	HL	C–DF	CFI
-----	Naehe des Geliebten	HL	D–EF	DIT
-----	Um Mitternacht	H	F–G	GSC
-----	Wanderers Nachtlied, 2	LH	F–F	GSC
Schumann	Alte Laute	HL	DF–DF	DIT
-----	Du bist wie eine Blume	HM	F–EF	GSC
-----	Intermezzo	HL	C–D	GSC

(Schumann)	Maerzveilchen	HL	C-C	DIT
-----	Marienwuermchen	HL	D-D	GSC
-----	Mondnacht	M	E-FS	GSC

Italian Songs of Limited Range

Coloratura, Lyric or Dramatic Soprano

Bassani	Posate, dormite la serenata	H	EF-F	GSC
Bononcini	Deh piu a me non v'ascondete	LH	EF-F	GSC
Caccini	Amarilli, mia bella	ML	C-D	GSC
Caldara	Sebben crudele	HML	E-DS	GSC
-----	Selve amiche, ombrose piante	HM	E-E	GSC
Cesti	Ah! quanto è vero (Il Pomo d'Oro)	HL	F-F	DIT
-----	Che angoscia che affanno (Il Pomo d'Oro)	HL	C-DF	DIT
Cimara	Fiocca la neve	LMH	G-G	GSC
Donaudy	O del mio amato ben	M	EF-F	RIC
Falconieri	Non più d'amore	HL	C-D	DIT
-----	Nudo arciero	HL	AF-AF	DIT
Gasparini	Caro laccio, dolce nodo	M	EF-EF	GSC
Handel	Rendi'l sereno al ciglio (Sosarme)	LH	EF-F	GSC
Legrenzi	Che fiero costume	HML	C-D	GSC
Lotti	Pur dicesti, o bocca bella	LMH	E-FS	GSC
Monteverdi	Lasciatemi morire	ML	D-D	DIT
Mozart	Vedrai, carino (Don Giovanni)	H	G-G	GSC
Paradies	M'ha preso alla sua ragna	M	EF-F	GSC
Pergolesi	Nina	HL	CS-D	DIT
Sadero	Stornello pugliese	M	F-F	GSC
Scarlatti, A.	Se Florindo è fedele	LM	EF-EF	GSC
Sgambati	Separazione	LMH	FS-G	GSC
Tosti	La Serenata	HLM	D-EF	GSC

Other Songs of Limited Range

Coloratura, Lyric or Dramatic Soprano

Bantock	Easter hymn	M	FS-F	CHE
Beethoven	A prayer	M	EF-F	BIR

302

Buck	The Virgin's lullaby	HL	B–CS	GSC
Chopin	Lithuanian song	ML	C–C	GSC
Cui	The statue at Czarskoe-Selo	HM	DF–EF	DIT
Dvořák	Songs my mother taught me	HM	E–E	GSC
Edmunds	Praise we the Lord	HL	D–D	ROW
Franck	O Lord most Holy	LM	A–FS	BOS
Goodhall	The mountain	M	D–E	GAL
Gounod	There is a green hill far away	LMH	E–F	GSC
Grieg	I love thee	HML	E–F	GSC
-----	In the boat	LM	D–EF	DIT
-----	To Norway	M	E–F	DIT
Lynn	The magic night of Christmas	M	D–D	DIT
Martin	The Holy Child	HML	G–G	ENO
Neidlinger	The manger cradle	L	EF–F	GSC
Niles	Our lovely lady singing	M	EF–F	GSC
Rachmaninoff	To the children	MH	F–G	DIT
Reger	The Virgin's slumber song	MH	G–G	DIT
Reimann	Joseph tender, Joseph mine	M	F–F	GRA
Schubert	They sang that night in Bethlehem	LMH	EF–EF	GSC
Scott	The first Easter morn	LH	F–G	GSC
Tchaikovsky	A legend	M	D–E	GSC
Turina	Rima	H	A–A	AMP
Tuthill	Prayer for those at home	HL	C–D	BOH
Valverde	Clavelitos	MH	E–F	GSC
Vaughan Williams	And all in the morning	L	D E	GAL
Warlock	The first mercy	M	F–F	BOO
Warren	Christmas candle	HML	D–E	GSC

Operatic Duets

Coloratura, Lyric or Dramatic Soprano

Bellini	Mira o Norma (Norma)	S&A	RIC
-----	Oh ciel che tento (La Sonnambula)	S&Bs	RIC
-----	Prendi l'anel ti dono (La Sonnambula)	S&S	RIC
-----	Sola furtiva al tempio (Norma)	S&S	RIC

303

(Bellini)	Son geloso del zefiro (La Sonnambula)	S&T	RIC
Berlioz	Reine d'un jeune empire (Les Troyens)	S&A	CHO
Bizet	Parle moi de ma mère (Carmen)	S&T	†
Boito	Lontano, lontano (Mefistofele)	S&T	†
Borodin	Duet of Jaroslavna and Galitsky (Prince Igor)	S&Bs	†
-----	Duet of Jaroslavna and Igor (Prince Igor)	S&Br	BOO
Catalani	Deh vieni (Loreley)	S&T	RIC
-----	M'hai salvato (La Wally)	S&T	RIC
Charpentier	L'enfant serait sage (Louise)	S&Br	HEU
Cilea	Io son sua per l'amor (Adriana Lecouvreur)	S&A	SON
Debussy	Ah! ah! tout va bien (Pelleas et Melisande)	S&Br	DUR
-----	Duo de la fontaine (Pelleas et Melisande)	S&T	DUR
-----	Duo de la lettre (Pelleas et Melisande)	S&Br	DUR
Delibes	C'est le Dieu de la jeunesse (Lakmé)	S&T	HEU
-----	Dans la forêt près de nous (Lakmé)	S&T	BRO
-----	Lakmé c'est toi (Lakmé)	S&T	HEU
-----	Sous le dome épais (Lakmé	S&S or S&A	GSC
Donizetti	Al bel destin (Linda di Chamounix)	S&A	
-----	Mad Scene (Linda di Chamounix)	S&A or S&S	
-----	Sulla tomba che rinserra (Lucia di Lammermoor)	S&T	BRO
-----	Tornami a dir, che m'ami (Don Pasquale)	S&T	BRO
-----	Verranno a te sul l'aure (Lucia di Lammermoor)	S&T	BRO
Dvořák	Julie and Bohuse (The Jacobin)	S&Bs	
Gershwin	Bess you is my woman now (Porgy and Bess)	S&Br	CHA
Giordano	Vicino a te (Andrea Chenier)	S&T	AMP
Gluck	Duet, Act Three (Orfeo ed Euridice)	S&A	DUR

Gounod	Ange adorable (Roméo and Juliette)	S&T	GSC
-----	Le foi de son flambeau (Mireille)	S&T	CHO
-----	Non ce n'est pas le jour (Romeo and Juliette)	S&T	CHO
Halévy	Ah! pour celui qui m'atrahie (La Juive)	S&S	
-----	Si trahison ou perfidie (La Juive)	S&T	
Humperdinck	Abendsegen (Haensel und Gretel)	S&S or S&A	AMP
-----	Mir traumte ich hoert ein Rauschen (Haensel und Gretel)	S&S	
Janacek	They went away, you go too (Jenufa)	S&T	
Kodaly	This side of the Tisza River (Hary Janos)	S&Br	
Lalo	Dans mon coeur envivre (Le Roi d'Ys)	S&T	HEU
-----	En silence pourquoi souffrir? (Le Roi d'Ys)	S&S or S&A	HEU
Leoncavallo	A kiss (Zaza)	S&Br	SON
-----	Sei là? credea che te non fossi (I Pagliacci)	S&Br	GSC
-----	Silvio! a quest' ora (I Pagliacci)	S&Br	GSC
Mascagni	Suzel, buon di (L'Amico Fritz)	S&T	GSC
-----	Tu qui Santuzza (Cavalleria Rusticana)	S&T	GSC
Massenet	Ah! des Grieux (Manon)	S&T	GSC
-----	C'est le soir la brise pure (Le Roi de Lahore)	S&A	HEU
-----	C'est Thais l'idole fragile (Thais)	S&T	HEU
-----	Death of Don Quichotte (Don Quichotte)	S&Bs	HEU
-----	Duo de l'oasis (Thais)	S&Br	HEU
-----	Duo du clair de lune (Werther)	S&T	HEU
-----	Jean, je te revois (Herodiade)	S&T	HEU
-----	J'écris à mon père	S&T	HEU
-----	Lassez le doute (Le Cid)	S&T	HEU
-----	N'est-ce plus ma main (Manon)	S&T	GSC
-----	Nous vivrons à Paris (Manon)	S&T	GSC

(Massenet)	Pardon! mais j'étais là (Manon)	S&Bs	GSC
-----	Quand apparaissent les étoiles (Don Quichotte)	S&Br	HEU
-----	Te souvient-il du lumineux voyage (Thais)	S&Br	HEU
Meyerbeer	Dans la nuit (Les Huguenots)	S&Bs	
-----	Love Duet, Act 4 (Les Huguenots)	S&T	BRO
-----	Pour garder a ton fils (Le Prophet)	S&A	
Mozart	Ah, perdona al primo affetto (La Clemenza di Tito)	S&A	
-----	Aprite, presto aprite (Le Nozze di Figaro)	S&S	RIC
-----	Bei Maennern, welche Liebe (Die Zauberfloete)	S&Bs	GSC
-----	Cinque, dieci (Le Nozze di Figaro)	S&Br	RIC
-----	Crudel! perchè finora (Le Nozze di Figaro)	S&Br	DIT
-----	Giovanette, chè all'amore (Don Giovanni)	S&Br	GSC
-----	Ich gehe, doch rate ich dir (Abduction from Seraglio)	S&Br	
-----	Il core vi dono (Cosi fan tutte)	S&Br	INT
-----	Là ci darem la mano (Don Giovanni)	S&Bs or S&Br	GSC
-----	Pa, Pa, Pa, Pa, Papagena! (Die Zauberfloete)	S&Br	GSC
-----	Se a caso Madama	S&Bs or S&Br	RIC
-----	Sull'aria! (Le Nozze di Figaro)	S&S	GSC
-----	Via resti servita (Le Nozze di Figaro)	S&S	RIC
Offenbach	Belle Nuit-Barcarolle (Tales of Hoffman)	S&A	GSC
-----	J'ai le bonheur dans l'âme! (Tales of Hoffman)	S&T	GSC
Pergolesi	Lo conosco, a quegli occhietti (La Serva Padrona)	S&Bs	RIC
-----	Per te ho io nel core (La Serva Padrona)	S&Bs	RIC
Ponchielli	L'amo come il fulgor del creato (La Gioconda)	S&S	RIC
-----	Laggiù nelle nebbie remote (La Gioconda)	S&T	RIC

Puccini	Amoro sol per te (Tosca)	S&T	RIC
-----	Duo Tosca and Cavaradossi (Tosca)	S&T	RIC
-----	Tutti i fior (Madama Butterfly)	S&A	RIC
-----	Già! Mi dicon venal (Tosca)	S&Br	RIC
-----	O dolci mani (Tosca)	S&T	RIC
-----	Oh quanti occhi fisi (Madama Butterfly)	S&T	RIC
-----	O soave fanciulla (La Bohème)	S&T	RIC
-----	Sono andati? (La Bohème)	S&T	RIC
Rossini	Oh! che muso (L'Italiana in Algeri	S&Bs	
-----	Serbami ognor si fido (Semiramide)	S&A	
Saint-Saëns	Il faut pour assouvir ma haine (Samson et Dalila)	S&Br	DUR
Smetana	Faithful love (The Bartered Bride)	S&T	BOO
-----	I know a maiden fair Bartered Bride)	S&T	BOO
-----	With my mother (The Bartered Bride)	S&T	BOO
Strauss	Aber der Richtige (Arabella)	S&S	BOO
-----	Ist ein Traum (Der Rosenkavalier)	S&S	BOO
-----	Love Duet, Act 2 (Arabella)	S&Br	BOH
-----	Presentation of the rose (Der Rosenkavalier)	S&S	BOO
Tchaikovoky	Didst thou not hear (Eugene Onegin)	S&S	GSC
-----	Tis evening (Pique Dame)	S&A	GSC
Thomas	Doute de la lumiere (Hamlet)	S&Br	HEU
-----	O ma gaselle (La Caid)	S&Bs	HEU
Verdi	Ciel mio padre (Aida)	S&Br	RIC
-----	Dite alla giovine (La Traviata)	S&BR	GSC
-----	E il sol dell'anima (Rigoletto)	S&T	GSC
-----	Figlia a tal nomo io palpito (Simon Boccanegra)	S&Br	RIC
-----	Figlia! Mio padre! (Rigoletto)	S&Br	GSC

(Verdi)	Già nella notte densa (Otello)	S&T	GSC
-----	La Vergine degli angeli (La Forza del Destino)	S&Bs	RIC
-----	Libiamo, libiamo ne'lieti calici (La Traviata)	S&T	RIC
-----	Mira, di acerbe lagrime (Il Trovatore)	S&Br	DIT
-----	Ah che la morte ognora (Il Trovatore)	S&T	GSC
-----	O terra addio (Aida)	S&T	GSC
-----	Parigi o cara (La Traviata)	S&T	GSC
-----	Pura siccome un angelo (La Traviata)	S&Br	RIC
-----	Quando narravi (Otello)	S&T	RIC
-----	Tutte le feste al tempio (Rigoletto)	S&Br	RIC
-----	Un di felice (La Traviata)	S&T	GSC
-----	Veglia o donna (Rigoletto)	S&Br	GSC
-----	V'ho ingannato (Rigoletto)	S&Br	GSC
Wagner	Act 2, Duet (Parsifal)	S&T	GSC
-----	Das suesse Lied verhallt (Lohengrin)	S&T	GSC
-----	Heil dir, Sonne! (Siegfried)	S&T	GSC
-----	Ja, ihr seid es (Die Meistersinger)	S&T	GSC
-----	Love Duet, Act 2 (Tristan und Isolde)	S&T	GSC
-----	O sink' hernieder (Tristan und Isolde)	S&T	GSC
-----	Siegmund heiss' ich und Siegmund bin ich (Die Walkuere)	S&T	GSC
-----	Siegmund! Sieh' auf mich! (Die Walkuere)	S&T	GSC
-----	Wirst du des Vaters Wahl nicht schelten? (Der Fliegende Hollaender)	S&Br	GSC
Wolf-Ferrari	Il cor nel contento (Le Donne Curiose)	S&T	GSC

Operetta Duets

Coloratura, Lyric or Dramatic Soprano

Berlin	Let's take an old fashioned walk (Miss Liberty	S&Br	BER

(Berlin)	They say it's wonderful (Annie Get Your Gun)	S&Br	BER
-----	White Christmas (Holiday Inn)	S&Br	BER
Caryll	There's a light in your eyes (The Girl Behind the Gun)	S&T	CHA
Coward	I'll see you again (Bitter Sweet)	S&Br or S&T	HAR
Donaldson	You (The Great Ziegfeld)	S&Br	FEI
-----	You never looked so beautiful (The Great Ziegfeld)	S&Br	FEI
Forrest-Grieg	Strange music (Song of Norway)	S&Br	CHA
Friml	Charms are fairest when they're hidden (Katinka)	S&Br	GSC
-----	Indian love call (Rose Marie)	S&Br or S&T	HAR
-----	Love me tonight	S&Br or S&Bs	FAM
-----	Only a rose (The Vagabond King)	S&Br	FAM
-----	Rose Marie (Rose Marie)	S&Br	HAR
-----	Sympathy (The Firefly)	S&Br	GSC
Gershwin	Embraceable you (Girl Crazy)	S&Br	NEM
-----	Of thee I sing (Of Thee I Sing)	S&Br	BRO
-----	Someone to watch over me (Oh, Kay)	S&T	HAR
Hahn	C'était pas la peine (Ciboulette)	S&T	SAL
-----	Chanson de route (Ciboulette)	S&Br	SAL
-----	Comme frère et soeur (Ciboulette)	S&T	HEU
-----	Nous avons fait un beau voyage (Ciboulette)	S&T	HEU
Henderson	The best things in life are free (Good News)	S&Br	CRF
Herbert	Ah sweet mystery of life (Naughty Marietta)	S&Br	HAR
-----	All for you (Princess Pat)	S&Br or S&T	WIT
-----	Because you're you (The Red Mill)	S&Br	WIT
-----	Gypsy love song (The Fortune Teller)	S&Br or S&T	WIT
-----	I'm falling in love with someone (Naughty Marietta)	S&Br	WIT

309

(Herbert)	In old New York (The Red Mill)	S&Br	GSC
-----	In the isle of our dreams (The Red Mill)	S&T	WIT
-----	Kiss me again (Mlle. Modiste)	S&Br	WIT
-----	Love is a story that's old (The Madcap Duchess)	S&T	GSC
-----	Moonbeams (The Red Mill)	S&Br or S&T	WIT
-----	Rose of the world (The Rose of Algeria)	S&Br	WIT
-----	Sweethearts (Sweethearts)	S&Br	GSC
-----	Thine alone (Eileen)	S&Br or S&T	WIT
-----	To the land of my own romance (Enchantress)	S&Br	WIT
-----	When you're away (The Only Girl)	S&Br	
Heuberger	Im chambre separée (Der Opernball)	S&T	
Hirsch	Kiss me (Going Up)	S &Br	WIT
Jacobi	I'll be true to you (Apple Blossoms)	S&Br	HAR
-----	On the banks of the Bronx (Apple Blossoms)	S&Br	HAR
-----	You are free (Apple Blossoms)	S&Br	HAR
Johnstone	Can it be love at last (Fiddler's Three)	S&Br	WIT
Kalman	In the garden of romance (Miss Springtime)	S&Br	HAR
-----	Love's own sweet song (Sari)	S&Br	MAR
Kern	D'ya love me (Sunny	S&Br	HAR
-----	Look for the Silver Lining (Sally)	S&Br	HAR
-----	Make believe (Show Boat)	S&Br	CHA
-----	Why do I love you (Show Boat)	S&Br	HAR
-----	You are love (Show Boat)	S&T	CHA
Koschna	Every little movement (Madame Sherry)	S&Br	WIT
Lehar	Are you going to dance (The Count of Luxembourg)	S&Br	CHA
-----	Bist du lachendes glueck (The Count of Luxembourg)	S&T	BRO
-----	Es liegt in blauen Fernen (Gypsy Love)	S&T	BRO
-----	Hab nur dich allein (Zarewitsch)	S&T	GLO

(Lehar)	Lippen schweigen (The Merry Widow)	S&T	CHA
-----	Niemand liebt dich so wie ich (Paganini)	S&T	GLO
-----	Wer hat die Liebe uns ins Herz gesenkt (The Land of Smiles)	S&T	SHU
-----	You're in love (Gypsy Love)	S&Br	CHA
Messager	The swing song (Veronique)	S&Br	CHA
-----	Trot here and there (Veronique)	S&Br	CHA
Milloecker	Without your love (Mme. Dubarry)	S&T	CHA
Porter	Night and Day (Gay Divorcee)	S&Br	HAR
-----	Wunderbar (Kiss me Kate)	S&Br	CHA
-----	You're the top (Anything Goes)	S&T	BRO
Reinhardt	Day dreams (The Spring Maid)	S&Br	MAR
-----	Two little love bees (The Spring Maid)	S&Br	MAR
Rodgers	A Fellow needs a girl (Allegro)	S&BR	CHA
-----	Here in my arms (Dearest Enemy)	S&Br	HAR
-----	If I loved you (Carousel)	S&Br	WMS
-----	My heart stood still (Conncticut Yankee)	S&Br	HAR
-----	People will say we're in love (Oklahoma)	S&Br	WIL
-----	So far (Allegro)	S&Br	CHA
-----	This nearly was mine (South Pacific)	S&Br	WIL
-----	We kiss in a shadow (The King and I)	S&Br	BRO
-----	With a song in my heart (Spring is Here)	S&Br	HAR
Romberg	Auf wiedersehn (The Blue Paradise)	S&Br	GSC
-----	Deep in my heart dear (The Student Prince)	S&Br or S&T	HAR
-----	Golden days (The Student Prince)	S&T	HAR
-----	I bring a love song (Viennese Nights)	S&T	HAR
-----	Just we two (The Student Prince)	S&Br	HAR

311

(Romberg)	Lover come back to me (New Moon)	S&T	HAR
-----	Once upon a time	S&Br	WIT
-----	One alone (The Desert Song)	S&T	HAR
-----	One kiss (New Moon)	S&Br	HAR
-----	Serenade (The Student Prince)	S&Br S&T	HAR
-----	Silver moon (My Maryland)	S&Br	HAR
-----	Song of love (Blossom Time)	S&Br	FEI
-----	The desert song (The Desert Song)	S&T	HAR
-----	Wanting you (New Moon)	S&T	BRO
-----	Will you remember	S&Br or S&T	GSC
-----	Your land and my land (My Maryland)	S&T	SCH
Schwartz	Dancing in the dark (The Band Wagon)	S&Br	HAR
-----	High and low (The Band Wagon)	S&T	HAR
Straus, O.	A waltz dream (A Waltz Dream)	S&Br	BRO
-----	My hero (The Chocolate Soldier)	S&T	WIT
-----	The letter song (The Chocolate Soldier)	S&S	REM
Strauss, J.	Taeubchen, das entflattert ist (Die Fledermaus)	S&T	BOO
-----	Trinke, Liebchen, trinke schnell (Die Fledermaus)	S&T	BOO
Sullivan	None shall part us (Iolanthe)	S&Br	
Tierney	Castle of dreams (Irene)	S&Br	FEI
-----	If you're in love you'll waltz (Rio Rita)	S&Br	FEI
-----	Rio Rita (Rio Rita)	S&Br	FEI
-----	You're always in my arms (Rio Rita)	S&Br	FEI
Youmans	Sometimes I'm happy (Hit the Deck)	S&Br	HAR
-----	Tea for two (No, No, Nanette)	S&Br S&A	HAR

Oratorio, Mass or Cantata Duets

Coloratura, Lyric or Dramatic Soprano

Bach, J.S.	Beruft Gott selbst (Cantata 88)	S&A	
-----	Den Tod (Cantata 4)	S&A	NOV
-----	Die Armut so Gott auf sich nimmt - with violin (Cantata 91)	S&A	
-----	Du wahrer Gott und David's Sohn obbligati of 2 oboes (Cantata 23)	S&A	BRO
-----	Er kennt die rechten freun-den Stunden -violin or small choir (Cantata 93)	S&A	NOV
-----	Gedenk an Jesu bittern Tod -flute and english horn or violin and viola (Cantata 101)	S&A	
-----	Gottes Wort -English Horn or Viola (Cantata 167)	S&A	
-----	Herr du siehst - flute and oboe d'amore or 2 violins or violin, viola (Cantata 9)	S&A	
-----	Peasant Cantata	S&Bs	
-----	Wenn des Kreuzes bitter-keiten - flute and oboe or 2 violins or violin and viola (Cantata 99)	S&A	
-----	Wenn Sorgen auf mich dringen - violin or oboe d'amore (Cantata 3)	S&A	
-----	Wir eilen - cello obbligato (Cantata 78)	S&A	BRO
Berlioz	L'arrivée à sais (L'Enfance du Christ)	S&Br	CST
-----	L'etable de Bethlehem (L'Enfance du Christ)	S&Br	NOV
Debussy	Que vois je un pauvre voyageur (L'Enfant Prodigue)	S&T	DUR
Elgar	Doubt not Thy Father's care (The Light of Life)	S&A S&Br	NOV
Handel	Apollo and Daphne (Cantata)	S&Br	
-----	Come ever smiling liberty (Judas Maccabaeus)	S&S	NOV
	Every joy that wisdom knoweth (Solomon)	S&S	NOV
-----	From this dread scene (Judas Maccabaeus)	S&T	NOV

(Handel)	Hail Judea (Judas Maccabaeus)	S&S	NOV
-----	O Fairest of ten thousand (Saul)	S&A	NOV
-----	O lovely peace (Judas Maccabaeus)	S&S	NOV
-----	O lovely peace (Judas Maccabaeus)	S&T	NOV
-----	O never bow we down (Judas Maccabaeus)	S&S	
-----	O peerless maid (Joshua)	S&A	NOV
-----	Our limpid streams (Joshua)	S&A	NOV
-----	Zion now her head shall raise (Judas Maccabaeus)	S&S	NOV
-----	Smiling Freedom (Deborah)	S&A	NOV
-----	The Lord is my strength (Israel in Egypt)	S&S	NOV
-----	These labours past (Jephtha)	S&A	NOV
-----	Thou in Thy mercy (Israel in Egypt)	S&T	NOV
-----	Thrice blest be the King (Solomon)	S&S	NOV
-----	Traitor to love (Samson)	S&T	NOV
-----	Where do thy ardours (Deborah)	S&A	NOV
-----	Who calls my parting soul (Esther)	S&T	NOV
Haydn	Graceful consort (The Creation)	S&Bs	NOV
Mendelssohn	Help me, oh man of God (Elijah)	S&Br	GSC
-----	I waited for the Lord (Hymn of Praise)	S&A	GSC
-----	In His Hands (Psalm 95)	S&T	NOV
-----	My song shall be always Thy mercy (Hymn of Praise)	S&T	GSC
Pergolesi	Quando corpus morietur (Stabat Mater)	S&A	ECS
Rossini	Qui est homo (The Stabat Mater)	S&S	
Saint Saens	Benedictus (Christmas Oratorio)	S&T	GSC

British Song Duets

Coloratura, Lyric or Dramatic Soprano

Arne	On the transport of possessing (Suleiman and Zaide)	S&T	
Beethoven	Constancy	S&T	ECS
-----	Sweet power of song	S&S S&A	ECS
-----	Where flowers were	S&S S&A	ECS
Britten	Mother comfort	S&S	BOH
-----	Underneath the abject willow	S&T S&Br S&S	BOH
Elgar	Fly singing bird two violins	S&S	NOV
Henschel	Gondoliera	S&Br	DEI
Hughes	When thro' life unblest we rove	S&Br	BOO
Huhn	Be Thou exalted	S&T	GSC
-----	The hunt	S&Br or S&S	GSC
Keel	You spotted snakes	S&A	BOO
Lawes	The angler's song	S&S S&Br or S&A	ECS
Morley	Sweet nymph	S&A	ECS
Purcell	Ah the sweet delights of love	S&S	DRH
-----	Let us wander	S&A S&Br	AUG
-----	Lost is my quiet	S&Br or S&A	AUG
-----	My dearest, my fairest	S&Br	AUG
-----	Shepherd leave decoying	S&Br or S&A	AUG
-----	Sound the trumpet	S&Br or S&A	AUG
-----	We the spirits of the air	S&A	
Ronald	Down in the forest	S&T	BOH
-----	O lovely night	S&T	ENO
Somervell	Under the greenwood tree	S&Br or S&A	BOO
Thiman	A shepherd kept sheep	S&S	NOV
-----	Spring wind	S&A	BOO
Vaughan Williams	It was a lover	S&T	

French Song Duets

Coloratura, Lyric or Dramatic Soprano

Chaminade	Angelus	S&Br	GSC
Chausson	La nuit	S&A	HAM
-----	Reveil	S&S	HAM
Dalcroze	Le coeur de ma mie	S&T	FOE

315

Faure, G.	Pleurs d'or	S&Br or S&T	
-----	Puisqu'ici bas toute ame	S&T or S&S	HAM
Fevrier	Au jardin charmant	S&S	
Franck	L'ange gardien	S&A	
-----	O Lord most holy	S&Br or S&A	BOS
-----	The Virgin by the manger	S&A	GSC
Gounod	Benedictus	S&T	MOR
Milhaud	Prends cette rose	S&Br or S&T	
Paladilhe	Au bord de l'eau	S&A	HEU
Rameau	Les amants trahis - cello	S&Br	DUR

German Song Duets

Coloratura, Lyric or Dramatic Soprano

Brahms	Am Strande	S&A	PET
-----	Die Boten der Liebe	S&A	PET
-----	Die Meere	S&A	PET
-----	Die Schwestern	S&A	
-----	Four Duets for Soprano and Contralto	S&A	
-----	Guter Rat	S&A	PET
-----	Klaenge	S&A	
-----	Klosterfraeulein	S&A	PET
-----	Nun lass uns wandern	S&Br or S&T	DIT
-----	Phaenomen	S&A	
-----	Three duets for Soprano and Alto	S&A	
-----	Walpurgisnacht	S&S	PET
-----	Weg der Liebe, 1	S&A	PET
-----	Weg der Liebe, 2	S&A	PET
Cornelius	Ein wort der liebe	S&Br	PET
-----	Lied des Narren, 2	S&S	PET
Goetze	Calm as the night	S&Br	GSC
Hildach	Now thou art mine	S&Br	GSC
-----	Passage birds farewell	S&Br	GSC
Hindemith	Acht kanons	S&Br or S&T	
Mendelssohn	Autumn song	S&S	NOV
-----	Children blessed of the Lord	S&T	JCH
-----	Gruess	S&A S&S or S&Br	WOO
-----	I would that my love	S&S or S&A	NOV
-----	My bark is bound to the gale	S&Br or S&A	
-----	The Sabbath morn	S&S or S&A	NOV
-----	Zuleika and Hassan	S&T	NOV

Mozart	Caro, bell idol mio	S&T	
Reger	Schnee	S&A	
Rubenstein	Meeresabend	S&A	PET
Schuetz	Erhoere mich wenn ich rufe	S&S	BAR
-----	O lieber Herre Gott wecke uns auf	S&S	BAR
-----	Schaffe in mir Gótt	S&T	BAR
Schumann	Das Glueck	S&S	PET
-----	Familien Gemaelde	S&T	
-----	Fruehlinglied	S&S	PET
-----	In the woods	S&T or S&S	DIT
-----	Liebhabers Staendchen	S&T	PET
-----	Remembrance	S&T or S&S	DIT
-----	Schoen Bluemelein	S&A	PET
-----	So wahr die Sonne scheinet	S&T	
-----	Unter'm Fenster	S&A	

Italian Song Duets

Coloratura, Lyric or Dramatic Soprano

Carissimi	Rimanti in pace omai	S&T	
-----	Vaghirai pupille ardente	S&Br or S&T	
Clari	Cantando un di	S&Br or S&A	ECS
-----	Long live song	S&A	ECS
-----	Ma sordo e ogn'uno	S&T or S&S	ECS
-----	Non ti sdegnar	S&T or S&S	ECS
-----	Sventurato son	S&T or S&A	ECS
Donaudy	Amor s'apprende	S&T or S&S	RIC
Floridia	A lover's duet	S&Br	DIT
Handel	Ahi, nelle sorti umane	S&T or S&S	PET
-----	Beato in ver chi puo	S&A	PET
-----	Caro autor	S&Br or S&T	
-----	Fronda leggiera e mobile	S&S or S&A	PET
-----	No di voi nun vo fidarmi, 1	S&A	PET
-----	No di voi non vo fidarmi, 2	S&T or S&A	PET
-----	Quel fio che all'alba ride	S&T or S&S	PET
-----	Rimanti in pace omai	S&T or S&Br	
Legrenzi	Ficrezza si vaga	S&S or S&A	
Lully	Bel tempo che vola	S&S or S&A	ECS
Monteverdi	Bel pastor	S&T	PET
-----	Chioma d'oro - 2 violins	S&S	PET
-----	Io son pur vezzosetta pastorella	S&S	PET
-----	Chime dov'e il mio ben	S&A	
-----	O viva fiamma	S&S	PET
Pergolesi	Contrasti crudeli	S&S	ROM

Rossi	Vo fuggir lontan da te	S&S or S&A	PET
	2 violins		
-----	Volo ne tuoi degli occhi	S&S	PET
Steffani	Occhi perche piangete	S&A	

Other Duets

Coloratura, Lyric or Dramatic Soprano

Couperin	Venite exultemus domino	S&S or S&A	
	- organ		
Dargomijshky	Vanka Tanka	S&Bs	
Hoffman	I feel thy angel spirit	S&Br	GSC
Mendelssohn	They have taken away my	S&Br or S&A	ECS
	Lord		
Nabokov	La vita nuova	S&T	
Pergolesi	Salve Regina, 2	S&Br	ROM
-----	Salve Regina, 3	S&S	ROM
Perosi	Cantate Domino	S&T	
-----	Domine salvum me fac	S&T	
Rachmaninoff	Two partings	S&Br	BOO
Rubinstein	Der Engel	S&A	PET
-----	Im heilischen Land	S&S or S&A	PET

Trios

Coloratura, Lyric or Dramatic Soprano

Bizet	Melons! Coupons!	SSS	GSC
	(Carmen)		
Debussy	L'Enfant Prodigue	S&T&Br	DUR
	(Cantata		
Gounod	Anges purs, anges radieux	S&T&Bs	
	(Faust)		
-----	Il m'amie, Act 2 (Faust)	S&T&Bs	
Handel	The flocks-shall leave	S&T&Br	NOV
	(Acis and Galatea)		
-----	Thou sittest (Dettingen	S&T&B	NOV
	Te Deum)		
Haydn	Most beautiful appear	S&T&Bs	NOV
	(The Creation)		
-----	On Thee each living soul	S&T&Bs	NOV
	(The Creation)		
Menotti	Trio (The Consul)	S&A&Br	GSC
Mozart	Ah taci ingiusto core	S&Br&Bs	
	(Don Giovanni)		
-----	Due pupille amabili	S&S&Br	

(Mozart)	Ecco quel fiero istante	S&S&Br	
-----	Grazie agl'inganni toui	S&T&Br	
-----	Liebes Mandel wo is's Bandel	S&T&Br	
-----	Luci care, luci belle	S&B&B	
-----	Mandina amabile	S&T&Br	
-----	Mi lagnero tacendo	S&S&Br	
-----	Se lontan ben mio tu sei	S&Br&Bs	
Offenbach	Tu ne chanteras plus (Tales of Hoffman)	S&Ms&B	GSC
Ponchielli	Figlia che reggi il tremulo piè (La Gioconda)	S&A&T	RIC
Purcell	Saul and the witch of Endor	S&T&Br	BOO
Strauss, J.	Frank, you set my doubts at rest (Die Fledermaus)	S&T&Br	BOO
-----	To part is such sweet sorrow (Die Fledermaus)	S&T&Br	BOO
-----	When these lawyers don't believe (Die Fledermaus)	S&T&Br	BCO
Strauss, R.	Hab mir's gelobt inn Lieb zu haben (Der Rosenkavalier)	SSS	BOO
Tchaikovsky	Trio and couplets (Eugenc Onegin)	S&T&B	GSC
Verdi	Della citta all occaso (Un Ballo in Maschera)	S&A&T	
-----	Io muojo (La Forza del Destino)	S&T&Br	RIC
-----	Ma dimmi (Aida)	S&T&Br	GSC
-----	Qual volutta trascorrere (I Lombardi)	S&T&Br	RIC
-----	Te sol quest anima (Attila)	S&T&Bs	GSC
-----	Tu se Ernani (Ernani)	S&T&Br	
-----	Vieni o diletta (Aida)	S&A&T	
-----	Wie was entsetzen (Der Freischuetz)	S&S&T	

Contemporary Chamber Operas

Coloratura, Lyric or Dramatic Soprano

		(minutes)	
Allen	Mamselle Figaro	60 S, T, BS-BAR	WHB
Barab	Chanticleer	40 S, C, T, BR	BOO
-----	A Game of Chance	35 2S, M, BS-BR	BOO
-----	Reba	40 T, S, C, BR	BOO
-----	The Rajah's Ruby	45 2S, T, BR, BS, mute	BOO

319

Bartok	Bluebeard's Castle	66	S, BS-BR, speaker	BOO
Bucci	The Dress	30	3S, BR	CHA
Davis	The Sailing of the Nancy Belle	30	S, T, BS and cho	BOO
deBanfield	Lord Byron's Love Letter	70	3S, C, T	RIC
Delaney	A Very Special Date	20	BR, S, small boy	
DiGiovanni	Medea	60	S, C, T, B, & cho	SPA
Elkus	Tom Sawyer	60	S, C, BS	NOV
Engel	The Malady of Love	30	S, BR, 2 mutes	Manu-script
Floyd	Slow Dusk	38	S, M, T, BR	BOO
Gladstein	The Lockout	15	S, T	AMM
Haubiel	Sunday Costs Five Pesos	35	S, C, & T	CMP
Holst	Savitri	40	S, T, BS & women's cho.	GCS
Johnson	A Letter to Emily		S, M, BR & BS-BR	MER
Kastle	The Swing	13	S, BR & speaker	TEM
Kupferman	In a Garden	20	S, T, BS	MER
Lecocq	Kiss at the Door	20	S, T	MAR
Lochrem	A Letter to Emily	40	S, M, BR, BS-BR	MER
Low	Rapunzel	40	S, C, BR	SOU
Martin	The Marriage	90	S, M, T, BR	BOO
Menotti	The Old Maid and the Thief	55	2S, M, BR	RIC
-----	The Telephone	25	S, BR	GSC
Milhaud	Le Pauvre Matelot	60	S, T, BR, BS	MER
Moore	Gallantry	35	S, BR, M, T (dancers opt.)	GSC
Patacchi	The Secret	65	3S, BS-BR	ASB
Petit	The Game of Love and Chance	25	S, M, BR	MER
Poulenc	La Voix Humaine		sop. & telephone	RIC
Ratner	The Necklace	40	S, M, BAR	MER
Rieti	Don Perlimplin			HEU
Rosenthal	The Weeping Willow	45	S, T, BR, cho. and sp.	MER
Siegmeister	Miranda and the Dark Young Man	60	S, M, BAR, BS-BAR	TEM
Stravinsky	Les Noces	25	4 and cho.	GSC
-----	Mavra	30	S, M, C, T	BOO

320

Toch	Egon and Emily	15	Col-Sop. & speaker	AMP
Townsend	Lima Beans	25	S, T, BAR	MER
Weisgall	The Stronger	25	Col-Sop, BR & mute	PRE

Standard Chamber Operas

Coloratura, Lyric or Dramatic Soprano

Bach, J. S.	The Coffee Cantata	35	S, T, BR & quartet	GSC
-----	The Peasant Cantata	40	2S, BR, BS	CFI
Byrd	The Music Master		S, T, BR	AMI
Cadman	The Willow Tree	55	S, C, T, BR	MER
Chabrier	The Incomplete Education	45	S, T, BR	
Debussy	The Prodigal Son	50	S, T, BR	MER
Delibes	The Omlet		4, 2 sp	HEU
Donizetti	Il Campanello	50	S, T, BR	RIC
Gluck	Orfeo ed Euridice	120	3S, M, cho.	GSC
Mascagni	Zanetto	60	S, M or T	SON
Mas senet	Portrait of Manon	45	S, M, T, BR cho.	MER
Monteverdi	Orfeo	60	S, C, T, BS, sp	AMP
Mozart	Bastien and Bastienne	35	3	MAR
-----	The Impresario	60	2S, T, BS	GSC
Offenbach	Forty Winks	20	S, T, BS	
-----	Lady to Raffle	45	Three	MER
-----	Marriage by Lantern-light	35	2S, M, T	WIT
Pergolesi	Jealous Husband	100	S, M, T, BS	MER
-----	La Serva Padrona	42	S&BS & mute	
Purcell	Saul and the Witch of Endor	30	3 and cho.	BOO
Suppe	The Beautiful Galalea		S, T, &B	
Wolf-Ferrari	The Secret of Suzanne	45	S&BR & speaker	GSC

50560